Mapping Comprehensive Units to the **ELA Common Core Standards**
6–12

To the enlightened educators who challenge themselves to a new level of professional excellence—and, in the process, raise the bar for all students.

Mapping Comprehensive Units to the ELA Common Core Standards 6–12

Kathy Tuchman Glass

Foreword by Jim Knight

CORWIN
A SAGE Company

CORWIN
A SAGE Company

FOR INFORMATION:

Corwin
A SAGE Company
2455 Teller Road
Thousand Oaks, California 91320
(800) 233-9936
www.corwin.com

SAGE Publications Ltd.
1 Oliver's Yard
55 City Road
London EC1Y 1SP
United Kingdom

SAGE Publications India Pvt. Ltd.
B 1/I 1 Mohan Cooperative Industrial Area
Mathura Road, New Delhi 110 044
India

SAGE Publications Asia-Pacific Pte. Ltd.
3 Church Street
#10-04 Samsung Hub
Singapore 049483

Acquisitions Editor: Carol Chambers Collins
Publisher: Lisa Luedeke
Developmental Editor: Julie Nemer
Editorial Assistant: Francesca Dutro Africano
Permissions Editor: Jennifer Barron
Project Editor: Veronica Stapleton Hooper
Copy Editor: Talia Greenberg
Typesetter: C&M Digitals (P) Ltd.
Proofreader: Dennis W. Webb
Indexer: Sheila Bodell
Cover Designer: Michael Dubowe

Printed in the United States of America

A catalog record of this book is available from the Library of Congress.

ISBN: 9781452268620

This book is printed on acid-free paper.

SUSTAINABLE FORESTRY INITIATIVE
Certified Chain of Custody
Promoting Sustainable Forestry
www.sfiprogram.org
SFI-01268
SFI label applies to text stock

13 14 15 16 17 10 9 8 7 6 5 4 3 2 1

Contents

Additional materials and resources related to *Mapping and Designing Units to the ELA Common Core Standards, 6–12* can be found at http://www.corwin.com/mappingela6-12

List of Figures

Chapter 6: Skills, Activities, Formative Assessments, and Resources

Chapter 7: Differentiated Instruction

Foreword

Kathy Glass's new book, *Mapping Comprehensive Units to the ELA Common Core Standards 6-12*, is an essential tool for anyone interested in translating the Common Core Standards into teaching practices. How people use this book, however, will profoundly affect whether or not this opportunity for change leads to positive improvements for children.

WHY THIS BOOK IS IMPORTANT

Teachers, administrators, and educators who guide professional learning will struggle to be effective if they do not have a deep understanding of what the Common Core entails and how it can be understood. Many people have told me they need a resource that can help them make sense of this new set of expectations and what they mean. For language arts, social studies, science, and other content area teachers invested in implementing the ELA Common Core in grades 6-12, this is that book. Kathy Glass walks us through a clearly delineated process for implementing this new initiative and helps us understand how to turn ideas into action.

In part, what Kathy does is provide us with a concise, easy-to-understand introduction to the Common Core, clarifying, for example, the differences between fiction and non-fiction texts, and argumentative, informative, and narrative writing. She then introduces readers to components of a curriculum unit map—along with numerous templates, tables, and examples—to illustrate how to fashion (or revise) a unit using the standards and key concepts embedded in them.

Kathy's book also helps district leaders develop a shared vocabulary around the Common Core by providing clear, accessible descriptions of critical features of unit design. Powerful professional learning occurs when teachers develop a shared meaning of essential concepts. Kathy's book makes it much easier for teachers to engage in the simple act of not only talking about teaching but doing the work to become great teachers.

Perhaps most important, Kathy helps us understand how to put the standards into action. She explains how to write guiding questions, create various types of assessments, and plan lessons that are differentiated so as to support learning for all students. In summary, Kathy shows us how to focus on what is essential in the standards, how to write essential understandings and accompanying essential questions, how to identify and teach knowledge, skills, and understandings to all students, and how to assess whether or not students have learned the targeted unit goals.

Used effectively, this book can be a powerful tool for improving instruction. However, to get the most out of Kathy's work, educational leaders need to consider at least two vital issues.

One: Involve Teachers in the Thinking. Professionals, by definition, use their education, intelligence, and creativity to make thousands of unique decisions based on the individual needs of the people they serve, which, in the case of teachers, is students. For that reason, having a few educators create a Common Core plan, and then expecting every other teacher to implement the plan likely won't work given what we know about professionalism.

Thomas Davenport explained this clearly in his 2005 book, *Thinking for a Living: How to Get Better Performance and Results from Knowledge Workers.* When knowledge workers such as teachers, principals, and coaches are not given the opportunity to reflect and think for themselves, they usually resist change. Doing the thinking for professionals and telling them what they must do is not a great change strategy. Davenport writes:

> Knowledge workers don't like to be told what to do, and they also don't like to see their jobs reduced to a series of boxes and arrows ….Thinking for a living engenders thinking for oneself. Knowledge workers are paid for their education, experience, and expertise, so it is not surprising that they take offense when someone else rides roughshod over their intellectual territory. (p. 15)

A better plan, as I have written in *Unmistakable Impact: A Partnership Approach to Dramatically Improving Instruction* (2011), is to involve all teachers in intensive learning teams where all teachers collaboratively create guiding questions, learning maps, assessments, and other curriculum elements such as those that Kathy Glass describes so well in this book. Intensive learning teams organize collaborative learning so teachers have a real voice in planning, thinking deeply about their content, and developing curriculum tools that they are committed to using. If teachers are simply told what to do, they may comply, but they are usually not enthusiastic about plans. When teachers actively help create instructional plans, they are much more likely to implement those plans.

Two: Provide Follow-Up. In the shelves in classrooms across our nation right now, there are thousands of binders filled with curriculum maps. Why haven't they been used? The answer is simple: Teachers often have no follow-up to help them implement practices. No matter how outstanding a workshop or meeting might be, without follow-up, practices usually don't get implemented (Cornett & Knight, 2008). Learning a new approach and translating it into practice requires more than deep thought; it requires ongoing, structured, helpful support. In other words, it requires instructional coaching.

Instructional coaches provide a second set of eyes, a second set of hands, to help teachers implement new practices. As I explain in *Unmistakable Impact* (2011), instructional coaches collaborate with teachers to set goals, provide clear explanations, model practices, provide partnership feedback, and offer ongoing support. Such follow-up is essential for translating Common Core ideas into teaching that helps students.

Like them or hate them, these new standards represent one of the most significant opportunities for improvement schools have faced in decades. This book will be a great help to anyone engaged in the act of translating the Common Core Standards into actual teaching practices. If schools use this book as a part of meaningful collaboration and coaching, these Standards can be a point of departure for real, positive change.

Jim Knight

Educational Consultant, Author, and President of Instructional Coaching Group

Acknowledgments

Julie Nemer's keen eye and brilliant commitment to this project made a significant impact on my finished book. Enormous thanks, Julie, for walking alongside me. I am deeply indebted to my editor, Lisa Luedeke, for giving me the gift of working with Julie. Once again, Veronica Hooper ensured that production ran smoothly and my manuscript was just right. Her attention to detail was astounding. Jim Knight graciously offered to write a Foreword even though he was probably dreaming in words after just finishing his own book.

Teachers have always motivated and informed me. Thanks to these stellar educators who imparted key input while I was typing away: Stephanie Newblanc, Debbie Hartwig, Alec MacKenzie, and Megan Mullaly.

In the K–5 version of this book, Corwin solicited the following reviewers to provide comments. Their insight and suggestions carried over to this book, as well, so I sincerely recognize their contributions: Rochelle DeMuccio, Arlene DeSiena, and Alesha M. Moreno-Ramirez.

I acknowledge those whose work has prompted me to ponder and grab hold with both hands, particularly Carol Tomlinson and H. Lynn Erickson. Through interactions with them and diving into their work, I've been inspired. In soaking up their wisdom, I have found new insights and ideas that I can share with educators so they can reach new heights.

I cannot envision what I would do without my invaluable husband, Mike. Every day I'm grateful for his constant support and thank him for his belief in me personally and professionally.

About the Author

Kathy Tuchman Glass consults nationally with schools and districts, presents at conferences, and teaches seminars for university and county programs delivering customized professional development. A former master teacher, she has been in education for over twenty years and works with administrators and teachers in groups of varying sizes from one on one to entire school districts, from kindergarten through high school. Her expertise revolves around areas affecting curriculum and instruction, such as implementation of the ELA CCSS or other standards-based curriculum using a backward design approach; differentiated tools, instructional strategies, and assessments; essential understandings and guiding questions to frame curriculum and instruction; pre-, formative, self-, and summative assessments; alignment of six-traits writing instruction and assessment to curriculum goals and CCSS; unit and yearlong curriculum maps; and text-dependent questions to facilitate close reading. By providing educators with practical application of research-based methods, she works to strengthen their teaching or coaching and extend their professional capacities to impact student achievement.

In addition to *Mapping Comprehensive Units to the ELA Common Core Standards, 6–12*, she has written *Mapping Comprehensive Units to the ELA Common Core Standards, K–5* (2012); *Lesson Design for Differentiated Instruction, Grades 4–9* (2009); *Curriculum Mapping: A Step-by-Step Guide to Creating Curriculum Year Overviews* (2007); and *Curriculum Design for Writing Instruction: Creating Standards-Based Lesson Plans and Rubrics* (2005). With Cindy Strickland, she has coauthored the *Staff Development Guide for the Parallel Curriculum* (2009). In addition, Kathy served as a differentiation consultant for Pearson Learning's social studies textbook series for K–5 (2013).

Originally from Indianapolis, Kathy resides in the San Francisco Bay Area. She can be reached through e-mail at kathy@kathyglassconsulting.com. Her website is www.kathy glassconsulting.com.

Introduction

If you are an educator in one of the states that has adopted the Common Core State Standards, you are undoubtedly preparing for change. Like other educators in your situation, you are embarking upon a new venture. As stated in the Center on Education Policy's *Common Core State Standards: Progress and Challenges in School Districts' Implementation* (Kober & Renter, 2011), "Most of these states are expecting, rather than requiring, districts to undertake such activities as developing new curriculum materials and instructional practices, providing professional development to teachers and principals, and designing and implementing teacher induction programs and evaluations related to the standards" (p. 1). It is therefore not surprising that you need some support in navigating your way through these new standards and in using them to create curriculum. That's where I can help. I wrote this book for teachers, curriculum designers or directors, administrators, professors in teacher credentialing programs, or anyone who plans to use the ELA Common Core Standards along with content area standards, as appropriate, to write meaningful and effective curriculum that can make a lasting impression on our charges.

WHAT TO EXPECT: UNIT MAP

Curriculum mapping allows educators to purposefully plan and outline what is taught in a given year. It allows for articulation across the grades and within each grade. As I write in my book *Curriculum Mapping: A Step-by-Step Guide for Creating Curriculum Year Overviews* (2007),

> A curriculum mapping document, as the name implies, maps everything—in all subject areas—that a teacher needs to cover in a given school year. The [map] accounts for all the content standards the district or state mandates, along with information that personalizes the document for each teacher. (p. 1)

Along with standards, curriculum maps can include key concepts, essential questions, skills, assessments, and more. Mapping a yearlong curriculum program allows educators to vertically and horizontally align their curriculum within a building and across the district. A map can uncover key learning that is repetitive, or missed entirely, so that educators become aware and accountable to students' learning.

Mapping the yearlong curriculum is advisable, and your school or district might be in the process of creating this kind of map or have plans to create one. However, teachers and curriculum designers need to understand the equally critical importance of creating a quality-driven unit map. That is the focus for this book: to guide readers to comprehensively map a unit of study using the ELA Common Core Standards. Whether or not schools or districts are in the process of a yearlong map, sooner or later teachers will need a comprehensive curriculum map for individual units. Creating maps will clarify the outcomes for learners and increase the quality and focus of instruction.

To aid in your creation of unit maps, this book includes a template with key components of a strong map and thorough explanations for each one. The chapters feature many examples of these components, such as enduring understandings, guiding questions, culminating assessments with rubrics, differentiation ideas, skills, activity ideas, and so forth, aligned to the ELA Common Core.

There is also a lesson design template that is a natural subsequent step to the unit map. You will find several comprehensive model lessons using this template. As you dive into the process of mapping a targeted unit, you will work closely with the Common Core Standards, and become intimate with them, as you carefully determine which to group together to form the basis for a unit. You will also use the skills embedded in the standards as a guide to identify the key conceptual understandings that will drive quality curriculum and engaging instruction. As you create your unit maps, I walk you through a clearly articulated process centering on key components of unit design. Here's a snapshot of what you will accomplish as you turn the pages of this book and work on various exercises:

- Group ELA Common Core Standards
- Identify what students should know
- Develop essential understandings
- Discern between essential unit and lesson guiding questions—and craft them
- Identify or create culminating assessments for students to demonstrate learning
- Preview prepared checklists and rubrics aligned to the Common Core Standards
- Consider ways to differentiate activities, assessments, and resources
- Distinguish activities from skills and record both
- Determine evidence of formative assessments
- Select appropriate resources

Truth be told, if you have done work with backward design, curriculum mapping, and differentiation, you will be familiar with much of what is presented here, but you should learn novel ideas or ways to approach what you have done in the past. My process for creating a map is akin to other methods and a compilation of successful work in the field from H. Lynn Erickson, Heidi Hayes Jacobs, Jay McTighe, Carol Ann Tomlinson, Grant Wiggins, and a host of other revered academicians. Like my cohorts, I have my own twist on this work; my strategies have evolved from years of being in the trenches and consulting with teachers regularly. And I have found this process and the examples I share resonate with them. As one New York City teacher commented, "You have an excellent ability to present material that can be 'overwhelming' into manageable chunks for success!" And from a teacher in Alaska, "Your ideas helped me see a new way of presenting information I didn't even realize. I was kind of 'stuck' in one way of thinking. Thank you!"

As a first step, I suggest you consider a targeted unit of study, print out the ELA Common Core Standards, gather together a textbook and readings or resources you might need for your unit, and begin to create a curriculum unit map with me. You can access my website at www.kathyglassconsulting.com for Microsoft Word formats of standards for each grade, 5–12, by clicking on the appropriate links in the "Download Resources" section. This will enable you to download them onto your computer and cut and paste standards more easily for curriculum mapping and lesson design. For a PDF version of all the standards, go to the Common Core State Standards Initiative website, www.corestandards.org/.

COMPANION WEBSITE: REPRODUCIBLES AND PRIMER ON THE ELA COMMON CORE

This book provides a multitude of reproducibles for classroom or professional use. These reproducibles are available on a companion website aligned to this book that you can download and print. Some reproducibles are in PDF format and others in Microsoft Word. The resources in Word are mostly handouts for student activities and various assessments (e.g., checklists, rubrics, etc.). You can download and adapt these figures to suit your particular grade level, or personalize and alter a specific assignment to meet students' needs. Throughout the book, you will see a mouse that indicates items that appear on this companion website. In some instances, a partial figure is included in the book and the entire figure is featured in the companion website.

In addition to reproducibles, you can access a Resource section in the online companion website. It provides an overview of the English language arts (ELA) Common Core (CC) Standards for 6–12 and is titled "A Brief Primer on the ELA Common Core Standards." Those of you familiar with the organization and contents of the standards might choose to skim this section or skip it altogether. Or some of you might prefer to access the original source and read the Common Core "Introduction" and appendices in their entirety. If so, go to the Common Core State Standards Initiative website (www.corestandards.org) and navigate to locate pieces of information you want to read verbatim.

To access this companion website that accompanies this book, go to http://www.corwin.com/mappingela6-12 and follow the directions.

1

Standards and Knowledge

> *Standards are the foundation upon which almost everything else rests—or should rest. They should guide state assessments and accountability systems; inform teacher preparation, licensure, and professional development; and give shape to curricula, textbooks, software programs, and more. Choose your metaphor: Standards are targets, or blueprints, or roadmaps. They set the destination: what we want our students to know and be able to do by the end of their K–12 experience, and the benchmarks they should reach along the way.*
>
> —Chester E. Finn, Jr., and Michael J. Petrilli (as cited in Carmichael, Martino, Porter-Magee, & Wilson, 2010, p. 1)

Those new to the Common Core (CC) Standards or who wish to have a refresher might read the Resource section of this book, "A Brief Primer on the ELA Common Core Standards," located on the companion website (http://www.corwin.com/mappingela6-12). Whether or not you read the primer for an overview of the CC Standards, Chapter 1 is the starting point for the process of creating a curriculum map that is linked to the standards. It culminates with two exercises:

1. Grouping standards

2. Using what you grouped to determine what you want students to know

These exercises are the launching pad for mapping an effective, concept-driven unit of instruction. The following is a snapshot of what this chapter includes:

- A cursory overview of the role of standards in general
- The major emphases of the ELA Common Core standards

- Concrete examples of types of fiction and nonfiction literature to help differentiate among them; specifics about what the genre of informational text entails and its distinguishing features
- Definitions of the Common Core text types—opinion/argument, informative/explanatory, narrative—along with ideas for writing prompts across content areas
- A commentary on the student writing samples that comprise Appendix C of the Common Core document
- Insights gleaned from the Common Core and ways to group and use them to guide instruction and collaborate with colleagues, especially for standards relating to grammar and conventions

THE PURPOSE OF STANDARDS

Standards get major attention in the world of education, and for good reason. They give teachers a starting point for teaching and can be a guiding light to help them plan goals for students. It is imperative to note that although standards provide a set of expectations, they do not diminish teachers' creative and professional capacity to plan curriculum and execute instruction, albeit instruction that is sound and based on research. Whether a school is public, charter, parochial, private, or blended, it is altogether prudent that educators have a guidepost for each year of instruction to deliver a comprehensive curriculum throughout the grade spans.

Standards alone will not guarantee that students will be successful. Using the blueprint metaphor from the beginning quote, an architect can design a detailed and magnificent building, but if the contractor cannot execute the plans, then how effective is the blueprint? Standards serve to guide expectations, but it takes insightful and skillful educators who make wise choices about what they teach and how they teach to really make an impact on students. You might have heard of the powerful trio—know, understand, do (KUD)—that is often mentioned in educational literature, as together the three form the basis for setting goals for effective teaching. Carol Tomlinson and Jay McTighe (2006) discuss this and state what really matters in teaching:

> Central to teaching is *what* we ought to teach—what we want students to know, understand, and be able to do. To be an expert teacher is to continually seek a deeper understanding of the essence of a subject, to increasingly grasp its wisdom. That understanding is key to a teacher's role in curriculum planning. It is difficult to imagine someone becoming a great teacher without persistent attention to that element of the art of teaching. (p. 12)

To expertly teach the CCSS, educators need to create a curriculum map that emanates from standards. This map should include the KUDs along with other components (e.g., activities, differentiation, resources) to be sure that each unit is quality driven and responsive to students' needs.

Our journey on unit mapping begins by getting familiar with the standards. The chapter then supports you in grouping standards and identifying what you want students to know from your selected standards.

KEY AREAS OF EMPHASIS IN THE ELA COMMON CORE STANDARDS

The following represents a detailed explanation of the major shifts of the new standards. It is critical that all stakeholders who implement the CC Standards be aware of them so curriculum and instruction align with these key points.

1. *Using content-rich nonfiction, particularly informational text, to build knowledge across content areas.* A key feature of the CC is that teachers from across disciplines incorporate literacy into their curriculum: " . . . the Standards define literacy expectations in history/social studies, science, and technical subjects, but literacy standards in other areas, such as mathematics and health education, modeled on those in this document are strongly encouraged to facilitate a comprehensive, schoolwide literacy program" (2010a, p. 6). Acquiring knowledge through informational text is paramount to this. (See the next section, "Understanding Fiction and Nonfiction Characteristics," for a detailed explanation of informational text.) As such, in K–5 classrooms, which are typically self-contained, the CC Standards require that teachers construct learning experiences that involve 50 percent literary text and 50 percent informational text. In the middle and high school grades, informational text is given greater attention as teachers of various disciplines incorporate reading opportunities in their planning and instruction (see Figure 1.1). Clearly, literacy is not solely the responsibility of ELA teachers. In fact, the Common Core states "because the ELA classroom must focus on literature (stories, drama, and poetry) as well as literary nonfiction, a great deal of informational reading in grades 6–12 must take place in other classes" (2010a, p. 5). Therefore, the Common Core emphasizes an interdisciplinary approach to literacy. For students to proficiently and independently read complex text and write coherently to prepare them for college and careers, teachers in other content areas need to have a role in their development and should expose students to quality, substantive informational texts.

Distribution of Literary and Informational Passages

Grade	Literary	Informational
4	50%	50%
8	45%	55%
12	30%	70%

FIGURE 1.1

Source: National Assessment Governing Board (2008).

2. *Reading, writing, and speaking centered on evidence from the text.* Students are asked to cull evidence from various sources to make sound arguments and communicate information. They are expected to write and even speak using their sources as the basis for making and supporting claims and conclusions and for sharing information. Teachers craft text-dependent questions so students can engage in rich discussions

and focus activities around close examination of a particular complex text. These kinds of questions point students directly to the text to determine and analyze authors' explicit and implied meanings. It is with this instructional practice that students will become more adept at extracting appropriate evidence to support an effective argument or informational piece. (See the section "Designing Text-Dependent Questions for Complex Text" in Chapter 3.) In fact, the CCSS for Mathematics point to writing and speaking evidentiary expectations, as students are asked to justify their conclusions and communicate them to others.

3. ***Increasing text complexity and focusing on academic vocabulary.*** Since the goal is for students to be college and career ready, teachers gradually increase the complexity of text that students encounter as they progress from grade to grade. The CC Standards refer to this as "a staircase of complexity," which is the role of Standard 10: "Whatever they are reading, students must also show a steadily growing ability to discern more from and make fuller use of text, including making an increasing number of connections among ideas and between texts, considering a wider range of textual evidence, and becoming more sensitive to inconsistencies, ambiguities, and poor reasoning in texts" (2010a, p. 8). If students need support, teachers scaffold instruction appropriately. As a key contributing factor to comprehending complex text, students need practice in building their general academic vocabulary or Tier Two words. These kinds of words appear in a variety of literary and informational texts (e.g., *determine, relative, formulate, admitted*), but are not specifically tied to a content area like domain-specific words (Tier Three words). The latter are treated as important (e.g., *mitosis, imperialism, lava*) since they are necessary to understand a new concept. As such, Tier Three words are emphasized repeatedly in targeted texts through repeated exposure and specialized treatment (e.g., highlighted, italicized, or bolded words; glossary entries, etc.). Tier Two words get short shrift because they "are not unique to a particular discipline and as a result are not the clear responsibility of a particular content area teacher. What is more, many Tier Two words are not well defined through contextual clues in the texts in which they appear and are far less likely to be defined explicitly within a text than are Tier Three words. Yet Tier Two words are frequently encountered in complex written texts and are particularly powerful because of their wide applicability to many sorts of reading" (2010b, p. 33). These words can be particularly challenging because their meanings vary based on the context in which they are used (e.g., *His fate was pre-determined. His determination spurred him on to win the award. The determining factor to his acceptance was his qualifications.*). If students cannot ascertain the meaning of academic words in context, teachers should offer support for these words when students require it. Teachers need to target academic vocabulary worthy of mastering and produce or obtain aligned materials so students can successfully expand their reading capacity as they advance through the grades.

UNDERSTANDING FICTION AND NONFICTION CHARACTERISTICS

With the CC Standards for the reading strand divided by literature and informational text and with attention to the latter text type, it is worthwhile for educators to have a clear definition of informational text. Furthermore, categorizing the different types or genres of literature makes the distinction among them clear.

Literature can be in prose or poetry form. *Prose* is standard written literature—which encompasses both fiction and nonfiction—and plays. Literature in verse form is referred to as *poetry*. All literature can be classified into two types: fiction and nonfiction. Fictional literature or narrative literary works contain content that is produced by the imagination and is not necessarily based on fact. It includes the five elements of literature: *setting, character, plot, point of view,* and *theme.* Some include *conflict* as part of these elements, but I include it with plot. Plot elements are represented by an inverted checkmark and include *introduction* (optional), *central conflict, rising action* (or *complications*), *climax* (or *crisis*), *falling action,* and *resolution* (or *denouement*). Fictional selections and some nonfiction also include a variety of literary elements, such as *foreshadowing, dialect, satire, irony, symbolism, tone,* and *mood,* as well as figurative language (e.g., *metaphor, simile, imagery*). In some instructional sources, I see a merging together of the aforementioned into one ball of wax; however, I prefer teaching to each of these three categories: (1) elements of literature (including plot elements), (2) literary devices, and (3) figurative language.

Nonfiction is an umbrella term that encompasses informational text. Biography, autobiography, and memoir are also considered nonfiction because they are predicated on known facts even if there are some instances where an author includes some fictional features such as setting or characterization. Autobiographies are written by a noteworthy person who writes his or her life story. Memoirs, also self-written, highlight a particular time or event of an individual's life (e.g., catastrophic event, winning an award, etc.). Nonfiction literature is opposite from fiction because text that falls under this category is informative and can include facts, details, anecdotes, and examples with analysis and illustrations. In addition, nonfiction can include features, such as a table of contents, glossary, index, captions, bold and italicized type, graphic aids like charts or diagrams, and so forth.

In the Common Core Standards, informational text is a focal point, so I want to be clear about what it encompasses. As stated in the "Revised Publishers' Criteria for the Common Core State Standards in English Language Arts and Literacy, Grades 3–12," Coleman and Pimentel state: "The Common Core State Standards require aligned ELA curriculum materials in grades 6–12 to include a blend of literature (fiction, poetry, and drama) and a substantial sampling of literary nonfiction, including essays, speeches, opinion pieces, biographies, journalism, and historical, scientific, or other documents written for a broad audience. . . . The standards emphasize arguments (such as those in the U.S. foundational documents) and other literary nonfiction that is built on informational text structures rather than literary nonfiction that is structured as stories (such as memoirs or biographies)" (2012, p. 5). No matter what grade you teach, the characteristics of informational text remain constant. In their book *Reading & Writing Informational Text in the Primary Grades,* Nell K. Duke and V. Susan Bennett-Armistead (2003) state that informational text has these distinctions:

- The primary purpose is to convey information about the natural and social world.
- It typically has characteristic features such as addressing whole classes of things in a timeless way that make these texts have a generalizing quality (e.g., *Sharks live in water; Objects appear in space*).
- The text comes in many different formats, including books, magazines, handouts, brochures, CD-ROMs, or an article from the Internet.
- The text may include a repetition of a topic or theme; descriptions of attributes; a compare/contrast or classification structure; technical vocabulary; realistic illustrations or photographs; labels and captions; navigational aids such as indexes, page numbers, and headings; and graphical devices such as diagrams, tables, and charts.

People read all types of informational texts that span an array of interest areas. Think of what you read and your purpose for doing so. If you are seeking ideas or facts about a topic hoping to glean information about what interests you or for research purposes, then you turn to an informational text. That might be a newspaper or magazine article, website with statistical information, or chapter book. So not only does informational text come in different formats and cross all sorts of terrain—geology, sports, animals, religion, politics, astronomy, sewing—it is organized in a variety of ways, too. Each source you use to collect information can be organized differently, such as comparison and contrast, cause and effect, sequential, description, or a combination of these structures. Depending upon what content area and grade you teach, you will expose students to specific types of informational text, such as science lab reports, legal documents, historical journals, literary analyses, research papers, automotive manuals, and so forth. Figure 1.2 provides examples of each text type and various formats; however, do not consider these lists finite. Students should be exposed to a variety of nonfiction literature with attention paid, particularly in the upper grades, to different types of informational formats across content areas.

DEFINITIONS OF THE COMMON CORE TEXT TYPES AND SAMPLE PROMPTS

Now let's move our attention from the reading strand to writing. Before grouping the standards, it is important to be familiar with the three different writing types emphasized in the CCSS so you can plan curriculum around them. Later in the book, when you focus on assessments, you can revisit the examples in this section to help you create writing assignments.

1. Opinion/argument

2. Informative/explanatory

3. Narrative

The Common Core Standards align with the National Assessment of Educational Progress framework that features a distribution of types of student writing for Grades K–12, as shown in Figure 1.3. As is evident, the emphasis is on argument and informational/explanation writing.

What follows is an explanation of these genres and some ideas for assignments tied to them that can help you get a better handle on these writing standards. But I forewarn you that they can be a bit confusing, so discuss and collaborate with colleagues to get a consensus on clear expectations for students. As the authors of Fordham Institute's "The State of State Standards—and the Common Core—in 2010" (Carmichael et al., 2010) assert, "One troublesome aspect of the writing standards is the persistently blurry line between an 'argument' and an 'informational/explanatory essay'" (p. 26). The authors of the Fordham Institute document admit that appended materials might provide some clarity but, in the end, state that "these new definitions are likely to confuse teachers, curriculum developers, and publishers" (p. 26). Appendix A of the Common Core Standards (National Governors Association [NGA], 2010b, pp. 23–24) provides a brief explanation of each genre, which I will share in this chapter and on which I will provide further elaboration to assist you in distinguishing one

Types and Formats of Fiction and Nonfiction

Fictional Literature (or Narrative Literature)	
Types	**Formats**
animal tales (fables, trickster tales, pourquoi)	chapter book
fairy tales	graphic novel
legends	novel
myths	novella
fantasy	picture book
historical fiction	play
mystery	short story
science fiction	
realistic fiction	
drama/plays	

Nonfiction (or Narrative Nonfiction or Literary Nonfiction)			
Types	**Formats**		
biography	chapter book	journal/diary	picture book
autobiography	feature story	photo essay	play
memoir			
informational	almanac	flyer/handout	observational notes
	book of statistics	Internet website	pamphlet
	brochure	journal/diary	photo essay
	CD-ROM	letter	picture book
	chapter book	magazine article	report
	encyclopedia	newspaper article	speech
	essay	technical manual	textbook
	field guide		

FIGURE 1.2

Distribution of Communicative Purposes

Grade	To Persuade	To Explain	To Convey Experience
4	30%	35%	35%
8	35%	35%	30%
12	40%	40%	20%

FIGURE 1.3

Source: National Assessment Governing Board (2008).

text type from another. Student writing examples are included in the Common Core's Appendix C; see my section "A Closer Look at Appendix C: Samples of Student Writing" in this chapter for a commentary.

There are instances in which text types are combined in a particular writing exercise, so when you group standards, you need to be mindful of this overlap. For example, a short story assignment would largely fall under the narrative realm. However, within the short story, students might create paragraphs that describe characters using the expository construction of topic sentence and supporting details found in an informational/explanatory text. Such a paragraph can begin with a topic sentence—*Mr. Hudson is a selfish man who cares only for himself*—and continue with pertinent information to support this impression: *When dining among company, he selects the choicest fare first and hastily grabs the last morsels left on a serving platter. At holiday time, despite his wealth, he purchases inexpensive items for others and expects costly gifts in return.* In fact, the Common Core raises this point and states that skilled writers oftentimes do blend the three text genres for a particular purpose, so it is important to be aware of this as you read further about the writing applications.

To begin, take a look at Figure 1.4, "ELA Common Core State Standards for Writing and Research: 5–12," which is a reformatted version of the writing and research standards (2010a) and can also be viewed and downloaded from the companion website to this book (http://www.corwin.com/mappingela6-12). It includes the exact writing standards by text type in linear fashion, so you can see the progression from grade to grade for each isolated genre. Grade 5 is included so that sixth-grade teachers know the expectations for the year prior to theirs. I also include research standards, since students should conduct research to provide evidence for their opinion/argument and informative/explanatory writing.

What Do Argument Texts Entail?

The Common Core calls for students to write opinion pieces in Grades K–5, preparing them for argument writing in Grades 6–12. This contrasts with some state standards, where this kind of writing is not expected until Grade 3 or later.

Many of you are familiar with persuasive writing, which is akin to—but not to be confused with—argumentation. Argument writing is predicated on clear reasons and relevant evidence and not on emotional appeal. The Common Core authors provide a distinction between persuasion and argument in Appendix A (2010b, pp. 23–24), which reads, in part, "A logical argument . . . convinces the audience because of the perceived merit and reasonableness of the claims and proofs offered rather than either the emotions the writing evokes in the audience or the character or credentials of the writer." To gain a better understanding of this text type, read the following:

- The "Opinion Pieces and Arguments" section of Figure 1.4, which shows a progression of these standards from grade to grade
- The "Research to Build and Present Knowledge" section of Figure 1.4 because students can gather research for their evidence in an argument
- Figure 1.5, "Definition and Application of Text Type: Argument," an excerpt from Appendix A of the Common Core that features a snapshot of the text type

The emphasis of this Common Core text type really picks up steam for students in middle and high school as they move from opinion pieces to argumentation in an effort to aptly

ELA Common Core State Standards for Writing and Research 5–12

Text Types and Purposes

	I. Opinion Pieces and Arguments
Grade 5	1. Write *opinion pieces* on topics or texts, supporting a point of view with reasons and information. a. Introduce topic or text clearly, state an opinion, and create an organizational structure in which ideas are logically grouped to support the writer's purpose. b. Provide logically ordered reasons that are supported by facts and details. c. Link opinion and reasons using words, phrases, and clauses. d. Provide a concluding statement or section related to the opinion presented.
Grade 6	1. Write *arguments* to support claims with clear reasons and relevant evidence. a. Introduce claim(s) and organize the reasons and evidence clearly. b. Support claim(s) with clear reasons and relevant evidence, using credible sources and demonstrating an understanding of the topic or text. c. Use words, phrases, and clauses to clarify the relationships among claim(s) and reasons. d. Establish and maintain a formal style. e. Provide a concluding statement or section that follows from the argument presented.
Grade 7	1. Write *arguments* to support claims with clear reasons and relevant evidence. a. Introduce claim(s), acknowledge alternate or opposing claim(s), and organize the reasons and evidence logically. b. Support claim(s) with logical reasoning and relevant evidence, using accurate, credible sources and demonstrating an understanding of the topic or text. c. Use words, phrases, and clauses to create cohesion and clarify the relationships among claim(s), reasons, and evidence. d. Establish and maintain a formal style. e. Provide a concluding statement or section that follows from and supports the argument presented.
Grade 8	1. Write *arguments* to support claims with clear reasons and relevant evidence. a. Introduce claim(s), acknowledge and distinguish the claim(s) from alternate or opposing claim(s), and organize the reasons and evidence logically. b. Support claim(s) with logical reasoning and relevant evidence, using accurate, credible sources and demonstrating an understanding of the topic or text.

FIGURE 1.4 *(Continued)*

FIGURE 1.4 (Continued)

	I. Opinion Pieces and Arguments
	c. Use words, phrases, and clauses to create cohesion and clarify the relationships among claim(s), counterclaims, reasons, and evidence. d. Establish and maintain a formal style. e. Provide a concluding statement or section that follows from and supports the argument presented.
Grades 9–10	1. Write **arguments** to support claims in an analysis of substantive topics or texts, using valid reasoning and relevant and sufficient evidence. a. Introduce precise claim(s), distinguish the claim(s) from alternate or opposing claims, and create an organization that establishes clear relationships among claim(s), counterclaims, reasons, and evidence. b. Develop claim(s) and counterclaims fairly, supplying evidence for each while pointing out the strengths and limitations of both in a manner that anticipates the audience's knowledge level and concerns. c. Use words, phrases, and clauses to link the major sections of the text, create cohesion, and clarify the relationships between claim(s) and reasons, between reasons and evidence, and between claim(s) and counterclaims. d. Establish and maintain a formal style and objective tone while attending to the norms and conventions of the discipline in which they are writing. e. Provide a concluding statement or section that follows from and supports the argument presented.
Grades 11–12	1. Write **arguments** to support claims in an analysis of substantive topics or texts, using valid reasoning and relevant and sufficient evidence. a. Introduce precise, knowledgeable claim(s), establish the significance of the claim(s), distinguish the claim(s) from alternate or opposing claims, and create an organization that logically sequences claim(s), counterclaims, reasons, and evidence. b. Develop claim(s) and counterclaims fairly and thoroughly, supplying the most relevant evidence for each while pointing out the strengths and limitations of both in a manner that anticipates the audience's knowledge level, concerns, values, and possible biases. c. Use words, phrases, and clauses as well as varied syntax to link the major sections of the text, create cohesion, and clarify the relationships between claim(s) and reasons, between reasons and evidence, and between claim(s) and counterclaims. d. Establish and maintain a formal style and objective tone while attending to the norms and conventions of the discipline in which they are writing. e. Provide a concluding statement or section that follows from and supports the argument presented.

Text Types and Purposes

	2. Informative/Explanatory Texts
Grade 5	2. Write *informative/explanatory texts* to examine a topic and convey ideas and information clearly. a. Introduce a topic clearly, provide a general observation and focus, and group related information logically; include formatting (e.g., headings), illustrations, and multimedia when useful to aiding comprehension. b. Develop a topic with facts, definitions, concrete details, quotations, or other information and examples related to the topic. c. Link ideas within and across categories of information using words, phrases, and clauses. d. Use precise language and domain-specific vocabulary to inform about or explain the topic. e. Provide a concluding statement or section related to the information or explanation presented.
Grade 6	2. Write *informative/explanatory* texts to examine a topic and convey ideas, concepts, and information through the selection, organization, and analysis of relevant content. a. Introduce a topic; organize ideas, concepts, and information, using strategies such as definition, classification, comparison/contrast, and cause/effect; include formatting (e.g., headings), graphics (e.g., charts, tables), and multimedia when useful to aiding comprehension. b. Develop the topic with relevant facts, definitions, concrete details, quotations, or other information and examples. c. Use appropriate transitions to clarify the relationships among ideas and concepts. d. Use precise language and domain-specific vocabulary to inform about or explain the topic. e. Establish and maintain a formal style. f. Provide a concluding statement or section that follows from the information or explanation presented.
Grade 7	2. Write *informative/explanatory* texts to examine a topic and convey ideas, concepts, and information through the selection, organization, and analysis of relevant content. a. Introduce a topic clearly, previewing what is to follow; organize ideas, concepts, and information, using strategies such as definition, classification, comparison/contrast, and cause/effect; include formatting (e.g., headings), graphics (e.g., charts, tables), and multimedia when useful to aiding comprehension. b. Develop the topic with relevant facts, definitions, concrete details, quotations, or other information and examples. c. Use appropriate transitions to create cohesion and clarify the relationships among ideas and concepts. d. Use precise language and domain-specific vocabulary to inform about or explain the topic. e. Establish and maintain a formal style. f. Provide a concluding statement or section that follows from and supports the information or explanation presented.

FIGURE 1.4 (*Continued*)

FIGURE 1.4 (Continued)

	2. Informative/Explanatory Texts
Grade 8	2. Write **informative/explanatory** texts to examine a topic and convey ideas, concepts, and information through the selection, organization, and analysis of relevant content. a. Introduce a topic clearly, previewing what is to follow; organize ideas, concepts, and information into broader categories; include formatting (e.g., headings), graphics (e.g., charts, tables), and multimedia when useful to aiding comprehension. b. Develop the topic with relevant, well-chosen facts, definitions, concrete details, quotations, or other information and examples. c. Use appropriate and varied transitions to create cohesion and clarify the relationships among ideas and concepts. d. Use precise language and domain-specific vocabulary to inform about or explain the topic. e. Establish and maintain a formal style. f. Provide a concluding statement or section that follows from and supports the information or explanation presented.
Grades 9–10	2. Write **informative/explanatory** texts to examine and convey complex ideas, concepts, and information clearly and accurately through the effective selection, organization, and analysis of content. a. Introduce a topic; organize complex ideas, concepts, and information to make important connections and distinctions; include formatting (e.g., headings), graphics (e.g., figures, tables), and multimedia when useful to aiding comprehension. b. Develop the topic with well-chosen, relevant, and sufficient facts, extended definitions, concrete details, quotations, or other information and examples appropriate to the audience's knowledge of the topic. c. Use appropriate and varied transitions to link the major sections of the text, create cohesion, and clarify the relationships among complex ideas and concepts. d. Use precise language and domain-specific vocabulary to manage the complexity of the topic. e. Establish and maintain a formal style and objective tone while attending to the norms and conventions of the discipline in which they are writing. f. Provide a concluding statement or section that follows from and supports the information or explanation presented (e.g., articulating implications or the significance of the topic).
Grades 11–12	2. Write **informative/explanatory** texts to examine and convey complex ideas, concepts, and information clearly and accurately through the effective selection, organization, and analysis of content. a. Introduce a topic; organize complex ideas, concepts, and information so that each new element builds on that which precedes it to create a unified whole; include formatting (e.g., headings), graphics (e.g., figures, tables), and multimedia when useful to aiding comprehension. b. Develop the topic thoroughly by selecting the most significant and relevant facts, extended definitions, concrete details, quotations, or other information and examples appropriate to the audience's knowledge of the topic.

2. Informative/Explanatory Texts

c. Use appropriate and varied transitions and syntax to link the major sections of the text, create cohesion, and clarify the relationships among complex ideas and concepts.

d. Use precise language, domain-specific vocabulary, and techniques such as metaphor, simile, and analogy to manage the complexity of the topic.

e. Establish and maintain a formal style and objective tone while attending to the norms and conventions of the discipline in which they are writing.

f. Provide a concluding statement or section that follows from and supports the information or explanation presented (e.g., articulating implications or the significance of the topic).

◆
◆
◆
◆
◆
◆

Text Types and Purposes

3. Narratives

Grade 5

3. Write *narratives* to develop real or imagined experiences or events using effective technique, descriptive details, and clear event sequences.

a. Orient the reader by establishing a situation and introducing a narrator and/or characters; organize an event sequence that unfolds naturally.

b. Use narrative techniques, such as dialogue, description, and pacing, to develop experiences and events or show the responses of characters to situations.

c. Use a variety of transitional words, phrases, and clauses to manage the sequence of events.

d. Use concrete words and phrases and sensory details to convey experiences and events precisely.

e. Provide a conclusion that follows from the narrated experiences or events.

Grade 6

3. Write *narratives* to develop real or imagined experiences or events using effective technique, relevant descriptive details, and well-structured event sequences.

a. Engage and orient the reader by establishing a context and introducing a narrator and/or characters; organize an event sequence that unfolds naturally and logically.

b. Use narrative techniques, such as dialogue, pacing, and description, to develop experiences, events, and/or characters.

FIGURE 1.4 (*Continued*)

FIGURE 1.4 (Continued)

	3. Narratives
	c. Use a variety of transition words, phrases, and clauses to convey sequence and signal shifts from one time frame or setting to another.
	d. Use precise words and phrases, relevant descriptive details, and sensory language to convey experiences and events.
	e. Provide a conclusion that follows from the narrated experiences or events.
Grade 7	3. Write *narratives* to develop real or imagined experiences or events using effective technique, relevant descriptive details, and well-structured event sequences.
	a. Engage and orient the reader by establishing a context and point of view and introducing a narrator and/or characters; organize an event sequence that unfolds naturally and logically.
	b. Use narrative techniques, such as dialogue, pacing, and description, to develop experiences, events, and/or characters.
	c. Use a variety of transition words, phrases, and clauses to convey sequence and signal shifts from one time frame or setting to another.
	d. Use precise words and phrases, relevant descriptive details, and sensory language to capture the action and convey experiences and events.
	e. Provide a conclusion that follows from and reflects on the narrated experiences or events.
Grade 8	3. Write *narratives* to develop real or imagined experiences or events using effective technique, relevant descriptive details, and well-structured event sequences.
	a. Engage and orient the reader by establishing a context and point of view and introducing a narrator and/or characters; organize an event sequence that unfolds naturally and logically.
	b. Use narrative techniques, such as dialogue, pacing, description, and reflection, to develop experiences, events, and/or characters.
	c. Use a variety of transition words, phrases, and clauses to convey sequence, signal shifts from one time frame or setting to another, and show the relationships among experiences and events.
	d. Use precise words and phrases, relevant descriptive details, and sensory language to capture the action and convey experiences and events.
	e. Provide a conclusion that follows from and reflects on the narrated experiences or events.
Grades 9–10	3. Write *narratives* to develop real or imagined experiences or events using effective technique, well-chosen details, and well-structured event sequences.
	a. Engage and orient the reader by setting out a problem, situation, or observation, establishing one or multiple point(s) of view, and introducing a narrator and/or characters; create a smooth progression of experiences or events.
	b. Use narrative techniques, such as dialogue, pacing, description, reflection, and multiple plot lines, to develop experiences, events, and/or characters.
	c. Use a variety of techniques to sequence events so that they build on one another to create a coherent whole.
	d. Use precise words and phrases, telling details, and sensory language to convey a vivid picture of the experiences, events, setting, and/or characters.
	e. Provide a conclusion that follows from and reflects on what is experienced, observed, or resolved over the course of the narrative.

	3. Narratives
Grades 11–12	3. Write **narratives** to develop real or imagined experiences or events using effective technique, well-chosen details, and well-structured event sequences. a. Engage and orient the reader by setting out a problem, situation, or observation and its significance, establishing one or multiple point(s) of view, and introducing a narrator and/or characters; create a smooth progression of experiences or events. b. Use narrative techniques, such as dialogue, pacing, description, reflection, and multiple plot lines, to develop experiences, events, and/or characters. c. Use a variety of techniques to sequence events so that they build on one another to create a coherent whole and build toward a particular tone and outcome (e.g., a sense of mystery, suspense, growth, or resolution). d. Use precise words and phrases, telling details, and sensory language to convey a vivid picture of the experiences, events, setting, and/or characters. e. Provide a conclusion that follows from and reflects on what is experienced, observed, or resolved over the course of the narrative.

◆

◆

◆

◆

◆

◆

Research to Build and Present Knowledge

Grade 5	7. Conduct short research projects that use several sources to build knowledge through investigation of different aspects of a topic. 8. Recall relevant information from experiences or gather relevant information from print and digital sources; summarize or paraphrase information in notes and finished work, and provide a list of sources. 9. Draw evidence from literary or informational texts to support analysis, reflection, and research. a. Apply Grade 5 Reading standards to literature (e.g., "Compare and contrast two or more characters, settings, or events in a story or a drama, drawing on specific details in the text [e.g., how characters interact]"). b. Apply Grade 5 Reading standards to informational texts (e.g., "Explain how an author uses reasons and evidence to support particular points in a text, identifying which reasons and evidence support which point[s]").
Grade 6	7. Conduct short research projects to answer a question, drawing on several sources and refocusing the inquiry when appropriate. 8. Gather relevant information from multiple print and digital sources; assess the credibility of each source; and quote or paraphrase the data and conclusions of others while avoiding plagiarism and providing basic bibliographic information for sources.

FIGURE 1.4 *(Continued)*

19

FIGURE 1.4 (Continued)

	9. Draw evidence from literary or informational texts to support analysis, reflection, and research.
	a. Apply Grade 6 Reading standards to literature (e.g., "Compare and contrast texts in different forms or genres [e.g., stories and poems; historical novels and fantasy stories] in terms of their approaches to similar themes and topics").
	b. Apply Grade 6 Reading standards to literary nonfiction (e.g., "Trace and evaluate the argument and specific claims in a text, distinguishing claims that are supported by reasons and evidence from claims that are not").
Grade 7	7. Conduct short research projects to answer a question, drawing on several sources and generating additional related, focused questions for further research and investigation.
	8. Gather relevant information from multiple print and digital sources, using search terms effectively; assess the credibility and accuracy of each source; and quote or paraphrase the data and conclusions of others while avoiding plagiarism and following a standard format for citation.
	9. Draw evidence from literary or informational texts to support analysis, reflection, and research.
	a. Apply Grade 7 Reading standards to literature (e.g., "Compare and contrast a fictional portrayal of a time, place, or character and a historical account of the same period as a means of understanding how authors of fiction use or alter history").
	b. Apply Grade 7 Reading standards to literary nonfiction (e.g., "Trace and evaluate the argument and specific claims in a text, assessing whether the reasoning is sound and the evidence is relevant and sufficient to support the claims").
Grade 8	7. Conduct short research projects to answer a question (including a self-generated question), drawing on several sources and generating additional related, focused questions that allow for multiple avenues of exploration.
	8. Gather relevant information from multiple print and digital sources, using search terms effectively; assess the credibility and accuracy of each source; and quote or paraphrase the data and conclusions of others while avoiding plagiarism and following a standard format for citation.
	9. Draw evidence from literary or informational texts to support analysis, reflection, and research.
	a. Apply Grade 8 Reading standards to literature (e.g., "Analyze how a modern work of fiction draws on themes, patterns of events, or character types from myths, traditional stories, or religious works such as the Bible, including describing how the material is rendered new").
	b. Apply Grade 8 Reading standards to literary nonfiction (e.g., "Delineate and evaluate the argument and specific claims in a text, assessing whether the reasoning is sound and the evidence is relevant and sufficient; recognize when irrelevant evidence is introduced").

Grades 9–10	7. Conduct short as well as more sustained research projects to answer a question (including a self-generated question) or solve a problem; narrow or broaden the inquiry when appropriate; synthesize multiple sources on the subject, demonstrating understanding of the subject under investigation.
	
	8. Gather relevant information from multiple authoritative print and digital sources, using advanced searches effectively; assess the usefulness of each source in answering the research question; integrate information into the text selectively to maintain the flow of ideas, avoiding plagiarism and following a standard format for citation.
	
	9. Draw evidence from literary or informational texts to support analysis, reflection, and research.
	
	   a. Apply Grades 9–10 Reading standards to literature (e.g., "Analyze how an author draws on and transforms source material in a specific work [e.g., how Shakespeare treats a theme or topic from Ovid or the Bible or how a later author draws on a play by Shakespeare]").
	
	   b. Apply Grades 9–10 Reading standards to literary nonfiction (e.g., "Delineate and evaluate the argument and specific claims in a text, assessing whether the reasoning is valid and the evidence is relevant and sufficient; identify false statements and fallacious reasoning").

Grades 11–12	7. Conduct short as well as more sustained research projects to answer a question (including a self-generated question) or solve a problem; narrow or broaden the inquiry when appropriate; synthesize multiple sources on the subject, demonstrating understanding of the subject under investigation.
	
	8. Gather relevant information from multiple authoritative print and digital sources, using advanced searches effectively; assess the strengths and limitations of each source in terms of the task, purpose, and audience; integrate information into the text selectively to maintain the flow of ideas, avoiding plagiarism and overreliance on any one source and following a standard format for citation.
	
	9. Draw evidence from literary or informational texts to support analysis, reflection, and research.
	
	   a. Apply Grades 11–12 Reading standards to literature (e.g., "Demonstrate knowledge of eighteenth-, nineteenth-, and early-twentieth-century foundational works of American literature, including how two or more texts from the same period treat similar themes or topics").
	
	   b. Apply Grades 11–12 Reading standards to literary nonfiction (e.g., "Delineate and evaluate the reasoning in seminal U.S. texts, including the application of constitutional principles and use of legal reasoning [e.g., in U.S. Supreme Court case majority opinions and dissents] and the premises, purposes, and arguments in works of public advocacy (e.g., *The Federalist*, presidential addresses]").

FIGURE 1.4

Definition and Application of Text Type: Argument

Definition
Arguments are used for many purposes—to change the reader's point of view, to bring about some action on the reader's part, or to ask the reader to accept the writer's explanation or evaluation of a concept, issue, or problem. An argument is a reasoned, logical way of demonstrating that the writer's position, belief, or conclusion is valid.
Grades K–5 Writing Applications
Although young children are not able to produce fully developed logical arguments, they develop a variety of methods to extend and elaborate their work by providing examples, offering reasons for their assertions, and explaining cause and effect. These kinds of expository structures are steps on the road to argument. In Grades K–5, the term *opinion* is used to refer to this developing form of argument.
Grades 6–12 Writing Applications
<ul><li>In English language arts (ELA), students make claims about the worth or meaning of a literary work or works. They defend their interpretations or judgments with evidence from the text(s) they are writing about.</li><li>In history/social studies, students analyze evidence from multiple primary and secondary sources to advance a claim that is best supported by the evidence, and they argue for a historically or empirically situated interpretation.</li><li>In science, students make claims in the form of statements or conclusions that answer questions or address problems. Using data in a scientifically acceptable form, students marshal evidence and draw on their understanding of scientific concepts to argue in support of their claims.</li></ul>

FIGURE 1.5

prepare them for college and careers. In Grades 7 and beyond, counterclaims are included as an element of a logical argument. Appendix A devotes a full page subtitled "The Special Place of Argument in the Standards" (2010b, p. 24) so that educators are aware of the research that states the critical value of argument not only in writing, but also in oral communication. After quoting several academics and theorists who assert that argument is paramount to college and career success, the authors of the Common Core conclude the section with this statement: "The value of effective argument extends well beyond the classroom or workplace. . . . Such capacities are broadly important for the literate, educated person living in the diverse, information-rich environment of the twenty-first century" (2010b, p. 25). It is also included in the Standards for Literacy in History/Social Studies, Science, and Technical Subjects, Grades 6–12. Therefore, students are expected to write an argument not only in language arts classes, but also across the content areas.

Arguments can be written in a wide variety of forms. They can be a book or film review, a petition, or a persuasive essay, speech, or letter. In Appendix C, there are seven samples of arguments written by students from Grades 6–12 that illustrate different forms argument can take. See my section "A Closer Look at Appendix C: Samples of Student Writing" in this chapter for commentary about the student samples in general.

A literary analysis, critique, or response to literature can also fall under the argument domain. When I taught or collaborated with others on response to literature, we didn't emphasize argumentation, which meant it was more an informational/explanatory essay. If, however, you would like to invite students to write a literary response aligned to argument, merely make it central to the writing focus. For example, students stake a claim about a theme that they feel emanates from a text and use evidence from the literature to support their assertion using a persuasive lens; or they argue that a character's attitudes fuel other characters' actions that ultimately shape the plot.

The CCSS ask that literacy skills be taught across the curriculum. To develop argument writing skills in science or social studies, students can take a stand about a controversial issue or topic and use textual evidence from primary and secondary sources to support their positions and address counterarguments. As appropriate for your student population and grade level, include rhetorical styles originating from the Greek philosopher Aristotle— *ethos, pathos, logos.* Particularly emphasize logos (logical appeal) for argumentation, as it is the means of persuasion through reasoning. In this realm, you can address deductive and inductive reasoning, as well as logical fallacies (e.g., hasty generalizations, either/or, over-simplification, etc.).

When you begin to design assessments, which are discussed in later chapters, you might decide to use one from Figure 1.6 that follows. If you do, make sure to incorporate the selected prompt within your targeted unit as opposed to assigning it in isolation. For example, when teaching a unit on ancient China, use the first social studies prompt and personalize it for this Asian civilization. For the second social studies prompt, first work with students to brainstorm a list of leaders involved in the unit you are studying, such as the Civil War (e.g., Jefferson Davis, Abraham Lincoln, Stephen Douglas, Charles Summer, Robert E. Lee, "Stonewall" Jackson, Ulysses S. Grant, Harriet Beecher Stowe, Frederick Douglass, etc.). Then, when you ask students to respond to the prompt, it will be folded into your unit goals. You might even use some of these prompts as oral exercises as a precursor to writing that focuses on an element of argument. Use this same concept of avoiding assigning remote prompts that don't have a connection to your curriculum to the other text types, as well.

Writing Prompts for Arguments

Social Studies	Various civilizations are credited with inventions that have served their people in history and have had lasting contributions even to today. Write an argument about an invention from the past that you think is the most useful today. Use credible informational texts to support your position with valid reasoning and relevant and sufficient evidence.
	Identify a leader who you think has made the most significant impact. Write a paper in which you provide a sound argument with clear reasons and relevant evidence. Use informational texts to support your argument, plus acknowledge and address counterclaims.

FIGURE 1.6 (*Continued*)

FIGURE 1.6 (Continued)

Social Studies	For a unit on the causes of the American Revolution, write an argument from the standpoint of a Tory, Loyalist, or Neutralist, persuading others to adopt this view. Use facts and examples from informational texts to support your position.
	Write a letter from the viewpoint of Native Americans to the president or settlers. In the letter, use evidence from informational texts to explain how you have been treated by the settlers who have tried to force you from your land. Include your cultural perspective on land usage and rights.
Science	Humans influence other species—for instance, through land use and pollution. Write an argument from the point of view of a species that is affected by humans. State your position and use evidence from informational text to defend your points. Include counterarguments from a human perspective and the weaknesses in them according to your chosen species.
	Write a letter to a politician in a foreign country arguing for actions to be taken to prevent the spread of infectious disease and the ramifications of inaction. Research to determine a country that could benefit from your letter. Include evidence from informational texts related to your topic that support your argument (e.g., viral/ bacterial transmission, vaccination programs, sanitation projects, mortality/morbidity rates, etc.).
	Conduct a peer review in which you evaluate the results of a scientific investigation. Analyze the procedures used, examine the evidence, and identify faulty reasoning using substantiated evidence to defend your position. Additionally, provide other explanations that could be made based on the investigation.
	Consider any of these questions as the basis for an argument. Use informational text to support your position: *Should sports figures be allowed to use steroids? Should there be a ban on using animals for testing chemicals and drugs? Is it okay to modify the environment for our benefit? Should the government spend money on space exploration? Why should schools include physical education and recess as part of the school day?*
Language Arts	Read a novel and watch a movie or play adaptation of it (e.g., *A Midsummer Night's Dream, Little Women, Anne Frank: The Diary of a Young Girl*). Write a critique in which you defend a claim about the literary form you prefer. Use details from both the book and movie or play to support your position.
	Read Mildred Taylor's *Roll of Thunder, Hear My Cry* or *The Land* or *Let the Circle Be Unbroken* and related informational text (e.g., racism, civil rights, inequality). State a claim about the theme of the text, and defend interpretations and judgments through evidence from the novel and historically significant informational text.
	Write a persuasive letter from the point of view of a character in one story to another character in the same story (or in another book) about something controversial that you did. Persuade this character that your actions were wise, and defend this position using details from the literary selection and other sources, as appropriate.
	Choose a form of figurative language (e.g., simile, metaphor, imagery, personification) and write from this perspective defending how your form is more effective than another type of figurative language. To defend your position, use evidence from a variety of literary works. Include a counterargument by acknowledging and addressing other forms of figurative language that might disagree with you.

Other	**Music.** After listening to a variety of musical works, choose a selection that provokes a reaction in you. Write a music review articulating your opinion on how this piece strongly moved you positively or negatively. Convince others of your position using appropriate elements of music (e.g., instrumentation, lyrics, dynamics, rhythm).
	Dance. Critique several dance performances and write a review about one in particular. Use vocabulary and concepts to discuss style, structure, and design to support your preference.
	Physical education. Read about various consumer physical fitness products or programs. Select one that you feel is optimal for good health. Defend your position by using sound reasoning and relevant evidence about fitness concepts and principles from informational text.

FIGURE 1.6

What Do Informative/Explanatory Texts Entail?

This writing type seems quite broad and can encompass myriad possibilities as students write to inform and explain in a variety of formats. For an overview, see the following excerpt in Figure 1.7, reprinted from Appendix A of the Common Core Standards, plus the grade-to-grade progressive view in the "Informative/Explanatory Texts" section of Figure 1.4. Also note "Research to Build and Present Knowledge" from Figure 1.4 because this writing can call upon students to research primary and secondary sources to cull examples, facts, definitions, quotes, and concrete details depending upon the grade.

Definition and Application of Text Type: Informative/Explanatory

Definition
Informational/explanatory writing conveys information accurately. This kind of writing serves one or more closely related purposes: to increase readers' knowledge of a subject, to help readers better understand a procedure or process, or to provide readers with an enhanced comprehension of a concept. To produce this kind of writing, students draw from what they already know and from primary and secondary sources. With practice, students become better able to develop a controlling idea and a coherent focus on a topic and more skilled at selecting and incorporating relevant examples, facts, and details into their writing. They are also able to use a variety of techniques to convey information, such as naming, defining, describing, or differentiating different types or parts; comparing or contrasting ideas or concepts; and citing an anecdote or a scenario to illustrate a point.

FIGURE 1.7 *(Continued)*

FIGURE 1.7 (Continued)

Writing Applications
Informational/explanatory writing addresses matters such as the following: • ***Types*** (What are the different types of poetry?) • ***Components*** (What are the parts of a motor?) • ***Size, function, or behavior*** (How big is the United States? What is an X-ray used for? How do penguins find food?) • ***How things work*** (How does the legislative branch of government function?) • ***Why things happen*** (Why do some authors blend genres?) Informational/explanatory writing includes a wide array of genres, including academic genres such as literary analyses, scientific and historical reports, summaries, and précis writing as well as forms of workplace and functional writing such as instructions, manuals, memos, reports, applications, and resumes. As students advance through the grades, they expand their repertoire of informational/explanatory genres and use them effectively in a variety of disciplines and domains.

FIGURE 1.7

The subtle differences between argument and informative/exploratory writing can be confusing between the two genres. The authors of the Common Core seem to have anticipated this; they provide the synopsis that follows in Figure 1.8 to help make the differences between the two easier to understand.

Argument and Explanation Text Types

Although information is provided in both arguments and explanations, the two types of writing have different aims.

• Arguments seek to make people believe that something is true or to persuade people to change their beliefs or behavior. Explanations, on the other hand, start with the assumption of truthfulness and answer questions about why or how. Their aim is to make the reader understand rather than to persuade him or her to accept a certain point of view. In short, arguments are used for persuasion and explanations for clarification.

• Like arguments, explanations provide information about causes, contexts, and consequences of processes, phenomena, states of affairs, objects, terminology, and so on. However, in an argument, the writer not only gives information but also presents a case with the "pros" (supporting ideas) and "cons" (opposing ideas) on a debatable issue. Because an argument deals with whether the main claim is true, it demands empirical descriptive evidence, statistics, or definitions for support. When writing an argument, the writer supports his or her claim(s) with sound reasoning and relevant and sufficient evidence.

FIGURE 1.8

Student writing samples for informative/explanatory writing (see Common Core Appendix C, 2010d) for Grades 6–12 include a research report, topical essays, process or procedural essays, literary analyses, a summary, and a short, constructed response. I highly recommend reviewing these samples to get a better understanding of the types of informative/ explanatory papers the designers endorse. Additionally, read my comments in this chapter's "A Closer Look at Appendix C: Samples of Students Writing" so you can view these student samples with a keener eye since they do not all represent stellar work.

In addition, informative/exploratory writing can include essays or reports that compare and contrast, explore a problem and solution, or describe cause and effect. The following list provides some other examples of informative/explanatory writing across content areas:

- *Types.* What are the different types of governments? Communities? Habitats? Rocks? Renewable energy? Leaders? Carbohydrates? String instruments? Musical genres? Maps? Bodies of water? Religions?
- *Components.* What are the parts of a plant? Cell? Government? Sentence? Culture?
- *Size, function, or behavior.* What is the size of our country? Oceans? Molecules? House of Representatives? What is a compass used for? Telescope? Microscope? How do an animal's physical traits help it to survive? How do people use natural resources to survive? How do the different forms of matter change from one form to another? How can people learn tolerance? How does the evolution and spread of religion create cultural diffusion?
- *How things work.* How does the system of checks and balances work? How does a law get passed? How does gravity influence the motion of celestial objects? How do infectious diseases spread? How do authors' choice of setting, words, images, and details convey tone? How does the digestive system work? How does the writing process improve an author's work?
- *Why things happen.* Why do natural events (e.g., floods, earthquakes, tornadoes) occur? Why do groups enter into conflict? Why do people persecute or take advantage of vulnerable populations? Why do civilizations fall? Why do characters change over time?

Some categories could prove worthwhile for a thought-provoking literary analysis assignment, as well. You could tailor any of these general questions to align with a particular drama, novel, or short story and instruct students to use textual evidence as support:

- *How do historical settings impact characters?*
- *How do characters behave who are selfish, compassionate, or humble?*
- *How does a character's behavior impact the plot (or other characters)?*
- *How and why do characters change over time?*
- *How does a narrator's point of view influence readers?*
- *Why does the author choose a particular literary device?*

The possibilities are vast. You might have students compare and contrast characters, settings, or themes across various works. You could extract a salient quote from the text and have students interpret or respond to it. Or you might ask students to change or invent a new setting and describe how the story would be different. Whatever writing you assign, students should use textual references for support. Clearly articulate the purpose of the writing and your expectations via a checklist or rubric prior to students beginning their tasks.

What Do Narrative Texts Entail?

The Common Core authors leave it up to educators to determine other creative expressions to teach in addition to narrative writing. As such, they do not include all forms of creative writing, such as poetry, in the text types. For a better understanding of what narrative entails, read Figure 1.9, which provides an overview of this writing type and is an excerpt from Appendix A (2010b, pp. 23–24) of the Common Core document. Also, see the grade-to-grade progressive view in the "Narratives" section of Figure 1.4. Lastly, take a gander at the Grade 8 narrative student sample in Appendix C titled "Miss Sadie" (2010d, pp. 52–54). In Grades 6–12, this is the only narrative sample provided.

Typically, the purpose of narrative writing—which can be found in novels, picture books, short stories, and plays—is to entertain or describe. As shown in Figure 1.9, narratives can also inform, instruct, or persuade. The following are some possibilities to get your creative energy flowing for narrative options. When assigning any of those listed below, remember to teach students the characteristics of narrative writing, such as setting, theme, sensory details, description, and dialogue, as needed. As always, whether students are writing an argument, informative/explanatory piece, or narrative, make sure you communicate the purpose for their writing and provide a checklist or rubric for clear expectations. Later in this book, you will find explanations and samples of checklists and rubrics.

Entertain. (1) Students write a short story about a real or an imagined character to entertain readers. This story could even be a mystery, science fiction, or fantasy piece. (2) If the

Definition and Application of Text Type: Narrative

Definition
Narrative writing conveys experience, either real or imaginary, and uses time as its deep structure. It can be used for many purposes, such as to inform, instruct, persuade, or entertain.
Writing Applications
• In ELA, students produce narratives that take the form of creative fictional stories, memoirs, anecdotes, and autobiographies. Over time, they learn to provide visual details of scenes, objects, or people; to depict specific actions (for example, movements, gestures, postures, and expressions); to use dialogue and interior monologue that provide insight into the narrator's and characters' personalities and motives; and to manipulate pace to highlight the significance of events and create tension and suspense. With practice, students expand their repertoire and control of different narrative strategies.   • In history/social studies, students write narrative accounts about individuals. They also construct event models of what happened, selecting from their sources only the most relevant information.   • In science, students write narrative descriptions of the step-by-step procedures they follow in their investigations so that others can replicate their procedures and (perhaps) reach the same results.

FIGURE 1.9

short story is tied to social studies, students can base the story on a historical setting and invent characters who behave, dress, and speak in a manner true to the chosen time period. (3) Students write a creation myth that provides an explanation for phenomena such as how the sky, earth, or death came to be.

Inform. (1) Students write an eyewitness account of an event in history to inform readers of what happened during a past noteworthy incident. The writer assumes the role of someone at the actual event watching it transpire. (2) Students write a biography of a current or historical figure, a leader, or a scientist to inform others about this person's accomplishments, influences, motivations, aspirations, and so forth. (3) Students write a personal journal or letter from the perspective of anyone past or living about a topic or event or process. Figures can include a historical figure, famous dancer, influential politician, inventor, business CEO, or scientist.

Instruct. (1) Students write a procedural account about how to conduct a science experiment, play a sport, organize an event, edit a paper, create a nutritional meal, balance a checkbook, use charcoal to create an image, and so forth. (2) Students write a descriptive letter to a character in a story giving advice about what this character should do about a problem the character faces.

Persuade. (1) Students write a memoir about a significant event in their lives and include a persuasive element along with narrative features. For example, if a student recounts an experience of riding a bike without a helmet and falling down and getting injured, he or she can persuade readers about the importance of bike safety in addition to using sensory details to describe the event and emotions associated with it. Or a student can write about a personal topic such as the death of a loved one, persuading others to appreciate those close to us more and describing the personal bonds. (2) After reading literature in which a character shows poor judgment, lacks integrity, commits a crime, or injures another emotionally, students can craft a convincing letter to the character to act more appropriately.

A CLOSER LOOK AT APPENDIX C: SAMPLES OF STUDENT WRITING

Appendix C contains an inventory of thirty-four student writing samples organized by grade level and writing type that "includes annotated samples demonstrating at least adequate performance in student writing at various grade levels" (2010a, p. 3). There is not a student sample for each of the three writing types per grade. Since the Common Core focuses on argument and informational/explanatory writing in upper grades, there is only one narrative sample in Grades 6–12 (Grade 8). Preceding each sample, there is an explanation of the circumstances of writing as well as a section titled "Annotation" following each writing sample that is the basis for my discussion here.

Each Annotation lists standards for a particular writing type along with verbatim words and phrases from the students' work associated with these particular standards. However, there is no rating or scoring that shows levels of proficiencies. Therefore, it seems unclear to me how the designers want teachers to interpret these samples to inform their teaching, especially in light of these opening comments: "Each of the samples exhibits **at least** the level of quality required to meet the Writing standards for that grade" (2010d, p. 2). And "The range of accomplishment within each grade reflects **differences in individual development**. . . ." (Bold typeface is my own emphasis.) It would be helpful to get more information so we can get an intimate look at the designers' impressions of what constitutes a level of proficiency within a grade level or grade span for each writing type. Instead, the Annotation provides modest evaluative comments instead of a more thorough critique. This is surprising, since the standards raise the bar and are meant to guide teachers. Plus, this quote from Coleman and Pimentel (2012) in "Revised Publishers' Criteria for the Common Core Standards in English Language Arts and Literacy, Grades 3–12" explicitly states that exemplary writing samples are needed: "Model rubrics for writing assignments as well as high-quality student samples should also be provided as guidance to teachers" (p. 11).

The examples provided in Appendix C introduce ambiguity where clarity is sorely needed. I can imagine teachers wondering, "So is this good enough? Is this really excellent?" I will elaborate and attempt to draw some conclusions by using two Grade 8 informational/explanatory student samples from Appendix C: "Football" (2010d, p. 47) and "The Old Man and the Sea" (pp. 49–50). The comments I provide are representative of the types of comments found in both the informative/explanatory and argument writing samples. "Football," an essay written in response to a favorite activity, was produced during one class period and revised on the following day after students worked with a partner to discuss revision suggestions. The essay "The Old Man and the Sea" was the result of a homework assignment in which students were asked to write a literary analysis based on the novel with the same title. With careful examination of the Annotation sections, I found an indication of some evaluation through omission or addition of certain standards and also places where there is editorializing and acknowledgement. Without the time and attention to detail, though, I doubt that educators would spot the following observations I have made:

- In both papers, the Annotation omitted this portion of standard W.8.2a: "[I]nclude formatting (e.g., headings), graphics (e.g., charts, tables), and multimedia when useful to aiding comprehension." I assume this is an intentional omission because the teacher did not expect this part of the standard as a criteria item for these assignments.
- Standard W.8.2b reads: "Develop the topic with relevant, well-chosen facts, definitions, concrete details, quotations, or other information and examples." In the "Football" paper, the term *well-chosen* is omitted in the Annotation; however, it is included in the "Old Man and the Sea" paper. I interpret this omission in "Football" and inclusion of this phrase in the other paper to mean that the writer for the "Old Man and the Sea" paper does indeed do a far better job at meeting this standard. I concur.
- Standard W.8.2c reads: "Use appropriate and varied transitions to create cohesion and clarify the relationships among ideas and concepts." In "Football," the word *varied* was omitted; however, there is a listing of many different transitions: *At times . . . The first time . . . After a while . . . During the game . . . For example . . . On offense, while playing receiver . . .* I'm wondering why "varied" was omitted in "Football" but not in the other eighth-grade sample since they both do accomplish this expectation.
- Standard W.8.2d reads: "Use precise language and domain-specific vocabulary to inform about or explain the topic." Each Annotation for these two samples includes a series of words that indicate precise language. However, "Football" also includes weak words (i.e., *fun, things, best*) that are not mentioned. I believe an acknowledgement that weak language is used should be included in the Annotation.
- This standard that is listed—"Demonstrates command of the conventions of standard written English"—seems to be a combination of Language Standards 1 and 2 for eighth grade. For both papers, the modifier "good" is inserted before "command." This gives an indication that mastery of conventions is not considered "exemplary," a word used in the Annotation for the Grade 9 student sample.

- Furthermore, there is a parenthetical remark in both the "Football" and "Old Man" papers that reads "with **some** errors that do not interfere materially with the underlying message" and "with **occasional** errors that do not interfere materially with the underlying message," respectively. The words I put in bold typeface seem to acknowledge a degree of proficiency.
- In "Football," the following is a parenthetical remark with regard to maintaining a formal style: "with occasional lapses into cliché and undefined terms." Nothing, though, is mentioned about the writer using the second-person pronoun *you*. I realize there are some different schools of thought on using first- or third-person pronouns in formal writing. In fact, the "Old Man" paper is written from the first-person point of view, which I can now assume is condoned in the Common Core. But the second-person pronoun *you?* That is clearly pushing it for me.
- No mention of title is given; however, I discourage students from using a title for a literary analysis that is the same as the novel.

As I have discussed, there are some inconsistencies and lack of clear directions for how teachers should use the commentary. Another point to emphasize is that teachers need to understand the conditions of each writing situation. This is imperative because if teachers do not pay attention to which papers are on-demand assessments versus those that were created with more time and resources, they might be misdirected when looking at the student samples and consequently not teach in accordance with the standards' expectations. Why? Because the Common Core expressly stresses grounding assertions and information on evidence from the text: "Students cite specific evidence when offering an oral or written interpretation of a text. They use relevant evidence when supporting their own points in writing and speaking, making their reasoning clear to the reader or listener, and they constructively evaluate others' use of evidence" (2010a, p. 7). However, "Football," an informative piece of writing, and "A Pet Story About My Cat . . . Gus" (2010d, p. 38), an argument, are both based on personal reflection and insight as opposed to writing that uses and cites sources. Both of these are the product of in-class assignments with limited time and access to resources, but this wasn't clearly stated, as was the case for "Video Cameras in the Classroom" (2010d, p. 40). The introductory comments for this latter piece explicitly indicate that time was not provided for students to research and embed source information. Therefore, teachers must consider the assignment parameters with regard to time constraints and access to outside materials even when the introductory comments are vague. If not, they might mistakenly accept that students do not need to include research and textual evidence, a key expectation in the Common Core. I infer from reading these particular samples that teachers are encouraged to assign informal prompts that call on students to use personal experience as precursory practice to satisfying these writing standards. Plus, they might issue these kinds of assignments as preassessments prior to launching into a more formal study of a particular writing type to diagnose students' current aptitudes in a genre. So, for teachers who are not well informed about the standards, I hope they are keen in surmising or reading the conditions for writing lest they misinterpret the intent of the rigor required of them.

All told, rating these student samples would have been helpful, for a number of reasons. First, teachers assess student work using all kinds of rubrics and scoring systems, so this is familiar terrain. Additionally, they would have a clear sense of what constitutes exemplary writing by pairing students' high-caliber work with associated standards. As it stands, there seems to be a contradiction of expecting teachers to have their students reach higher when some of these writing samples portray dubious quality and do not seem to align with the rigor of the Common Core. Furthermore, teachers could use the samples in more targeted ways during instruction by intentionally planning to use mediocre and also exemplary work for useful critique and comparison activities. With the current samples, there is no clear indication from the designers which ones are beyond or right on target with their expectations or which ones miss the mark. I concur with Calkins, Ehrenworth, and Lehman, who provide their opinion about a third-grade student sample called "Horses" (2010d, p.18): "As an exemplar of informational writing for third grade, this text does not intimidate. There is no unusual level of skill displayed, either in the detail, the structure, or the logic of the writing. The narrative exemplars, on the other hand, set a higher bar" (2012, p. 115). Although the comment speaks to a third-grade informative/explanatory sample and narratives rather than the whole inventory of student writing in Appendix C, there is acknowledgement of mediocrity in some samples. They also state the following, which are sentiments I agree with: "The Common Core suggests that students should not just lift quotes from texts and plop them into their opinion and argument writing, but instead analyze their sources of information with more and more nuance, and then use the analysis within their writing. Now, you might ask, 'What does this look like?' Unfortunately, again, the exemplar pieces provided in Appendix C do not reveal the level of complexity described here" (p. 135).

To be fair, this Appendix is not titled "Exemplary Student Work" but merely "Samples of Student Writing." "Exemplary" denotes writing that exceeds a basic level of proficiency at a given grade level for a particular writing application. I wish the Appendix had, though, assessed the samples they include so we would know which parts of a writing sample meet, exceed, or fall below expectations along with thorough explanations. It seems incomplete to lay out high level standards, as the Common Core does, but not provide commensurate examples. You might use the observations I have made about these eighth-grade samples as a guide for examining other samples.

IDENTIFYING AND ARTICULATING THE LANGUAGE STANDARDS ACROSS GRADES

The language strand includes conventions of standard English—grammar and usage, capitalization, punctuation, and spelling—plus knowledge of language and vocabulary acquisition and use, including figurative language. The authors of the Common Core make a point to state that even though language standards are relegated to their own strand, these skills are interwoven throughout reading, writing, speaking, and listening. Indeed, language skills are part and parcel of formal spoken English as well as formal written English. Therefore, when you group standards, it is imperative to consider which language standards complement a unit of instruction you are teaching. For example, if you are teaching a short story writing unit, you would want students to write dialogue. As such, it is important to include language standards for punctuating and capitalizing dialogue correctly along with how to treat related nondialogue sentences. As students write reports and essays requiring evidence from researched material, target standards related to using parentheses and quotation marks to appropriately give attribution as well as those associated with using a standard format for works cited.

In Figure 1.10, "Common Core State Standards Language Progressive Skills, by Grade," you will see selected, key Common Core Standards for this strand written in a continuum: "While all of the Standards are cumulative, certain Language skills and understandings are more likely than others to need to be retaught and relearned as students advance through the grades" (2010b, p. 29). I couldn't agree more. However, in looking at this table of progression and also at the comprehensive grade-by-grade standard expectations for this strand, I realize that teachers might have the same struggles I did when I taught ELA and that my clients also share: They might need more support. Allow me to explain.

Common Core State Standards Language Progressive Skills, by Grade

The following skills, marked with an asterisk (*) in Language standards 1–3, are particularly likely to require continued attention in higher grades as they are applied to increasingly sophisticated writing and speaking.

Standard	Grade(s) 3	4	5	6	7	8	9–10	11–12
L.3.1f. Ensure subject-verb and pronoun-antecedent agreement.	X	X	X	X	X	X	X	X
L.3.3a. Choose words and phrases for effect.	X	X	X	X	X	X	X	X
L.4.1f. Produce complete sentences, recognizing and correcting inappropriate fragments and run-ons.		X	X	X	X	X	X	X
L.4.1g. Correctly use frequently confused words (e.g., to/too/two; there/their).		X	X	X	X	X	X	X
L.4.3a. Choose words and phrases to convey ideas precisely.*		X						
L.4.3b. Choose punctuation for effect.		X	X	X	X	X	X	X
L.5.1d. Recognize and correct inappropriate shifts in verb tense.			X	X	X	X	X	X
L.5.2a. Use punctuation to separate items in a series.†			X					
L.6.1c. Recognize and correct inappropriate shifts in pronoun number and person.				X	X	X	X	X
L.6.1d. Recognize and correct vague pronouns (i.e., ones with unclear or ambiguous antecedents).				X	X	X	X	X
L.6.1e. Recognize variations from standard English in their own and others' writing and speaking, and identify and use strategies to improve expression in conventional language.				X	X	X	X	X
L.6.2a. Use punctuation (commas, parentheses, dashes) to set off nonrestrictive/parenthetical elements.				X	X	X	X	X
L.6.3a. Vary sentence patterns for meaning, reader/listener interest, and style.‡				X				
L.6.3b. Maintain consistency in style and tone.				X	X	X	X	X
L.7.1c. Place phrases and clauses within a sentence, recognizing and correcting misplaced and dangling modifiers.					X	X	X	X
L.7.3a. Choose language that expresses ideas precisely and concisely, recognizing and eliminating wordiness and redundancy.					X	X	X	X
L.8.1d. Recognize and correct inappropriate shifts in verb voice and mood.						X	X	X
L.9–10.1a. Use parallel structure.							X	X

FIGURE 1.10

*Subsumed by L.7.3a

†Subsumed by L.9–10.1a

‡Subsumed by L.11–12.3a

When I taught, standards guided me in determining what I was to teach. Like the Common Core, each standard was relegated to a particular grade level with the expectation that it would be taught and mastered in an appointed school year. Invariably, there were particular grammar and convention standards that seemed developmentally challenging or too difficult for students to master all in one year. For some standards, on the other hand, I could say with conviction that most of my students could achieve proficiency within the school year. It is true that the Common Core includes gradual progression for some standards, but not necessarily a complete flow of support from grade to grade. So for the more challenging and lofty ones, where there is no indication of preparation, teamwork in the school might be advantageous so that teachers in the grade level prior might introduce them. This way, when students come into a classroom, they might be familiar with the vocabulary of a standard even if they are unclear or forgot how to actually demonstrate clear understanding. For example, teaching complex sentences requires knowledge of subordinating conjunctions, independent and dependent clauses, and also commas if the sentence begins with the dependent clause. It would be helpful if students were exposed to examples and the terminology of this skill in the grade prior to the one listed in the standard. The grade-level teachers responsible for this standard would then repeat and formally teach complex sentences so students could identify and write them with proficiency. They would know that students had some introductory lessons and familiarity with the skill in the previous grade which helps inform their teaching and supports student proficiency. So for the more rigorous and complicated standards that teachers and students find daunting to learn, welcome the support of colleagues for the sake of student achievement and build in articulation as I suggest. Keep reading.

To teach challenging standards, it occurred to me in consulting and working with teachers that a continuum to show progression and teamwork for introducing and mastering grammar and conventions would be needed. The Common Core State Standards Language Progressive Skills, by Grade (Figure 1.10) attempts to accomplish this goal, but I went a bit further in my Language Continuum in Figure 1.12 so teachers could see exactly what is incumbent upon them to teach in a particular grade to help students achieve mastery in a particular skill across a grade span. This figure includes every Common Core language standard from Grades 5–12 with some complementary writing standards. The line items that are shaded reflect additional expectations I thought should be included even though they aren't in the Common Core document. In augmenting standards that I think are noteworthy and important to teach, I have followed the suggestions of the designers of the Common Core to use their grade-level standards as a framework and my professional judgment for additions. Following is a list to show how I have categorized Figure 1.12. An excerpt of the figure is printed in this chapter so you can see the format and what to expect of the entire document; go to the companion website (http://www.corwin.com/mappingela6-12) to view it in its entirety:

- grammar
- sentence structure
- punctuation
- capitalization
- spelling
- knowledge of language
- vocabulary acquisition

With the help of many teachers along the way, we created the symbol key featured in Figure 1.11 to accompany Figure 1.12. As shown, a symbol is assigned to each grade-level standard—introduction (bullet), ongoing instruction (arrow), proficiency (asterisk). Most all of the standards span no more than three grade levels. Those with a three-year learning span are for the more complicated standards, and I recommend designing instruction as follows:

- A *bullet* signifies an introductory year and means teachers provide the first exposure students will have to this standard. They will teach the vocabulary associated with the standard, show examples of it in writing, and ask students to practice the skill.
- If an *arrow* is shown in a particular grade level, teachers will be aware that students have had some instruction in the year prior and will continue to hone this skill or concept in the next grade. Therefore, this teacher continues instruction to help students learn terminology, identify the standard in published and student work, and practice writing according to this standard.
- In the final phase, indicated by an *asterisk,* teachers are aware it is their responsibility to have students gain proficiency.

As noted, most standards will have no more than a three-year grade-level span; therefore, you will typically not find the same symbol two straight years in a row. My rationale is that if a standard needs four years, then it is too sophisticated and should be introduced in a later grade, or the standard might need to be separated. For example, Language Standard L.8.1a for eighth grade reads: "Explain the function of verbals (gerunds, participles, infinitives) in general and their function in particular sentences" (2010a). This standard can be addressed on separate days and even within different units of study in a school year. The same principle can apply with this jam-packed Language Standard L.9–10.1b in high school: "Use various types of phrases (noun, verb, adjectival, adverbial, participial, prepositional, absolute) and clauses (independent, dependent, noun, relative, adverbial) to convey specific meanings and add variety and interest to writing or presentations" (2010a).

There are instances, though, when you see asterisks in more than three grades or an asterisk alone in a grade. I've done this for those standards that are repeated verbatim in many grade spans, such as the standard about spelling correctly, which is listed in multiple grades, or many listed under vocabulary acquisition and use. In these grades where there are repeated asterisks, teachers should conduct formal lessons with the goal of achieving proficiency in that grade for more sophisticated content as students progress from one grade to the next. Note that for Grade 5 standards where there are only asterisks, this indicates that instruction was given in previous grades.

Symbol Key

> **SYMBOL KEY:**
>
> - ● introduce skill, strategy, concept, etc.
> - → continue to teach knowing students received instruction at an introductory level the previous year
> - ∗ seek to gain proficiency at an intermediate level for 90% of students

FIGURE 1.11

You will also see standards on the continuum where there is a bullet and asterisk in the same grade because a standard could be introduced and mastered in a given school year. It is important to note that I was mindful to use an asterisk to indicate proficiency where the Common Core Standards show them at a particular grade level. I then used my professional judgment to determine if I thought the standard could be mastered in a given school year, needed two years to learn, or was a more challenging standard that required three years. If you use this continuum, consider your student population and revise grade-level expectations as you deem appropriate, while still being cognizant of the target year for Common Core Standards. After all, students will be assessed against these standards in the appointed grade level.

Language Continuum

		Grade(s)					
		5	6	7	8	9–10	11–12
GRAMMAR							
PRONOUNS	Ensure that pronouns are in the proper case (subjective, objective, possessive) (L.6.1a).	●	*				
	Use intensive pronouns (e.g., *myself, ourselves*) (L.6.1b).	●	*				
	Recognize and correct inappropriate shifts in pronoun number and person (L.6.1c).	●	*				
	Recognize and correct vague pronouns (e.g., ones with unclear or ambiguous antecedents) (L.6.1d).	●	*				
VERBS/VERBALS/VERB TENSE	Form and use the perfect (e.g., *I had walked. I have walked. I will have walked.*) verb tenses (L.5.1b).	●/ *					
	Use verb tense to convey various times, sequences, states, and conditions (L.5.1c).	*					
	Recognize and correct inappropriate shifts in verb tense (L.5.1d).	*					
	Explain the function of verbals (gerunds, participles, infinitives) in general and their function in particular sentences (L.8.1a). [**Verbals:** Words that come from verbs but act like other parts of speech.]			●	*		
	Form and use verbs in the active and passive voice (L.8.1b). [**Active:** *The student completed the homework.* **Passive:** *The homework was completed by the student.*]			●	*		
	Form and use verbs in the indicative, imperative, interrogative, conditional, and subjunctive mood (L.8.1c).		●	→	*		

	Grade(s)					
	5	6	7	8	9–10	11–12
GRAMMAR						
Recognize and correct inappropriate shifts in verb voice and mood (L.8.1d).			●	*		
Use verbs in the active and passive voice and in the conditional and subjunctive mood to achieve particular effects (e.g., emphasizing the actor or the action expressing; expressing uncertainty or describing a state contrary to fact) (L.8.3a).			●	*		

SYMBOL KEY:

- ● introduce skill, strategy, concept, etc.
- → continue to teach knowing students received instruction at an introductory level the previous year
- * seek to gain proficiency at an intermediate level for 90% of students

		Grade(s)					
		5	6	7	8	9–10	11–12
	SENTENCE STRUCTURE						
SENTENCE TYPES AND STRUCTURE	Expand, combine, and reduce sentences for meaning, reader/listener interest, and style (L.5.3a).	*					
	Use sentence beginning variety (e.g., start with dependent clause, prepositional phrase, adverbs [softly/quickly], subjects [noun, pronoun, proper noun]; etc.).	*					
	Vary sentence patterns for meaning, reader/listener interest, and style (L.6.3a).	●	*				
	Choose among simple, compound, complex, and compound-complex sentences to signal differing relationships among ideas (L.7.1b).	●	→	*			
	Use parallel structure (L.9–10.1a).				●	*	
	Vary syntax for effect, consulting references (e.g., Tufte's *Artful Sentence*) for guidance as needed; apply an understanding of syntax to the study of complex texts when reading (L.11–12.3a).				●	→	*

FIGURE 1.12 (*Continued*)

FIGURE 1.12 (Continued)

		Grade(s)					
		5	**6**	**7**	**8**	**9–10**	**11–12**
	PUNCTUATION						
MISCELLANEOUS PUNCTUATION	Use underlining, quotation marks, or italics to indicate titles of works (L.5.2d).	*					
	Use punctuation (commas, parentheses, dashes) to set off nonrestrictive/parenthetical elements (L.6.2a).		●/*				
	Use punctuation (comma, ellipsis, dash) to indicate a pause or break (L.8.2a).			●	*		
	Use an ellipsis to indicate an omission (L.8.2b).				●/*		
	Use semicolon (and perhaps a conjunctive adverb) to link two or more closely related independent clauses (L.9–10.2a).					●/*	
	Observe hyphenation conventions (L.11–12.2a).						●/*
	Follow a standard format for citation (W.7–12.8).			*	*	*	*

FIGURE 1.12

If you peruse Figure 1.12 and believe some standards are missing, they might be included in earlier grades. You can consult the Common Core standards document, or see the Language Continuum aligned to Grades K–5 that I created for my book *Mapping Comprehensive Units to the ELA Common Core Standards, K–5*. To *cross reference* your current state standards with the Common Core, conduct a search of the Common Core using the Adobe tool search engine. To access the tool do the following:

- Access the ELA Common Core Standards.
- Right-click the Adobe tool search engine. The Adobe Reader toolbar will appear on the left-hand side of your screen.
- Click on the binoculars icon and type a search word, like appositive. (By the way, *appositive* is not included in the CCSS.)
- See a list of entries appear if the targeted words are in the document.
- Click on each one to reveal the full standards associated with your search word(s).

Implementing the "Language Continuum" (Figure 1.12) can be a very useful document for teachers' planning, and it can help prevent unnecessary repetition from grade to grade.

Many teachers may not be in the habit of reviewing the standards for the grades preceding and following theirs. Using this continuum as a guide for planning at the building or district level will assist teachers as they work to target their instruction more narrowly. It will also encourage reliance on support among colleagues to more aptly service students.

A fully editable version of Figure 1.12 is available on this book's companion website so you can make adjustments as you deem necessary. Have this continuum—or an edited version you work on with colleagues—easily accessible so when you prepare curriculum for your year, you can use this school document to plan accordingly.

EXERCISE 1: WHAT IS THE BEST WAY TO GROUP STANDARDS?

In this section I will walk you through the first task in creating a unit map. At the end of Exercise 1 (grouping standards), you will have a compilation of standards recorded for a targeted unit of study. In Exercise 2, later in the chapter, you will use your standards to identify the knowledge you want students to glean from these standards.

Unit Focus and Template

To begin, you will need a unit in mind that you wish to create. As you read this book, you'll design a unit map step by step since the best way to learn this process is to roll up your sleeves and dive in. Once it is complete, you will use it as the basis for lesson design. Think of a unit that involves the ELA CC Standards. The unit can be for a language arts class, of course, but it could also be for a social studies or science class as long as it involves reading and culminates in a writing piece or a project that has a writing component.

A unit of study constitutes a subdivision of instruction within your course. You can think in terms of representative topics, such as a unit on China in the Middle Ages. In science, it might be Forces and Motion. In health, it could be Diet and Nutrition. You can also teach a thematic unit or an interdisciplinary one. Instead of teaching ancient civilizations one at a time (e.g., ancient Rome, India, China, Japan, etc.), you might teach using a thematic approach (e.g., economic influences, social structures, spread of religion, etc.). An interdisciplinary unit on conflicts and persecution can pertain to World War II topics in social studies, related literature (e.g., *Anne Frank: Diary of a Young Girl*, *Night*, *When the Emperor Was Divine*), and science (atomic theory, genetics related to Aryan supremacy).

To begin to design your own unit, you will first complete the top part of the unit template that follows (see Figure 1.13). Ultimately, you'll finish an entire unit map as you complete exercises in this book. First, choose one of these options to obtain the entire unit template:

1. Photocopy a hard copy from Figure 4.1 in Chapter 4.

2. Go to this book's companion website (http://www.corwin.com/mappingela6-12), follow the directions online, and print or download Figure 4.1 onto your computer.

3. Go to my website (www.kathyglassconsulting.com), click on "Unit Template" on the right-hand side of the home page, and print or download it onto your computer.

4. Use Figure 4.1 as a guide to create your own template.

Unit Template Excerpt 1

Unit: _____

Subject: _____ Grade: _____ Timing: _____

ELA Common Core Standards	Knowledge
Content Area Standards: _____ (if applicable)	**Knowledge**

FIGURE 1.13

Considerations for Grouping Standards

When you group and record standards on your template, although they are organized by strand, the unit as a whole incorporates expectations *across* selected strands. Below are points to consider when you begin grouping standards for your unit:

- When you teach a writing domain, it isn't just a writing unit. Reading and writing are invariably intertwined. Students need to be exposed to a wide variety of student and published writing as part of the instruction in a particular genre. Immersing students in models, or mentor texts, will help students become familiar with and internalize the features of the genre, and ultimately understand expectations for the unit. So you will record reading standards even if writing a major paper is the culminating assessment.

- If reading will drive your unit, particularly in social studies, science, or any discipline where students are acquiring content knowledge, writing can be assigned throughout the unit as a way for students to demonstrate what they learn.

- Speaking and listening standards can be incorporated into any unit, as students will probably engage in discussion and debate no matter what the content area.

- Technology and media standards are embedded throughout the CCSS, so make sure to include these key expectations as appropriate for your unit.

- Be on the lookout for opportunities to group standards when teaching certain content. For example, when students write an argument or informational report, they'll conduct research to gather evidence. Most likely they will select pertinent quotes to support their assertions. When quoting from informational text, they'll need to know how to use quotation marks to indicate the words of an author and then use parentheses for the citation. If they construct a literary analysis, they will also need to have these skills to properly cite quotes from a work of literature. Do you expect students to vary their sentence beginnings to avoid redundancy? If so, you might conduct a few lessons on beginning sentences with dependent clauses, prepositional phrases, adjectives, adverbs, and subjects. Therefore, you will need to group and record pertinent standards from the language strand for these kinds of expectations.

Grouping Standards: Two Approaches

There are a couple of ways to approach the task of grouping standards for your targeted unit. The best method depends on your comfort level with the unit content you're about to map and on your personality style.

Option 1: A New or Unfamiliar Unit

If the unit is relatively new for you, and you've not taught it before, the first option might be to go directly to the standards and group them from the start. Reading the various standards from the different ELA strands and from content area standards (e.g., social studies, science, health, etc., as applicable) and selecting ones that make sense to pull together can help you formulate ideas about what the whole unit might comprise. You might conduct this exercise with a textbook or other resources in front of you to use as a guide to content knowledge you might wish to include in the unit.

Option 2: Mapping a Familiar Unit

Maybe you fall into one of the following categories:

- You're comfortable with the content and are already thinking of a culminating assessment.
- You've taught the unit before but are thinking of a new direction.
- You'd like to discuss the overarching expectations with colleagues so you are all on the same page.

If so, the second option might be a better approach for you.

Because the standards are organized by strands, grouping them can feel like compartmentalization, and not an accurate mirror of how we teach. Although you probably have students read or listen and then practice writing, these actions overlap and intertwine, and ultimately your entire unit will be a holistic piece with these literacy elements interwoven. Therefore, this approach involves conducting a stream-of-conscious free write or brainstorm before grouping specific standards. This helps me consider the whole of the unit, as well as the interconnectedness of the standards, and can lead to what feels like a more natural, holistic approach to this work.

Let's say, for example, that your targeted unit is narrative writing. You want students ultimately to produce a narrative piece, specifically a short story, by the end of the unit. Think about your expectations for students in this short story unit and your ideas for a culminating product, even if it's a rough idea. Jot down some ideas, perhaps using an organizational structure (e.g., web, outline, etc.); mull them over in your head; or have a conversation with a colleague. I imagine your notes, monologue, or conversation would include something like the following:

For a short story, I want students to include the elements of literature in their writing: character, setting, plot, and point of view. In reading, I want them to identify all of these elements, including theme. I don't think they necessarily need to state the theme prior to writing their own stories, but they surely would need to brainstorm a plot diagram, plus include the characters and setting. I want them to describe in detail at least one character. I want to know what that character looks like and also personality traits for this character. They should be able to support a trait instead of just writing that so-and-so is vicious or compassionate. I want to know what has led this character to exhibit this trait. What motivates him/her? What obstacles does s/he encounter? What impact do his/her actions have on other characters? I also want them to write using imagery so readers can fully experience the places and characters. Dialogue is a necessity, too, and I expect them to use narration. Instead of a simple plot, I want them to incorporate multiple plot lines to develop a more sophisticated story than they have in prior grades. Reading and writing are interconnected as they read and analyze stories from various authors and identify these elements in the literature. When they write their own stories, I want them to vary their sentence structures and use rich vocabulary and figurative language. I will give them time to progress through the writing process. . . .

And so on. After this brainstorm or free write, you can turn to the standards and begin to identify and group appropriate ones. Or you can do this while you have a conversation with colleagues or yourself.

Whatever approach you choose, you will eventually enter the standards on the unit template and group them by strands. You can do this in any of the following ways:

- By cutting and pasting standards from the Common Core website (http://www .corestandards.org/ELA-Literacy), which is in PDF format.
- By cutting and pasting from a Word version of the standards found on my website (www.kathyglassconsulting.com) under the link "ELA Common Core Standards 6–8 or 9–12 (Word)."
- By writing down the letters and numbers associated with each standard and entering them on the unit template (e.g., W.8.1 = writing strand, Grade 8, Standard 1).

Once you have entered your standards, return to this book and continue reading to learn how to identify knowledge items; then move onward to Exercise 2.

DEFINITION AND EXAMPLES FOR KNOWLEDGE

Designing a quality unit of instruction entails focusing on outcomes; this means focusing on what we want students to know, understand, and be able to do by the completion of the unit. Below, I explain what constitutes a "knowledge item" and then suggest an exercise in which you record *knowledge* associated with the grouped standards for your unit. First, we need a common definition:

KNOWLEDGE is the factual information that students use as the foundation for gleaning overarching concepts; specifically, knowledge includes *facts, dates, people, places, examples,* **and** *vocabulary/terms of a given unit*.

Note: Some vocabulary words or terms might fall under *concepts,* which I will discuss later.

Standards do not explicitly state all that you might include in the knowledge list, particularly in the content areas. It is up to you to consider each standard and use your professional judgment to determine what a standard means for your subject area and classroom.

In addition to using standards to compile your list, you may wish to have books and other resources and materials at hand. It can also be helpful to consult colleagues as you work to generate knowledge items.

Figure 1.14 provides examples of standards and a corresponding list of knowledge items. The key is to determine the factual knowledge that is embedded in each standard, and then consider what is important to *teach* in order to meet the standard. Note that the list items do not begin with a verb (verbs will be used later, when you describe skills and activities). Rather, you are merely listing items related to your content. To review, that includes:

- facts
- dates
- people
- places
- examples
- vocabulary/terms

If you are a content area teacher, your list of standards should be a combination of ELA and content area standards. For example, if students will write an argument piece about the Civil War, include standards for ELA and social studies. If, however, you are an English teacher and your students are writing an informational paper about a work of literature, then the ELA Common Core standards are enough.

Identifying What Students Should Know

READING	Knowledge
1. Read closely to determine what the text says explicitly and to make logical inferences from it; cite specific textual evidence when writing or speaking to support conclusions drawn from the text.	• **Terms:** *counterclaim/counterargument, reasons, textual evidence, thesis, argument, claim,* vocabulary specific to topic, *plagiarism, inference* • Purpose of argument writing, formats of argument writing, persuasive vs. argument • Author's perspective • Main idea/supporting details from multiple sources
2. Determine central ideas or themes of a text and analyze their development; summarize the key supporting details and ideas.	• **Organizational structure of arguments:** intro with thesis, body paragraphs with reasons (topic sentences) and evidence, strongest argument last body paragraph, conclusion
4. Interpret words and phrases as they are used in a text, including determining technical, connotative, and figurative meanings, and analyze how specific word choices shape meaning or tone.	• **Thesis:** stakes claim, construction of thesis statement, all topic sentences must relate to thesis • **Counterclaims:** separate paragraph or woven into body

FIGURE 1.14 (*Continued*)

FIGURE 1.14 (Continued)

	Knowledge
COLLEGE AND CAREER READINESS (CCR) ANCHOR STANDARDS	

5. Analyze the structure of texts, including how specific sentences, paragraphs, and larger portions of the text (e.g., a section, chapter, scene, or stanza) relate to each other and the whole.

6. Assess how point of view or purpose shapes the content and style of a text.

8. Delineate and evaluate the argument and specific claims in a text, including the validity of the reasoning as well as the relevance and sufficiency of the evidence.

9. Analyze how two or more texts address similar themes or topics in order to build knowledge or to compare the approaches the authors take.

WRITING

1. Write arguments to support claims in an analysis of substantive topics or texts using valid reasoning and relevant and sufficient evidence.

4. Produce clear and coherent writing in which the development, organization, and style are appropriate to task, purpose, and audience.

5. Develop and strengthen writing as needed by planning, revising, editing, rewriting, or trying a new approach.

8. Gather relevant information from multiple print and digital sources, assess the credibility and accuracy of each source, and integrate the information while avoiding plagiarism.

9. Draw evidence from literary or informational texts to support analysis, reflection, and research.

Knowledge:

- Transitional words and phrases
- **Evidence from multiple sources:** facts, data, statistics, examples, other information
- Credible and reliable sources, search terms
- **Quotes:** selection of salient quotes and other information
- Formal style
- Oral debates; expression of ideas
- **Conventions/grammar:** proper in-text citations, works cited format, titles
- **Writing process:** prewriting, drafting, editing, revising, publishing

		Knowledge
HISTORY/SOCIAL STUDIES STANDARDS: EARLY HUMANKIND	**SPEAKING AND LISTENING** 1. Prepare for and participate effectively in a range of conversations and collaborations with diverse partners, building on others' ideas and expressing their own clearly and persuasively. **LANGUAGE** 1./2. Demonstrate command of the conventions of standard English. (ELA Common Core State Standards, 2010)	

	EARLY HUMANKIND
	
	6.1 Students describe what is known through archaeological studies of the early physical and cultural development of humankind from the Paleolithic era to the agricultural revolution.
	
	  1. Describe the hunter-gatherer societies, including the development of tools and the use of fire.
	
	  2. Identify the locations of human communities that populated the major regions of the world and describe how humans adapted to a variety of environments.
	
	  3. Discuss the climatic changes and human modifications of the physical environment that gave rise to the domestication of plants and animals and new sources of clothing and shelter.
	
	(California Department of Education History–Social Studies Content Standard, 2009, p. 23)
		• Terms: *archaeology, anthropology, environment, climate, socialization, hominid, domestication, agricultural revolution*
		• Types of hominid groups:
		  o Australopithecus Afarensis or "Southern Ape"
		  o Homo Habilis or "Handy Man"
		  o Homo Erectus or "Upright Man"
		  o Homo Sapiens Neanderthalensis or "Neanderthal Man"
		  o Homo Sapiens Sapiens or "Doubly Wise Man"
		• Time periods of each hominid group
		• Physical characteristics
		• Tools and their purposes
		• Socialization: family/community living, communication systems, rituals
		• Location of communities
		• Migration patterns
		• Diet

FIGURE 1.14 (*Continued*)

FIGURE 1.14 (Continued)

		Knowledge

HISTORY/SOCIAL STUDIES STANDARDS: CIVIL WAR	**The Civil War**
	
	• USI.35 Describe how the different economies and cultures of the North and South contributed to the growing importance of sectional politics in the early 19th century.
	• USI.36 Summarize the critical developments leading to the Civil War.
	• USI.37 On a map of North America, identify Union and Confederate states at the outbreak of the war.
	• USI.38 Analyze Abraham Lincoln's presidency, the Emancipation Proclamation (1863), his views on slavery, and the political obstacles he encountered.
	• USI.39 Analyze the roles and policies of various Civil War leaders and describe the important Civil War battles and events.
	
	(Massachusetts Department of Education History and Social Science Curriculum Framework, 2003, pp. 70–71)
		• Terms (and concepts): *secession, sectionalism, emancipation, abolitionist, interdependence*
		• Geography
		• Growth of sectional differences: agrarianism/slavery versus capitalism/industrial growth; southern Protestantism versus northern Puritans, etc.
		• Catalysts leading to war:
		  ○ Increasing tensions: *Dred Scott* decision, John Brown's raid, *Uncle Tom's Cabin*, Lincoln-Douglas debates, etc.
		  ○ Efforts to compromise: Missouri Compromise, Compromise of 1850, Kansas-Nebraska Act
		• Civil War leaders:
		  ○ Political leaders: Jefferson Davis, Alexander Stephens, Abraham Lincoln, Stephen Douglas, Charles Summer, etc.
		  ○ Military leaders: Robert E. Lee, "Stonewall" Jackson, Ulysses S. Grant, William Tecumseh Sherman, etc.
		  ○ Abolitionist leaders: William Seward, Harriet Beecher Stowe, Frederick Douglass, etc.
		• Lincoln's speeches: Emancipation Proclamation, "House Divided," Gettysburg Address
		• Battles and military strategy: Antietam, Vicksburg, Gettysburg, etc.
		• States that seceded from the Union and those that did not

HEALTH: DRUG USE AND ABUSE	**Health Standard 9.** Understands aspects of substance use and abuse
	
	1. Knows conditions that may put people at higher risk for substance abuse problems
	
	2. Knows factors involved in the development of a drug dependency and the early, observable signs and symptoms
	
	3. Knows the short- and long-term consequences of the use of alcohol, tobacco, and other drugs
		• Vocabulary: *drug dependency, tolerance level, denial, cirrhosis, lung cancer, emphysema, low self-esteem, paranoia, depression, apathy, domestic violence*
		• Types of drugs
		• Factors that put people at risk for higher substance abuse problems:
		  ○ substance abuse risk
		  ○ genetic inheritability
		  ○ frustration tolerance
		• Signs and symptoms of drug dependency: tolerance level, drug-seeking behavior, loss of control, denial

	Knowledge
5. Knows community resources that are available to assist people with alcohol, tobacco, and other drug problems (Grades 6–8) *Source:* Kendall, 2011. Copyright 2011, McREL. Reprinted by permission of McRel.	• Possible consequences of alcohol, tobacco, drug use: ○ physical/tobacco and drug use: shortness of breath, lung cancer, emphysema ○ physical/alcohol use: cirrhosis ○ psychological/alcohol use: low self-esteem, depression, apathy ○ psychological/drug use: low self-esteem, paranoia, depression, apathy ○ social/drug and alcohol use: crime, domestic violence, loss of friends ○ social/tobacco use: loss of friends • Personal resources: school, community, faith-based • Online, print, video resources
Science Standard 10. Understands forces and motion 4. Understands effects of balanced and unbalanced forces on an object's motion (Grades 6–8) *Source:* Kendall, 2011. Copyright 2011, McREL. Reprinted by permission of McRel.	• Vocabulary: force, net force, unbalanced force, inertia, mass, action, reaction, friction, equilibrium, acceleration • Isaac Newton: 17th-century scientist, Newton's Three Laws of Motion • Equilibrium versus state of motion • Effects of balanced and unbalanced forces on an object's motion • Fact: If more than one force acts on an object along a straight line, then the forces will reinforce or cancel one another depending on their direction and magnitude. • Fact: Unbalanced forces, like friction, will cause changes in the direction and speed of an object's motion.

Side label: SCIENCE: BALANCED AND UNBALANCED FORCES

FIGURE 1.14

EXERCISE 2: HOW ARE STANDARDS USED TO DETERMINE WHAT STUDENTS SHOULD KNOW?

Now you are ready to look at your standards and catalog your own list that represents what you want students to know about the content you are teaching in a given unit. Here are some tips for entering this factual information on the unit template:

- **Consider your audience**. If it is just for your own personal use, you may prefer to be brief. For instance, if you want students to know the basic steps in the writing process, you can merely write *writing process.*

- **Enter details if colleagues will view this document.** For example, include *planning, drafting, editing, revising, publishing,* or even a definition of each step in the writing process. In some districts, teachers put their work on a district server or share with a number of colleagues, so adding detail is important for everyone to be clear about what your unit entails. Detail also ensures that all who write curriculum from your outline are operating from the same frame of reference.

- **Remember that you are making a list.** Avoid sentences unless you enter a statement of fact. Basic facts might be helpful for colleagues for planning purposes and should ultimately be communicated to students (e.g., *Unbalanced forces, like friction, will cause changes in the direction and speed of an object's motion. As part of President Andrew Jackson's removal policy, the Cherokee Nation was forced to leave its lands and march in a deadly journey called "The Trail of Tears" that cost thousands of lives.*).

Using your standards as a guide, along with other resources that can help you identify factual information for your targeted unit, record what you want students to know onto the unit template. To complete this exercise, make sure to review the definition of knowledge on pages 42 and 43 and refer to additional examples of knowledge that are listed in Figure 1.14. If you would like further examples, view the unit map example in Chapter 4.

At the end of this chapter, you should have completed the following:

1. Downloaded or copied the unit template

2. Targeted a unit of study as the basis for a curriculum map

3. Grouped standards for this unit

4. Identified what students should know at the completion of the unit

LOOKING AHEAD

Now that the standards and knowledge are entered on your unit map template, you are ready to move ahead. In the next chapter, we will explore essential understandings and guiding questions—critical components of any high-quality unit.

2

Essential Understandings

> When curriculum and instruction require students to process factual information through the conceptual levels of thinking, the students demonstrate greater retention of factual information, deeper levels of understanding, and increased motivation for learning.
>
> —H. Lynn Erickson (2007, p. 2)

What I am about to share with you in this chapter is a significant gift that educators can bring to the classroom. It had a pivotal impact on my own teaching and one that will yield enormous benefits for your students by strengthening their critical thinking and problem-solving skills. This gift is the strategy of teaching with essential (or enduring) understandings. It is wildly impactful for students—empowering them to connect concepts and knowledge across grades and subjects and giving them the perspective to apply what they have learned to their immediate world and the greater world at large. If you follow what I suggest in the pages ahead, I guarantee it will transform your teaching or the teaching of those you may mentor.

The obvious by-product of using essential understandings is a more meaningful learning experience for students. As mentioned in Chapter 1, KUDs—what we want students to know, understand, and do—form the basis for a unit of instruction and emanate from standards. It is imperative that teachers present and teach the factual information (know) and skills (do), but the end goal is to have students use them to make sense of a greater realization (understanding). Therefore, this chapter addresses the unit map component of essential understandings. It is challenging work, but once you grasp the overall *what* and *why* and then delve into the *how,* you'll see the benefits.

THE NATURE AND CRITICAL IMPORTANCE OF ESSENTIAL (OR ENDURING) UNDERSTANDINGS

You might have heard the term *enduring understandings* from Wiggins and McTighe's (1998) prominent work *Understanding by Design.* They also use the phrase *big ideas,* which is a term that appears in many textbooks, too. Others (including me) use the phrase *essential understandings* (Erickson, 2007). But no matter what the terminology may be, these understandings or big ideas share a common denominator: They are conceptually based statements that teachers invent or borrow and use as a guiding light to design curriculum and instruction that derive from standards. As Wiggins and McTighe (1998) state, "*Enduring* refers to the big ideas, the important understandings, that we want students to 'get inside of' and retain after they've forgotten many of the details. . . . Enduring understandings go beyond discrete facts or skills to focus on larger concepts, principles, or processes" (p. 10).

So why should teachers spend the time to create essential understandings? Many academic experts have espoused the virtues and efficacy of using understandings and guiding questions as a driving force in instruction. There are too many to name here; however, those that stand out for me are H. Lynn Erickson, who popularized concept-based instruction; the aforementioned Grant Wiggins and Jay McTighe, who are known for their work in backward design; and Carol Ann Tomlinson, who is at the forefront of differentiation. Erickson crystallizes the relationships between concepts and facts. In her work, she discusses the "synergistic interplay between the factual and conceptual levels of thinking" (Erickson, 2007, p. 2) as a pathway to intellectual growth. In a nutshell, the idea is that most people don't remember a litany of facts. However, if you tie them to concepts so there is a home base and an opportunity to make connections, then people are much more likely to retain these facts.

I can explain it best by giving you a concrete example. Let's say you are teaching the Civil War. As a guide about what to teach, you look to the standards, which might look like an excerpt from the Massachusetts curriculum framework shown in Figure 2.1 (Massachusetts Department of Education, 2003).

Massachusetts History and Social Science Curriculum Framework: The Civil War

The Civil War
- USI.35 Describe how the different economies and cultures of the North and South contributed to the growing importance of sectional politics in the early 19th century.
- USI.36 Summarize the critical developments leading to the Civil War.
- USI.37 On a map of North America, identify Union and Confederate states at the outbreak of the war.
- USI.38 Analyze Abraham Lincoln's presidency, the Emancipation Proclamation (1863), his views on slavery, and the political obstacles he encountered.
- USI.39 Analyze the roles and policies of various Civil War leaders and describe the important Civil War battles and events.

FIGURE 2.1

Source: Adapted from Massachusetts Department of Education (2003).

There is a lot of factual material that students would need to know in order to meet these standards. Here is a preliminary list: growth of sectional differences (e.g., agrarianism/ slavery versus capitalism/industrial growth, southern Protestantism versus northern Puritanism, etc.); catalysts leading to war, such as increasing tensions (e.g., *Dred Scott* decision, John Brown's raid, *Uncle Tom's Cabin,* Lincoln-Douglas debates, etc.) and efforts to compromise (e.g., Missouri Compromise, Compromise of 1850, Kansas-Nebraska Act); the Civil War political leaders (e.g., Jefferson Davis, Alexander Stephens, Abraham Lincoln, Stephen Douglas, Charles Summer, etc.), military leaders (e.g., Robert E. Lee, "Stonewall" Jackson, Ulysses S. Grant, William Tecumseh Sherman, etc.), and abolitionist leaders (e.g., William Seward, Harriet Beecher Stowe, Frederick Douglass, etc.); Lincoln's speeches; the battles (e.g., Antietam, Vicksburg, Gettysburg); states that seceded from the Union and those that did not; and so forth. There are also many terms students would need to know, such as *agrarian, industrialist, sectionalism,* and *secession.* All of this is critically important information for students to know when they are learning about this period in history, and it must be included in the knowledge piece explained in Chapter 1. However, it still represents a mere collection of facts.

To help students make sense of this factual information, we need to create overarching conceptual statements. These statements will provide students with the context they need in order to understand the broader relevance of the pertinent facts. It is through creating essential understandings that we also discern what the standards mean and what we really want our students to take away. As educators, we must study these standards carefully in order to develop approaches to teaching the material that will ensure that students leave a particular unit of study with a deep level of understanding. Consider the following examples of essential understandings, which could be tied to some of the social studies standards and facts cited earlier:

- Differences in cultural, political, and economic systems can foster sectional tensions that can escalate into acrimony and result in conflict.
- Political sectionalism and unwillingness to compromise can lead to conflict.
- Individuals can make powerful contributions for targeted groups of people that might lead to change, growth, and survival.
- Leaders' perspectives, personality traits, and actions can shape events and impact people's political opinions and involvement, thereby generating change.
- Disparate views of political leaders can contribute to unavoidable conflict, which impacts individuals and groups.
- Location and topography influence strategic military maneuvers and decisions that contribute to the development and outcome of battles.
- To position their armies for victory, military leaders must understand the political dynamics so they can develop a strategy that fully considers their economic advantages and military strengths.

ESSENTIAL UNDERSTANDINGS AS STATEMENTS OF CONCEPTUAL INTENT

The exercise of creating or finding the right essential understanding will allow you to focus on what you want students to understand as indicated by the standard. In that way, it will serve as a statement of your own conceptual intent. Since you will use the understandings to write, find, or revise curriculum, it's important that these statements clearly articulate the goals for the unit, as they will form the basis for your teaching.

Why aren't there one or two universal essential understandings for each standard? There are many reasons for teachers to craft different essential understandings for the same standard. It might be that teachers interpret the same standard slightly differently because they naturally view it through their own individual lens, they want to go beyond the standard, they have various rich resources at their disposal to use, and so forth. In addition, there might be more than one essential understanding that makes sense for each standard. If there is a subtle difference between two or more essential understandings, then choose the one that clearly indicates the direction for your teaching. You don't want overlap; this is because each essential understanding should stand alone. In other cases, however, the standard might be hefty and require two essential understandings to cover different aspects of it. Or you might have two understandings aligned to a particular standard because they represent two directions that a standard can take, and you might teach to both.

The following questions might help you as you begin to think about how you will find or design essential understandings for your class:

- *What do you want your students to really remember long after they have forgotten the discrete facts?*
- *What is your goal for student understanding based on the standards?*
- *What is the essence of this particular unit of study?*
- *What differentiated resources will you use to illuminate the standards?*
- *What reading materials are at your disposal?*
- *Are you team teaching with other staff members who will address parts of these standards?*
- *How can you merge content areas in a meaningful way in a core classroom?*
- *How can you help students transfer the knowledge they learn across subjects and grades?*
- *How can you help students make various connections, including text-to-text and text-to-world?*

Let's review concrete examples and special considerations in the sections that follow before we embark on the step-by-step process of crafting your own essential understandings.

EXAMPLES OF ESSENTIAL UNDERSTANDINGS ALIGNED TO THE ANCHOR STANDARDS FOR READING

What follows are essential understandings that I wrote to align with the ten College and Career Readiness Anchor Standards for Reading. Prior to reviewing them, consider this quote from highly acclaimed literacy researchers Irene Fountas and Gay Su Pinnell (2001): "Reading for meaning—*comprehension*—is the goal of every reading episode as well as of our teaching. We want students not only to understand what they read but also to enjoy texts, interpret them, and apply their learning from reading to other areas. . . . Reading is the construction of meaning. Without understanding, there is no reading. Everything about reading is directed toward making meanings that are infused with active curiosity, emotion, and satisfaction" (pp. 302, 322). The kinds of comprehension required in the Common Core Standards echo Fountas and Pinnell's statements. In their book *Pathways to the Common Core*, Lucy Calkins and her colleagues also elucidate the very sophisticated expectations embedded in the reading standards:

> The grade level specifics for informational reading follow the same logic as those for literature. The difference lies in the kind of comprehension involved. When reading informational texts, the standards focus readers on the work of analyzing the claims texts make, the soundness and sufficiency of their evidence, and the way a text's language and craft may reveal points of view; the emphasis is investigating ideas, claims, reasoning, and evidence, rather than themes, characters, figurative language, and symbolism. The level of analysis called for by the information reading standards is no higher than that called for in literature—the Common Core standards for reading literature demand extremely sophisticated reading practices. (2012, pp. 75–76)

With these quotations in mind, take a look at my essential understanding examples in Figure 2.2. Of course, these are merely my interpretations, and your essential understandings might look a bit different. As you read them, begin to reflect on the following considerations for crafting effective essential understandings. Doing so will help prepare you for the upcoming exercise in which you write these kinds of statements for your targeted unit.

- *Concepts.* When creating essential understandings, consider the concept or word that serves as an umbrella term that encompasses the facts. A concept is "a mental construct that frames a set of examples sharing common attributes . . . concepts are timeless, universal, abstract, and broad" (Erickson, 2002, p. 164). Concepts are expressed as nouns and can be one or two words, such as *theme, writing process, global economy, figurative language,* or *persuasion.* Put another way, the New York State Department of Education (1999) provides this definition: "Concepts represent mental images, constructs, or word pictures that help people to arrange and classify fragmented and isolated facts and information" (p. 8). In Figure 2.2, look for the concepts in some of my essential understandings; you won't find any proper nouns because concepts are defined as timeless, universal, abstract, and broad. Figures 2.3 and 2.4 also include lists of concepts in various subject areas. Some concepts listed in the figures are not as complex as others, and sometimes I use gerunds for concepts (e.g., summarizing, comparing and contrasting). However these words represent key ideas, too. The capitalized words in the following literature examples feature examples of concepts:

    o CHARACTERS can change over time through EVENTS, SETTING, or INTERACTION with other characters, which can, in turn, shape the PLOT.
    o Writers intentionally craft DIALOGUE TAGS to enhance the spoken words of CHARACTERS to convey TONE and ACTION.

Essential Understandings Aligned to the College and Career Readiness Anchor Standards for Reading

CCR Anchor Standards	Essential Understandings
Read closely to determine what the text says explicitly and to make logical inferences from it; cite specific textual evidence when writing or speaking to support conclusions drawn from the text (2010a, R.CCR.1).	• People cite concrete evidence from a text to support their analyses of what the text says explicitly and inferentially.
Determine central ideas or themes of a text and analyze their development; summarize the key supporting details and ideas (R.CCR.2).	• Summarizing allows readers to briefly articulate the substance of a work to facilitate overall comprehension. • Proficient readers engage in an ongoing process of extracting information from a text and tracking the development of central ideas to comprehend the whole of a text.
Analyze how and why individuals, events, and ideas develop and interact over the course of a text (R.CCR.3).	• Characters' motivations, circumstances, and interactions with others drive plot development. • Analyzing the development and interactions of individuals, events, and ideas allows readers to arrive at insights and conclusions.
Interpret words and phrases as they are used in a text, including determining technical, connotative, and figurative meanings, and analyze how specific word choices shape meaning or tone (R.CCR.4).	• Readers can uncover an author's meaning and tone by interpreting and analyzing salient words and phrases.
Analyze the structure of texts, including how specific sentences, paragraphs, and larger portions of the text (e.g., a section, chapter, scene, or stanza) relate to each other and the whole (R.CCR.5).	• Readers analyze the structure of a text to locate information, determine how parts are related, and construct overall meaning. • Authors structure texts to organize content, develop ideas, and help facilitate comprehension.
Assess how point of view or purpose shapes the content and style of a text (R.CCR.6).	• A character's or narrator's point of view can expose readers to cultural awareness and an appreciation for diversity. • Proficient readers assess the author's point of view or purpose and the use of rhetorical devices to determine how it shapes the content and style of the text. • Acknowledging and addressing counterclaims contribute to the strength of an argument and the ability of authors to successfully convince others of their point of view.

CCR Anchor Standards	Essential Understandings
Integrate and evaluate content presented in diverse formats and media, including visually and quantitatively, as well as in words (R.CCR.7).	• People evaluate and integrate content in various formats and media to gain clarity about a topic and communicate a complete account.
Delineate and evaluate the argument and specific claims in a text, including the validity of the reasoning as well as the relevance and sufficiency of the evidence (R.CCR.8).	• Readers evaluate an author's argument by examining valid reasoning and relevant and sufficient evidence in order to determine the validity of the claim.
Analyze how two or more texts address similar themes or topics in order to build knowledge or to compare the approaches the authors take (R.CCR.9).	• Readers analyze multiple texts on similar themes or topics to build knowledge and to compare authors' approaches. • Readers glean a more thorough and accurate account of a subject matter or issue by comparing and contrasting multiple texts on the same topic.
Read and comprehend complex literary and informational texts independently and proficiently (R.CCR.10).	• Students develop skills and strategies necessary to appreciate literature through independently and proficiently reading, comprehending, and writing about complex text. • Students develop content knowledge through independently and proficiently reading, comprehending, and writing about topics found in complex informational text.

FIGURE 2.2

English Language Arts Concepts

Online Resources Included

Reading for Literature		
• genre (e.g., fantasy, mystery, biography, memoir, etc.) • literary devices (e.g., allusion, suspense, tone, foreshadowing, dialect, mood, symbolism) • elements of literature (i.e., character, plot, setting, theme, point of view)	• words/phrases/language • figurative language (e.g., simile, metaphor, personification, sensory detail/imagery) • reading strategies (e.g., questioning, inference, retelling, summarizing, prediction, monitoring and clarifying, visualization, connection)	• narrator/narration • persuasion • illustrations/visuals • cause/effect • culture • diversity • interactions • motivation • pattern • perception • perspective

FIGURE 2.3 *(Continued)*

FIGURE 2.3 (Continued)

Reading for Literature		
<ul><li>central message/moral/ theme</li><li>hero/heroine</li><li>protagonist/antagonist</li><li>exposition</li><li>problem/solution</li><li>conflict</li><li>sounds of language (e.g., rhythm, rhyme, meter, repetition, alliteration, onomatopoeia)</li></ul>	<ul><li>metacognition</li><li>audience</li><li>author/writer</li><li>writer's style</li><li>voice</li><li>purpose</li><li>reader</li></ul>	<ul><li>relationships</li><li>sequence</li><li>structure</li><li>transformation</li></ul>
Reading for Informational Text		
<ul><li>claim/proposition/position</li><li>main topic/key details</li><li>idea/concept</li><li>thesis/topic sentence</li><li>evidence/reasons/support</li><li>structure/organization</li><li>comparison/contrast</li><li>similarities/differences</li><li>procedure</li><li>chronology</li><li>sequence/time</li><li>cause/effect</li></ul>	<ul><li>problem/solution</li><li>relationship</li><li>interaction</li><li>interpretation</li><li>integration</li><li>argumentation</li><li>persuasion</li><li>stereotype</li><li>fact/opinion</li><li>illustrations/visuals/images</li><li>author's purpose</li><li>author/writer</li></ul>	<ul><li>writer's style</li><li>voice</li><li>perspective/point of view</li><li>words/phrases/ language</li><li>reading strategies (see "Reading for Literature")</li><li>metacognition</li><li>text features</li><li>research</li><li>credibility</li><li>search tools (e.g., key words, sidebars, hyperlinks)</li></ul>
Writing		
<ul><li>text types (e.g., argument, informative/ explanatory, narrative)</li><li>audience</li><li>purpose (e.g., to persuade, describe, inform, etc.)</li><li>bias</li><li>viewpoint/perspective</li><li>perception</li><li>elements of literature (see "Reading for Literature")</li><li>reasons/evidence</li></ul>	<ul><li>thesis/topic sentence</li><li>structure/organization</li><li>sequence/logical order</li><li>comparison/contrast</li><li>cause/effect</li><li>transitions</li><li>fact/opinion</li><li>writing process (e.g., prewriting, drafting, editing, revising, publishing)</li><li>research/information</li><li>bibliography/works cited</li></ul>	<ul><li>investigation</li><li>analysis/reflection/ interpretation</li><li>summarizing/paraphrasing</li><li>word choice/language</li><li>writer's style</li><li>writer/author</li><li>reader</li><li>plagiarism</li><li>see "Language"</li></ul>

Language	
• grammar and usage • sentence structure • conventions (i.e., capitalization, punctuation, spelling) • language • vocabulary acquisition	• word relationships • word nuances • words/phrases • figurative language • references (e.g., thesaurus, dictionary, etc.) • expression
Speaking and Listening	
• collaborative conversations • collaborative discussions • communication • main ideas/supporting details • facts/details • formal versus informal discourse • viewpoint/perspective	• comprehension (e.g., questioning, clarifying, retelling, summarizing, paraphrasing) • active listening • oral communication (e.g., volume, pitch, intonation, phrasing, pace, modulation, facial expressions, verbal cues, gestures) • visual displays
Foundational Skills for Reading	
• word recognition • word analysis • phonics	• print features • reading accuracy • reading fluency

FIGURE 2.3

Content Area Concepts

Science	Social Studies	Math
adaptability	change	algebra
change	citizenship/democracy	data analysis
conservation	civilization	estimation
diversity	conflict	function
energy	culture	geometry
environment	diversity	logical reasoning
equilibrium	economy	measurement
evolution	exploration	number
genetics	geography/climate	operation
gravity	government systems	order
light	immigration/migration	pattern

FIGURE 2.4 *(Continued)*

FIGURE 2.4 (Continued)

Science	Social Studies	Math
magnetism	imperialism	probability
matter	interdependence	proportions
organism	justice	quantity
scale and structure	nationalism	ratio
scientific method	politics	statistics
systems	religion	symmetry
	social systems	

Visual Arts	Health	Macroconcepts (broad, interdisciplinary concepts)
aesthetic	body system	change
balance	diet	community
color	disease	connection
contrast	drug	form
form	exercise	function
line	family	identity
pattern	hygiene	interdependence
perspective	illness	movement
shadow	nutrition	order
shape	puberty	pattern
texture	wellness	perspective
unity		structure
		system

FIGURE 2.4

- *Number of concepts.* Each essential understanding should forge a relationship between at least two concepts; oftentimes there are more than two.

- *Verbs.* Look at the verbs used to connect the concepts in each literature essential understanding that you read earlier; verbs are in italics for easy reference in these examples:

  o CHARACTERS can *change* over time through EVENTS, SETTING, or INTERACTION with other characters, which can, in turn, *shape* the PLOT.
  o Writers intentionally *craft* DIALOGUE TAGS to *enhance* the spoken words of CHARACTERS to *convey* TONE and ACTION.

In *Concept-Based Curriculum and Instruction for the Thinking Classroom* (2007), Erickson suggests that essential understandings should not include forms of the verb *to be*, such as *is*, *are*, *was*, or *were*. While essential understandings that use forms of the verb *to be* are not incorrect, they are invariably more sophisticated when they are rewritten using stronger verbs. One reason they are higher level is that some verbs can be converted to concepts, which means the verbs give more mileage for conceptual intent. Consider *cooperate* as a verb doubling for the concept *cooperation,* or *discriminate* for *discrimination.* Finally, the verbs in essential understandings should be in the present tense. All told, verbs can turn a mediocre essential understanding into a stronger one. Weak example: *Conflict can be a result of societies dividing individuals into groups based on their background.* Stronger: *Societies might discriminate against groups of people based on their background, which can foster discord and erupt in conflict.* Review Figure 2.2 and locate the strong verbs in the essential understandings.

- *Importance factor.* One of the main points of establishing essential understandings and teaching around them is to have students come to realize an enduring truth. If you keep this end goal in mind while constructing your essential understandings, you will have successfully addressed what I call the importance factor. Figure 2.5 illustrates this idea. The examples in the left column are weak not just because of the verbs *to be;* they also seem incomplete in terms of what teachers want students to really understand and viscerally grasp. To merely state that *paragraphs are organized in a logical order in an informative paper* begs the questions, *Who cares? Why should students know this? What about it is important?* Plus, it is more a statement of fact than an essential understanding. If, however, I write *why* organization matters, then I've succeeded in writing a more sophisticated and complete essential understanding. So to answer the question, *Why is it worth knowing that paragraphs are organized logically?* I can respond, *Logically organizing paragraphs in a sequential fashion facilitates comprehension.* Let's try the second example: *Why is it worth knowing that context clues are what readers use to help understand words?* Because *using context clues provides readers with a means for deciphering unknown words, which supports overall comprehension.*

Strong Versus Weak Essential Understandings I

Weak Essential Understandings	Stronger Essential Understandings
Paragraphs are organized in a logical order in an informative paper.	Logically organizing paragraphs in a sequential fashion facilitates comprehension.
Context clues are what readers use to help understand unfamiliar words.	Readers use context clues as a means for deciphering unknown words, which ultimately aids in overall comprehension.
It is important for writers to be aware of purpose and audience when they begin their writing project.	Knowing the purpose and audience at the outset of writing guides authors to incorporate the appropriate elements for a specific genre and focus on a target audience in their work.

FIGURE 2.5

- *Transfer value.* As adults, we make connections and transfer knowledge repeatedly when we watch or listen to news reports, read editorials, encounter novel situations, and so forth. It actually helps us make sense of the world or gain deeper insights. In the same way, we need to create learning experiences for students so they can make similar connections and become more global, critical thinkers. When you write or find profound and worthwhile essential understandings to represent what is important for students to retain beyond a course of study, you have successfully taken the idea of "transfer value" into account. If you stay on course with using these essential understandings to guide your students' instruction, you will prime them to make key connections and transfer information to broaden their thinking. When students say something like the following, they have "arrived," and you have aided them on their journey:

- *A few years ago I read the book* Sacrifice, *set in Salem, Massachusetts, in 1692. The panic of witchcraft affected the characters as townspeople turned against each other. I also better understand the terror and ignorance of characters and their motivations in* The Crucible *now that I'm reading literature with a similar plotline and historical setting.*

- *Religious intolerance seems to be a recurring theme in history and even ironic. We learned before that one reason early settlers came to the New World was to practice religious freedom, but yet there was religious intolerance in many of the colonies. Then we learned that religious intolerance was evident all throughout history—Spanish Inquisition, pogroms in Russia, Holocaust. Now we continue to learn about religious intolerance all over the world today. It doesn't seem that we've learned too much from our past mistakes.*

In addition to reviewing the essential understandings in Figure 2.2 with the aforementioned bullets in mind, think about or discuss with colleagues how some essential understandings can apply to different units of instruction across grades and subjects.

SPECIAL CONSIDERATIONS: TIME, INTELLECTUAL GROWTH, CLUSTERING

In the upcoming Exercise 3, "How Do Educators Create (or Revise) Essential Understandings?," you will have a chance to practice writing and revising your own essential understandings. Before we delve into this exercise, I want to mention a few additional points for you to consider as you are working:

- *Time.* It is important to know the amount of time you have available to teach your targeted unit and find or craft essential understandings that take this factor into account. If you have three weeks for a unit, you do not want five statements; that wouldn't be sufficient time to explore them all thoroughly. By the same token, avoid using more than six essential understandings for a comprehensive unit because that is probably about the maximum number you can aptly cover for a six- to eight-week unit. This is generally the case, but not always. So keep in mind how many understandings you will create based on the time you have at your disposal to teach your targeted unit.

- *Intellectual growth.* When you build or revise essential understandings, be aware that as students advance through the grades, the essential understandings should be commensurate with their growth and development and serve to continuously challenge them. You know that essential understandings are expressly written to form a relationship between at least two concepts that emanate from standards to articulate what students should understand. Therefore, there will undoubtedly be some of the same concepts from grade to grade, and it is important to determine what you want students to glean as they become more adept learners. Note that there are many different ways that an essential understanding can be written using the same concepts.

For example, students will revisit *character* and *setting* repeatedly throughout their schooling. Following are several understandings that can be used with these two concepts for various grades and literary units of study. Some clearly overlap, so teachers can choose the language they prefer; others are more sophisticated, for older and advanced students:

o Settings can shape and transform characters' beliefs, feelings, and actions.
o Settings can facilitate growth and change for characters, thereby impacting the plot.
o Authors suggest settings through characters' dialectical and speech patterns.
o Settings can create a mood or atmosphere that impacts characters' motivations and actions.
o Settings can symbolize the emotional state of characters and propel the plot forward.
o Settings that provide a cultural context can foster character identity and newfound perspectives.
o Historical settings can influence the interactions among main and subordinate characters, which can impact the plot and contribute to the theme.
o Complex characters develop through their interactions with other characters and reactions to settings.

As students learn and apply more sophisticated reading strategies with more complex text, it is critical that they be required to apply and synthesize these—and, of course, other—concepts at a higher level. If teachers were to create the same understandings from the elementary school years into high school using the same concepts, the bar for students would be set too low for them to demonstrate higher learning and growth as they mature. Given two concepts, there are myriad ways to write essential understandings; so devise and choose appropriate ones based on your student population and the considerations I've shared.

- *Clustering.* As mentioned previously, essential understandings serve to foster critical thinking and problem solving, and to help students make connections and transfer knowledge. To support this goal, think about using the same essential understandings over two or three grade levels. As students approach different and more complex subject matter, topics, and texts, encourage them to see the relationships by using the same understandings for grade clusters (e.g., 3–5, 6–8, 9–10, 11–12). For example, you might use something like this for Grades 7 and 8: *Intolerance leads to unspeakable actions, which can desensitize communities.* It could pertain to units of study within and across these grades, such as the Crusades during a study of Medieval Europe, the conquistadors who destroyed civilizations, the Salem witch trials, the Trail of Tears, and slavery.

Review Figure 2.2, which has the essential understandings aligned to the CCR Anchor Standards for Reading. Could any of those serve for a tight cluster of grades? Teaching this way also supports the notion of curriculum mapping. Educators can build upon prior knowledge and introduce appropriately challenging material through horizontal articulation across subjects and units of study in the same grade, plus vertically between different grade levels. When essential understandings guide instruction and when there is an intentional fluid progression of skill building and conceptual focus, students can more easily see connections and transfer knowledge from subject to subject and grade to grade.

CONSTRUCTING YOUR OWN ESSENTIAL UNDERSTANDINGS

Chapter 1 guided you through two exercises: (1) "What Is the Best Way to Group Standards?" and (2) "How Are Standards Used to Determine What Students Should Know?" At this juncture, you will embark upon Exercise 3: "How Do Educators Create (or Revise) Essential Understandings?" It includes step-by-step directions to help you practice creating your own essential understandings. I must admit, creating rigorous, meaningful essential understandings is challenging work. There is a process to follow that I delineate, and I find that those who abort it and jump ahead do not necessarily create the most enriching statements. Invariably, they end up forging ahead only to find that if they had started with Step 1 they would have had a stronger end result. Therefore, I suggest following each step in order. After this exercise and the next one in Chapter 3 for essential unit and guiding questions, you will have completed the components shown in Figure 2.6, "Unit Template Excerpt 2." The number of lesson guiding questions listed in the figure that follows is merely an example. You will determine how many are needed to best accommodate your unit goals.

Unit Template Excerpt 2

Unit: _____

Subject: _____ Grade: _____ Timing: _____

ELA Common Core Standards		Knowledge
Content Area Standards: _____ (if applicable)		Knowledge
Essential Understandings	**Essential Unit Guiding Questions**	**Lesson Guiding Questions**
1.	1.	Lesson (L) 1.1: L 1.2:
2.	2.	Lesson (L) 2.1: L 2.2: L 2.3:
3.	3.	Lesson (L) 3.1: L 3.2:

FIGURE 2.6

EXERCISE 3: HOW DO EDUCATORS CREATE (OR REVISE) ESSENTIAL UNDERSTANDINGS?

STEP 1: Assemble Materials

Before beginning, lay out the tools you'll need for your targeted unit.

- English language arts (ELA) Common Core Standards that you grouped (Chapter 1, Exercise 1) and entered on the unit template
- The knowledge list you created (Chapter 1, Exercise 2), which should also be on the unit template
- Textbook, materials, and resources tied to the unit
- Laptop or paper and pencil

. . . and a little chocolate wouldn't hurt.

STEP 2: Find and Make a List of Concepts Embedded in the Standards

- Review the standards on your unit template and systematically make a list of all the concepts that are in each standard on a separate sheet of paper or a new page on the computer.
- Use Figure 2.3, "English Language Arts Concepts," and Figure 2.4, "Content Area Concepts" (as applicable), to assist with this task.

As you might have noticed earlier when you previewed Figure 2.3, the concepts are categorized based on the ELA Common Core headings (e.g., Reading Standards for Literature, Reading Standards for Informational Text, etc.). This figure also provides some concepts in more than one category since there is a great deal of overlap. Figure 2.4 includes a column for macroconcepts. Basically, these are overarching megaconcepts that can be used across subjects and grades. Because they are broad and encompass many concepts, they are typically used for crafting interdisciplinary units. However, feel free to use them for your unit, as needed, even if you are addressing one content area.

If you see concepts in either Figure 2.3 or Figure 2.4 that are related to your grouped standards but are not stated explicitly in the standards, feel free to include them. Also, you might find concepts that you listed in the *knowledge* component; it is fine to record these again on your concept list. You will need this list of concepts that you generate for the next step, so keep it handy. If you typed the list on a computer, I suggest you print it out.

STEP 3: Brainstorm Statements

- Keep your tools out for reference and gather the concepts you generated in Step 2.
- Consider the age and readiness level of your students and—above all—the essence of what you want them to glean from this unit.
- Look at your concept list, and begin brainstorming statements that include relationships between at least two concepts. Truly brainstorm by avoiding any conversation or critiquing as you list statements; know that in the next step you will edit and revise to find just the right verb or collapse statements that appear too similar. To get started, you

might have a conversation with colleagues (or yourself) about the key takeaways from the unit using this beginning frame: *Students will understand that. . . .* What follows this phrase should be a complete sentence rather than a fragment. Check that this is the case by removing the sentence starter to see if what you have left is a complete thought.

Another suggestion is to use a formula to write essential understandings. Take a look at the types of formulas shown in Figure 2.7 and choose what works for you or modify what I have suggested. Note that concepts can be embedded in a phrase, such as *understanding purpose and audience, comparing and contrasting texts, formulating ideas,* and *punctuating sentences.* Remember that at this point you are brainstorming, so merely write down statements; you'll have an opportunity to revise them in the following step. I even advocate teaching students how to articulate a theme for a reading selection or craft a thesis statement using one or both of the constructions I'm sharing here.

Ideas for Formulating Essential Understandings

CONCEPT +	VERB(S) +	CONCEPT +	ANSWER: So what? Why is this important? How? What about it?
Communities	change and grow	throughout time	by the cultural and religious contributions of people who live there.
Music	can serve	as a political, social, and cultural vehicle	for fostering change, action, and solidarity.
Writers	make more	convincing arguments	
	and support	explanations more clearly	when they cite salient quotes from a text to support their assertions and analyses.

CONCEPTUAL PHRASE +	ANSWER: So what? Why is this important? How? What about it?
To counter unjust leaders and support righteousness,	individuals might courageously help others to survive.
To gain both general knowledge and discipline-specific expertise,	people read a wide range of quality materials and refine and share what they glean through writing and speaking.
To present an argument that effectively convinces others,	writers must articulate a clear position, evaluate and use evidence to support it, and address counterclaims.
Knowing the purpose and audience at the outset of writing	allows authors to incorporate the appropriate elements for a specific genre and focus on a target audience.

CONCEPTUAL PHRASE +	ANSWER: So what? Why is this important? How? What about it?
Engaging in physical activity and eating nutritional meals	promote optimal health, which can contribute to longevity.
Evaluating and choosing multiple credible sources	enable writers to identify effective reasons and sound evidence to support their assertions.

FIGURE 2.7

A word to the wise: If you are using your state or district document as a guide, or even a published textbook that claims to include big ideas or enduring understandings, be sure that the essential understandings you find from these resources follow the criteria I have explained. Many times I find resources that purport to include essential understandings, but in actuality are providing statements of fact; these are better suited for the knowledge section of your unit template.

STEP 4: Revise the Brainstormed Statements

Revise the statements you have brainstormed. As you do so, avoid overlap. Combine similar statements and/or wordsmith them to arrive at one essential understanding that can stand alone. If some statements subsume others, then merge them or just keep one statement that is the strongest. As a brief example, what follows are similar statements to think about or discuss with colleagues. You could select, merge, or rewrite any of them to arrive at the one that best represents what you want students to understand about the literary work:

- Settings impact characters' actions.
- Settings shape and transform characters.
- Settings can change characters.
- Characters evolve as they encounter various settings.
- Settings can facilitate growth and change for characters, thereby impacting the plot.

Also keep in mind the considerations that were discussed earlier in this chapter and that I reemphasize here: verbs, importance factor, and transfer value.

- *Verbs.* Use Figure 2.8, "Verbs That Show Relationships," to revise your statements so that there are no forms of the verb *to be* to connect concepts. In addition, make sure you write present-tense verbs. Once you write past-tense verbs, you have grounded your statement with an event, situation, or person from the past. You want your statements to potentially be used in different situations across time.

Verbs That Show Relationships

act	elicit	initiate	recommend
activate	employ	institute	reconcile
ascertain	enable	integrate	reduce
build	encourage	interact	regulate
change	energize	interpret	reinforce
construct	enhance	introduce	relate
contrast	establish	invent	resolve
contribute	estimate	lead to	respond
control	evolve	manage	restore
convert	examine	manipulate	revitalize
cooperate	expand	map	separate
correspond	explain	model	sequence
create	expound	modify	shape
decipher	express	motivate	share
define	facilitate	offer	show
demonstrate	formulate	organize	simplify
describe	foster	originate	solve
design	generate	perform	stimulate
determine	guide	persuade	structure
develop	identify	point to	suggest
devise	illustrate	precipitate	support
differentiate	impact	prevent	transfer
direct	improve	produce	transform
discriminate	incorporate	promote	transition
display	increase	prompt	translate
disseminate	induce	propel	transmit
distinguish	infer	propose	uncover
distribute	influence	provide	use
dominate	inform	provoke	utilize
drive	inhibit	question	

FIGURE 2.8

- *Importance factor.* Make sure your essential understandings answer the question of why the content is important to learn or what makes it so salient. These examples—along with others in this chapter and elsewhere in the book—will help elucidate this point:

- *Individuals might courageously help others to survive* does not provide information about why individuals are prompted to stick their necks out. This shows a more comprehensive understanding: *To counter unjust leaders and support righteousness, individuals might courageously help others to survive.*
- *The structures and behaviors of living organisms help them adapt to their environments.* This doesn't answer the question *why?* A stronger statement would include this at the end: *so they can survive.*
- Try this: *People cause changes to the environment.* What about it? So what? This reflects a deeper essential truth: *People cause changes to the environment, which can impact organisms' survival and reproduction.*
- Consider math: *People can display the same data in different ways, which may lead to various interpretations and conclusions.* If the statement were merely *People can display the same data in different ways*, it would not be complete in furnishing the essence of the unit goal.
- Any subject matter is ripe for creating essential understandings. An art teacher might make the point of why considering others' perceptions about artwork is a central principle in her teaching: *People can listen to someone's beliefs and reasoning about a work of art to gain a new perspective and perhaps a greater appreciation for the art piece.*

- *Transfer value.* The goal is to prime students to connect and transfer what they learn within and across grades and even subjects; therefore, it is important to create conceptually based, general statements that can allow for this transference. If you are too specific and insert, for example, Navajo, Amelia Earhart, the Versailles Treaty, Hester Prynne, or the Mississippi River, they cannot make these connections. Instead, replace any proper nouns with general concepts. When you create your lesson guiding questions featured in the next chapter, you will address the specifics of the unit and include the pertinent factual knowledge. Plus, this specific information should be addressed in the knowledge component. The glory of essential understandings is that they are enduring, so refrain from using proper nouns or past-tense verbs, as illustrated in Figure 2.9.

Strong Versus Weak Essential Understandings 2

Weak Essential Understandings	Red Flags	Stronger Essential Understandings
Virginia communities have a long history and have changed greatly from the time of the early explorers to today.	• *Virginia* shouldn't be used because it is a proper noun; the statement would only work for this state. • The verbs could be stronger. • Although there are concepts—*community, history, explorers*—there are other concepts that should be included that contribute to change. What is really worth knowing is why communities change, a question that isn't fully addressed.	Communities change and grow throughout time by the cultural and religious contributions of the people who live there.

FIGURE 2.9 *(Continued)*

FIGURE 2.9 (Continued)

Weak Essential Understandings	Red Flags	Stronger Essential Understandings
In *The Hundred Dresses*, Maddie realizes that standing by while Wanda is bullied makes her an accomplice and just as guilty of bullying Wanda as the girls who taunt her.	• The essential understandings should be void of proper nouns: *The Hundred Dresses*, Maddie, Wanda. • The statement is specific to a work of literature even though it contains global concepts.	Those who witness an act of bullying and fail to take action perpetuate cruel and unacceptable behavior, thereby serving as accomplices in persecuting others.

FIGURE 2.9

STEP 5: Record Your Essential Understandings

- Once you have crafted your essential understandings, logically sequence them based on how you will teach the unit. You will see two places on the unit template for entering essential understandings. (See Chapter 1, Exercise 1, for options on how to access the unit template if you haven't done so already.)
- On page 1 of the unit template, list all of the essential understandings and associated questions so you can see an outline of the whole unit.
- Note that page 2 and the similarly formatted pages that follow are dedicated to each essential understanding and other template components that will be discussed in the chapters that follow.

SHARING ESSENTIAL UNDERSTANDINGS WITH YOUR STUDENTS

So should teachers share essential understandings with their students? The essential understandings basically give away what you want all students to realize, so if you show or read them, it is most effective to do so near the end of the unit. Also, keep in mind that educators write essential understandings to gain clarity about the direction of a unit and its outcomes based on standards. They serve to keenly identify targeted goals prior to teaching. As such, they are written in adult language, so not all students can decipher them. Unit guiding questions, which are the subject of the next chapter, are intentionally written in language suitable for students' age and readiness and used during teaching. If you wanted to also share essential understandings, do not water them down. Instead, write them for you—the professional—then substitute difficult vocabulary for age-appropriate language. Show the connections among the questions the students explored throughout the unit and the associated essential understandings. Also, you might choose to conduct one of the following exercises through discussion or writing. Any would help to further foster the goal of having students engage in thinking critically and making connections.

Option 1

In small groups or as a class, have students brainstorm a list of lessons and activities they have completed during the unit. Then ask them to work in pairs or trios to create general statements about what they learned based on the list they generated. Tell them their statements cannot include proper nouns. You can help guide them to take the factual information from the lessons and see if they can arrive at a larger understanding. Promote conversation through these kinds of questions:

- *Why did we learn about this?*
- *Can you make any connections between this unit and other units we have studied?*
- *Can you make connections about life based on what you learned?*
- *Did you learn how to solve any problems through our work in this unit? How so?*
- *Can you think of a theme based on what we studied much like you would consider the theme or central message of a text?*

Option 2

- Write each factual piece of information that was presented in the unit on a separate card. Gather the fact cards together to make a set.
- Distribute a set of fact cards to each small group. Have the groups categorize the cards in a way that makes sense.
- Ask students to carefully study all the cards in one category at a time. At the top of each category, have them write a general statement on a blank card that does not include any of the proper nouns that are on the teacher-prepared fact cards they grouped.
- Have each group share and discuss these generalizations with the whole class. You can then reveal the essential understandings and see if any are similar to what students created as a springboard for discussion.

Option 3

- As a class, generate a list of the different lessons and activities students completed in the unit.
- Distribute concept cards to small groups—for example, *diversity, patterns, conflict, friendship,* and so on.
- Instruct groups to identify the concept cards that are associated with what they learned, and use these concepts to create general statements to share with the class.

LOOKING AHEAD

One significant goal for students on the journey toward deep understanding is to make connections and transfer knowledge. Using essential understandings and guiding questions help support students in this endeavor. In Chapter 3, you will learn more about guiding questions—specifically, the difference between unit and lesson guiding questions, why these questions are so important, how to go about creating them for your students, and ways to use them during instruction. I also define and share a process for creating text-dependent questions to facilitate close reading of complex text.

3

Guiding Questions

The essential question is conceptual commitment. When a teacher or group of teachers selects a question to frame and guide curriculum design, it is a declaration of intent. In a sense you are saying, "This is our focus for learning. I will put my teaching skills into helping my students examine the key concept implicit in the essential question."

—Heidi Hayes Jacobs (1997, p. 27)

When I was teaching, I was great at finding activities and assessments from colleagues, on the Internet, in a textbook, or through other resources. And I would spend time creating, revising, finding, and then finally teaching them. Even though I felt what I delivered was engaging and educationally sound, I sometimes forgot to tell students the *purpose* of what they were doing to make it wholly meaningful for them, as well. If I had used questions to set the stage for intentional work, what I was teaching would have been much more effective. It's a winning combination not only to deliver compelling instruction, but also to alert students to the overriding goal of each learning opportunity so they are clear about the outcomes and intent. Through the use of essential guiding questions, you can do just that. Guiding questions are carefully crafted and provocative, and they usher students through a unit of study in a thoughtful way that focuses on key learning goals and exploration. As you read this chapter, you will distinguish between different types of questions and their purposes for curriculum design and instruction.

THE IMPORTANCE OF GUIDING QUESTIONS

Each activity, each lesson, each reading assignment, each assessment should be focused around a guiding question so teachers have a commitment to what they are teaching. As such, students have a purpose for what they are expected to accomplish.

Consider the following two scenarios. In which situation do you think students would likely engage more deeply with key concepts and retain factual knowledge?

1. Students are studying the concept of movement, both literally and figuratively. Literally, they focus on settlement in the Americas and the physical movement associated with relocating from one place to another. Through literature, they experience figurative movement as characters change and grow. They are exposed to a variety of photographs and video excerpts; they read differentiated nonfiction and historical fiction materials; and they engage in activities and assignments such as cooperative jigsaws, graphic organizers, informal debates, and oral and written responses to essays and journal prompts.

2. In addition to what is articulated in Scenario 1, students are asked to focus on these questions, which are tied to everything they do throughout the thematic unit on movement:

   • Why do people move?
   • How can movement lead to positive growth and change?
   • How can movement create conflict and opportunity?

The obvious answer is Scenario 2. When students know why they are completing an activity, reading an excerpt, watching a video clip, working with a computer software program, or listening to a lecture, they are apt to glean more. The second scenario includes a list of essential guiding questions that students would be exposed to throughout the unit and would then need to address in a summative assessment to demonstrate understanding.

Guiding questions—along with essential understandings—are powerful together as they both contribute to meaningful learning opportunities. Consider these essential understandings linked to the guiding questions above:

   • Movement can create discontent and conflict, which might lead to negative consequences for individuals or groups.
   • People who avoid change might become stagnant and miss valuable opportunities.
   • Movement provides an opportunity for individuals to experience new situations and ideas that cause them to grow and change emotionally and intellectually.

SHARING GUIDING QUESTIONS WITH YOUR STUDENTS

Guiding questions articulate the purpose for learning and promote students' self-discovery, so these questions should be clearly visible for students when you are teaching every unit. While the language for essential understandings is often sophisticated, guiding questions should be pointed, succinct, and provocative. They should be written so students understand them. See examples of pairings of essential understandings and unit questions in Figure 3.1. Notice that the language for essential understandings is not only more complex, but that it also reveals the answers to the guiding questions that form the basis for teaching.

Possible Essential Understandings and Unit Questions

Essential Understandings	Essential Unit Questions
Readers generate and respond to purposeful questions associated with a text to delve deeply into an author's work to explore surface and hidden meanings.	How does questioning enhance comprehension?
Writers who employ a systematic series of steps defined in the writing process produce optimal results.	How does the writing process benefit writers?
Military leaders who capitalize on economic advantages and military might can position themselves for victory.	How can military leaders position themselves for victory?
Historical settings provide a unique backdrop that can change characters by fueling their actions and beliefs, thereby impacting the plot.	How can historical settings impact characters?

FIGURE 3.1

THE DIFFERENCES BETWEEN ESSENTIAL UNIT AND LESSON GUIDING QUESTIONS

There are two sets of guiding questions. What have been introduced thus far are what I call *essential unit guiding questions.* They are overarching, derived from the essential understandings, and are transferrable. Because they are conceptually based, many of the questions can apply to other units of study within and across grades and even provide commentary about life. For example, the essential unit guiding question *How can movement create conflict and opportunity?* can be relevant to the historical time period of the first settlers arriving in our country. The same guiding question can also pertain to a multitude of other situations, such as the Irish who emigrated to the United States during the Potato Famine, the Chinese who came to work during the Gold Rush in California, or recent immigrants from Central and South America. The question can also apply to figurative movement, such as changing one's mindset to embrace and grapple with new ideas.

Essential unit questions help students make connections and bridge what they learn to new situations and content. Teachers use these types of questions at specific points during the unit and in the culminating summative assessment so students can demonstrate their understanding of the whole unit. Lesson guiding questions are necessary to address the factual knowledge that builds the foundation for understanding the more complex essential unit guiding questions. In language arts, for instance, students might read a novel, short story, or play. You would surely want them to know the characters' names and their personalities, identify the specific settings, retell the plot, explain the theme or central message, define and identify tone, and so forth. Therefore, you would fashion lesson guiding questions to focus students' attention on these specific aspects of the reading. By asking students these factual questions associated explicitly with content, you are setting the stage for them to eventually grasp the greater unit guiding questions, such as *How does the setting influence characters? How do obstacles facilitate change? Why do civilizations fall?* Once armed with the factual information, students can investigate responses to the unit questions, which are called *essential unit* guiding questions because they represent the overall essence of the content.

See Figure 3.2, "Argumentation Writing Standards With Essential Understandings and Guiding Questions," for a sample of argumentation writing standards, essential understandings, and essential unit and lesson guiding questions working together to form a comprehensive orchestration of the outcomes. Use what I have as a guide and adjust accordingly as long as you maintain the integrity of standards-based, effective unit design. You might adjust the order of what I have in the figure to reflect how you feel the unit should logically flow. If you teach a lower grade, I might provide more than what you need, so revise the line items to suit your teaching style and grade-level standards.

To provide you with additional examples of how standards, essential understandings, and the two levels of guiding questions work together, also read Figure 3.3, "Essential Understandings and Guiding Questions Aligned to Selected CCR Anchor Standards for Reading." Since I have used the anchor standards for this figure, refer to your grade-level Common Core Standards and revise the guiding questions as appropriate. In addition, personalize the lesson guiding questions to associate with specific text you are reading in class. To this point, I include some blank spaces to indicate where you can insert a title. I also suggest that you add text-dependent questions to the lesson guiding questions; see the upcoming section on text-dependent questions for guidance.

DESIGNING TEXT-DEPENDENT QUESTIONS FOR COMPLEX TEXT

Text-dependent questions, as the name suggests, are questions designed around a specific text that prompt readers to use the actual text to respond. These are not questions that rely on students to use their personal opinions and experiences to respond. Rather, text-dependent questions require readers to keenly examine the content of a text and its structure in order to uncover rich meaning.

Close reading of complex texts is mandatory for students who need to meet the Common Core Standards for Reading. These standards call on students to collect evidence, build knowledge, and glean insight from myriad reading materials that expressly include complex text. Specifically, this strand of standards focuses on the competencies of analysis, evaluation, and inferential thinking.

To support students in meeting these rigorous standards, either find or craft text-dependent questions that are pertinent to a difficult reading selection. This will give your students the opportunity to grapple with the text on a more intimate level in order to decipher both surface and hidden meanings. David Coleman and Susan Pimentel, coauthors of the Common Core, explain the nature of high quality text-dependent questions as follows:

> High quality text-dependent questions are more often text specific rather than generic. That is, high quality questions should be developed to address the specific text being read, in response to the demands of that text. Good questions engage students to attend to the particular dimensions, ideas, and specifics that illuminate each text. Though there is a productive role for good general questions for teachers and students to have at hand, materials should not over rely on "cookie-cutter" questions that could be asked of any text, such as "What is the main idea? Provide three supporting details." Materials should develop sequences of individually crafted questions that draw students and teachers into an exploration of the text or texts at hand. (2012, pp. 6–7)

Argumentation Writing Standards With Essential Understandings and Guiding Questions

Common Core Writing Standards	Essential Understandings	Essential Unit Guiding Questions	Lesson Questions
Produce clear and coherent writing in which the development, organization, and style are appropriate to **task, purpose, and audience** (2010a, W.9–10.4).	**PURPOSE/ AUDIENCE/STYLE** The purpose and audience for writing shape the content, structure, and style of an author's work.	**UNIT INTRODUCTION** How do purpose and audience influence an author's work?	• Why do people write? What are purposes for various writing types? Who are the audiences for each type? • What are the elements and structure of an argument?
Establish and maintain a formal **style** and objective **tone** while attending to the norms and conventions of the discipline in which they are writing (W.9–10.1d).		How do I write with the proper style and tone?	• What is my purpose for writing an argument? Who will read it? • How do I maintain a formal style and objective tone in my paper? Why is this important?
Introduce precise claim(s), distinguish the claim(s) from alternate or opposing claims, and create an organization that establishes clear relationships among claim(s), counterclaims, reasons, and evidence (W.9–10.1a).	**INTRODUCTION** Introductions provide context for an argument and give writers an opportunity to make a favorable impression on readers.	How can I write an effective introduction for my argument?	• What does an introduction for an argument include? • What is a debatable topic or issue I can use as the basis for my argument? What claim can I make? • How can I write a thesis statement to stake a claim? Where should I include my thesis in my introduction? • What strategies can I use to begin my argument so I get my reader's attention? For example, what quotes, anecdotes, background information, or definition of key terms should I use?

FIGURE 3.2 (*Continued*)

FIGURE 3.2 (Continued)

Common Core Writing Standards	Essential Understandings	Essential Unit Guiding Questions	Lesson Questions
• Write arguments to support claims in an analysis of substantive topics or texts, using valid **reasoning** and relevant and sufficient **evidence** (W.9–10.1). • Draw **evidence** from literary or informational texts to support analysis, reflection, and research (W.9–10.9). • Gather relevant information from **multiple** authoritative print and digital **sources**, using advanced searches effectively; assess the usefulness of each source in answering the research question; **integrate information** into the text selectively to maintain the flow of ideas, avoiding **plagiarism** and following a standard format for **citation** (W.9–10.8). • Produce clear and coherent writing in which the **development, organization,** and style are appropriate to task, purpose, and audience (W.9–10.4). • Introduce precise claim(s), distinguish the claim(s) from alternate or opposing claims, and create an **organization** that establishes clear relationships among claim(s), counterclaims, reasons, and evidence (W.9–10.1a).	**REASONS/ EVIDENCE** Writers provide clear reasons and relevant evidence culled from multiple, reliable sources to strengthen an argument. **ORGANIZATION/ DEVELOPMENT** A well-organized and developed argument facilitates the flow of ideas and promotes understanding. **CREDIBILITY/ ATTRIBUTION** With proper attribution, writers selectively integrate credible and accurate information from multiple sources to construct a sound argument.	How can I organize and develop a logical argument? How can I evaluate the credibility of my sources and give proper citation?	**REASONS** • How can I support my claim with logical reasoning (logos)? What does deduction and induction mean? Which reasoning technique is most effective for my argument? • How do my reasons link to the thesis? **EVIDENCE** • What sources can I use to gather relevant evidence? • What evidence should I use from these sources to support my reasons? • How can I interpret my evidence to explain what it means? How do I know if I should paraphrase or summarize information or use quotes, statistics, findings, facts, examples, or anecdotes? • When will I know if I have enough evidence? • What is the best way to logically organize my reasons and supporting evidence to make a sound argument? • What are indicators that a source is credible? • How might the tone or style of the writing impact its credibility? • What are characteristics of unreliable sources? • What is plagiarism? • How do I properly reference sources I use? • What punctuation is needed for in-text citations? • What is the standard format for citation?

Common Core Writing Standards	Essential Understandings	Essential Unit Guiding Questions	Lesson Questions
Write arguments to support claims in an analysis of substantive topics or texts, using **valid reasoning** and relevant and sufficient evidence (W.9–10.1).	**FALLACIES** Logical fallacies (e.g., hasty generalizations, circular reasoning, either/or fallacy, etc.) undermine the strength of an argument, causing readers to disavow the claim and supporting evidence.	How can logical fallacies affect my reasoning?	• What are examples of fallacies? • How do I avoid fallacies which undermine the logic of my argument?
Use words, phrases, and clauses to **link the major sections of the text**, create cohesion, and clarify the relationships between claim(s) and reasons, between reasons and evidence, and between claim(s) and counterclaims (W.9–10.1c).	**TRANSITIONS** To assist readers in following a coherent argument, writers use transitions to form logical connections among ideas and clarify relationships among sections.	How do transitions help readers follow the logic of my argument?	• Why do writers use transitions? • How can I use transitions to form logical connections and clarify relationships between sections of my argument? • What transitional words and phrases can I use to create cohesion within each paragraph?
Develop claim(s) and **counterclaims** fairly, supplying evidence for each while pointing out the strengths and limitations of both in a manner that anticipates the audience's knowledge level and concerns (W.9–10.1b).	**COUNTERCLAIMS** Writers who anticipate and address opposing viewpoints exhibit deep understanding of an issue, which strengthens the overall argument.	Why and how do I address counterarguments?	• What are the opposing viewpoints to my claim? Why should I address them? • How do I acknowledge and address them? • Where do I insert counterarguments in my paper?

FIGURE 3.2 (Continued)

FIGURE 3.2 (Continued)

Common Core Writing Standards	Essential Understandings	Essential Unit Guiding Questions	Lesson Questions
Provide a **concluding** statement or section that follows from and supports the argument presented (W.9–10.1e).	**CONCLUSION** Writers create conclusions for an argument to leave a lasting impression on readers and compel them to act or change their views.	How can I effectively conclude my argument paper?	• How can I summarize the main points of my argument? • What can I include that might compel readers to act? • What strategies that I used for writing my introduction would work for my conclusion?
Develop and strengthen writing as needed by planning, revising, editing, rewriting, or trying a new approach, focusing on addressing what is most significant for a specific purpose and audience (W.9–10.5).	**WRITING PROCESS** Employing the writing process enables writers to challenge their own ideas and make necessary edits, which can lead to an improved and stronger argument.	How do writers use the writing process to help produce optimal results?	• What are the steps in the writing process? • How do I use each step to develop and strengthen my argument? • Revising Ideas: What information can I delete that is trivial or irrelevant? What sections do I need to reorder for clarity or to make a stronger argument? Can I substitute weaker words for stronger ones? Does my introduction need to be more compelling? Do I need to rewrite any repetitive sentence beginnings? Do I need to add to my conclusion to leave a stronger impression on readers? • Editing/proofreading Ideas: Are my punctuation marks in the right place especially for referencing sources? Are all of my words spelled correctly? Have I indented where I should?

FIGURE 3.2

Essential Understandings and Guiding Questions Aligned to Selected CCR Anchor Standards for Reading

CCR Anchor Standards	Essential Understandings	Unit Guiding Questions	Lesson Questions
Read closely to determine what the text says explicitly and to make logical inferences from it; cite specific textual evidence when writing or speaking to support conclusions drawn from the text (2010a, R. CCR.1).	• People cite concrete evidence from a text to support their analysis of what the text says explicitly and inferentially.	• Why do people cite textual evidence?	• What textual evidence can I use from this reading to support my analysis about ____? • What are inferences? • What inferences can I make about ____ that can support my thesis?
Determine central ideas or themes of a text and analyze their development; summarize the key supporting details and ideas (R.CCR.2).	• Summarizing allows readers to succinctly articulate the substance of a work to facilitate overall comprehension. • Proficient readers engage in an ongoing process of extracting key information from a text and tracking the development of central ideas to comprehend the whole of a text.	• How and why do people summarize?	• Why do people summarize reading material? • What are the organizational structure and elements of a summary? • How do I write a summary? • How often should I summarize as I read? • How can a written or oral summary help me to better understand what I'm reading?

FIGURE 3.3 (Continued)

FIGURE 3.3 (Continued)

CCR Anchor Standards	Essential Understandings	Unit Guiding Questions	Lesson Questions
Analyze how and why individuals, events, and ideas develop and interact over the course of a text (R.CCR.3).	• Characters' motivations, circumstances, and interactions with others drive plot development.	• How do characters impact the plot?	• Who are the characters in the story _____? • What is the distinction between types of characters (e.g., dynamic, static, stock)? What kind of character is _____? What evidence supports this? • What are the methods of characterization? Give examples of each for selected characters. • How do selected characters of this story impact events? What evidence from the story supports my impressions? • How do characters or individuals interact? What conclusions can I draw from these interactions?
	• Analyzing the development and interactions of individuals, events, and ideas allows readers to arrive at deeper insights and new perspectives.	• How can readers analyze text?	• Who are the key figures of this text? What are the significant events? • What provokes a change in individuals or events? How does the change impact others or society? • What new insights or beliefs can readers have after analyzing this text?
Assess how point of view or purpose shapes the content and style of a text (R.CCR.6).	• Proficient readers assess how the author's point of view or purpose and the use of rhetorical devices shape the content and style of the text.	• How does point of view or purpose shape a text?	• What is point of view? What is the author's point of view or purpose in this text? • What are rhetorical devices? How does the author use rhetorical devices to support his or her point of view or purpose?

CCR Anchor Standards	Essential Understandings	Unit Guiding Questions	Lesson Questions
(see previous row)	• Acknowledging and addressing counterclaims contribute to the strength of an argument and the authors' ability to successfully convince others of their point of view.	• How do writers establish a credible point of view?	• How does the author's point of view or purpose shape the content and/or style of this reading? • What counterclaims does the author acknowledge? Does the author address each one? Do they contribute to the strength of the argument? How so?
Delineate and evaluate the argument and specific claims in a text, including the validity of the reasoning as well as the relevance and sufficiency of the evidence (R.CCR.8).	• Readers assess the strength of an argument by evaluating the validity of a writer's reasoning and the relevancy and sufficiency of evidence.	• How can readers evaluate an author's argument?	• What is the author's position or claim? Is it clearly stated? • What reasons does the author give to support his or her position? Are they valid reasons? Does each reason support the position? • What evidence can I find that supports each reason? Is there enough evidence to convince me of the author's position? What additional evidence do I need? • Does the author cite sources for evidence? Do they seem to be credible sources? How do I know? • Do I support the author's position? Why or why not?

FIGURE 3.3

Text-dependent questions should not only be specific to targeted reading, but should also prompt students to think critically about what they have read. They should compel students to reach inside the text to answer the questions you have posed. Avoid asking questions that students can respond to without ever having read the material. Rather, ask probing questions that require them to carefully examine the text and, as a result, come to some greater realization or deeper understanding. Figure 3.4 juxtaposes questions that are not dependent on the text alongside those that are, so you can get a sense of the difference between the two.

Figure 3.6 features an explanation of a process that you can follow to craft or revise your own text-dependent questions, along with corresponding examples. Keep in mind that my questions in some steps in this figure are general in nature so that you can use them as a guide to build your own text-dependent questions. *Teachers should definitely personalize the questions so they are expressly associated with a particular text that is the center of instruction.* These are the steps that are illustrated in the figure:

Step 1: Develop essential understandings around the text.

Step 2: Identify what is noteworthy about the text.

Step 3: Create a final assessment.

Step 4: Target vocabulary, sentence syntax, and text structure.

Step 5: Recognize key details.

Step 6: Delve into challenging areas of the text.

Step 7: Arrange questions in appropriate order for instruction.

In Steps 4, 5, and 6, I remind readers to consider the Common Core Standards. Specifically, make sure you are aware of which grade-level standards apply to your targeted text and devise text-dependent questions and tasks accordingly (see Figure 3.5 for examples). It might

Not Text-Dependent Versus Text-Dependent Examples

Not Text-Dependent	Text-Dependent
In "Casey at the Bat," Casey strikes out. Describe a time when you failed at something.	What makes Casey's experiences at bat humorous?
In "Letter from a Birmingham Jail," Dr. King discusses nonviolent protest. Discuss, in writing, a time when you wanted to fight against something that you felt was unfair.	What can you infer from Dr. King's letter about the letter that he received?
In "The Gettysburg Address" Lincoln says the nation is dedicated to the proposition that all men are created equal. Why is equality an important value to promote?	"The Gettysburg Address" mentions the year 1776. According to Lincoln's speech, why is this year significant to the events described in the speech?

FIGURE 3.4

Source: Achieve the Core (www.achievethecore.org).

be that as you carefully read and annotate the text (Step 2) to prepare for writing your questions, you revise the list of standards that you had planned to apply to a given unit.

Ideally, you should aim to conduct classroom experiences that allow time for students to frequently and independently delve deeply into appropriately challenging text around these types of questions. However, do not completely abandon the notion of students' background knowledge and their ability to make personal connections, as there is still a place for these insights at a certain point during discussion. David Coleman, coauthor of the CC Standards, explains his experience building text-dependent questions as follows:

> It is not simple work because you're trying to define questions that not only are text dependent but worth asking, worth exploring, that deliver richly, that as you look at the text more closely you see more and more in it because that's the true source of excitement and interest. And I would say, to be clear, that once you've deeply taken in what exactly [Dr. Martin Luther] King meant and didn't mean by *tension* and you've immersed yourself in that, then it might be very interesting after such a close encounter to then say, *How does that resemble or not resemble what I've experienced or seen in others?* . . . [S]o it's more a matter of priority and giving more time for the text to breathe and be the first source of investigation than eliminating any kind of further connection. (Coleman, 2011)

Examples of Text-Dependent Questions Aligned to Standards

Common Core Standards	Text-Dependent Questions and Tasks*
Describe characters in a story (e.g., their traits, motivations, or feelings) and explain how their actions contribute to the sequence of events (2010a, RL.3.3).	• (Q3) Opal says, "She looked sad and old and wrinkled." What happened to cause Miss Franny to look this way? • (Q4) What were Opal's feelings when she realized how Miss Franny felt? • (Q5) Earlier in the story, Opal says that Winn-Dixie "has a large heart, too." What does Winn-Dixie do to show that he has a "large heart"?
Draw evidence from literary or informational texts to support analysis, reflection, and research (W.8.9).	• (Q10) In what ways is Douglass saying slaveholders are like robbers? Find and explore the structure of the sentence that gives voice to this idea most clearly.
Interpret figures of speech (e.g., hyperbole, paradox) in context and analyze their role in the text (L.11–12.5a).	• (Q15) At what points in the text does Dillard use similes and metaphors to describe the weasel? Why does she choose figurative language to do this?

FIGURE 3.5

*Achieve the Core, http://achievethecore.org.

Although the Common Core Standards do not include information about making text-to-self connections or accessing prior knowledge, there is a time when this might be fruitful. As Coleman and Pimentel note, "Student background knowledge and experiences can illuminate the reading but should not replace attention to the text itself" (2012, p. 7). With regard to text-to-text connections, they expect students to make these kinds of links between reading materials as long as this work does not supplant careful reading of the targeted text (p. 8).

In addition to the examples in Figure 3.6, review Lesson 2 in Chapter 8, where text-dependent questions for Sandra Cisneros's story "Eleven" are embedded within the lesson on characterization. I encourage you to consider the discussion in this section as you devise lesson guiding questions in the exercise at the end of this chapter. Use a combination of text-dependent and lesson guiding questions for your unit, as appropriate.

Designing Text-Dependent Questions

STEP 1: Develop Essential Understandings Around the Text

Explanation	When teachers identify the essential understandings that incorporate the key ideas of any text, they are clear-minded about what they want students to understand. Identifying this critical component helps guide teachers in fashioning effective text-dependent questions and also the final assessment. These essential understandings represent what the whole text is about, so it serves as a thematic statement. Since more than one theme emanates from a work, consider creating several such statements. The examples that follow show a combination of understandings for nonfiction or fiction texts. Fashion ones that work for your particular reading selections. To create your essential understandings around your text, you can use the process I detail in Chapter 2's Exercise 3. During that exercise, you were asked to generate a list of concepts. Use the concepts in Figures 2.3 and 2.4 to create essential understandings for your targeted text in various content areas. For literature, you might need to consider others, such as *alienation, charity, courage, diversity, fear, hope, immortality, isolationism, maturation, perseverance, prejudice, selfishness, tolerance,* and so forth.
Examples	<ul><li>The evolution and spread of religion can affect communities by influencing social structures and political beliefs.</li><li>Effective leaders can help unite disparate groups to achieve a unified goal by using compromise and strategy.</li><li>Artistic and literary contributions of civilizations influence and permeate contemporary society.</li><li>Sometimes the truth needs to remain secret to protect people.</li><li>Those who witness bullying and fail to take action perpetuate cruel and unacceptable behavior, thereby serving as accomplices in persecuting others.</li><li>The courage to break free of familiar ways creates freedom and self-confidence.</li><li>The structures and behaviors of living organisms help them adapt to their environments so they can survive.</li><li>Temperature determines the density of water which dictates the survival of organisms in certain environments.</li></ul>

◆ ◆ ◆ ◆ ◆

STEP 2: Identify What Is Noteworthy About the Text; Be Mindful of Standards

Explanation	Take note of what makes the text challenging, intriguing, stylistic, or worthy of investigation. See the examples in this step for the kinds of text you might identify; this list is not finite. Take out the text you're going to teach. Have a tool in hand so you can annotate, highlight, or use sticky notes to identify important concepts, a writer's style, a particular literary device, a salient passage, or something to point out to students that warrants further examination. You will use these notations later to create text-dependent questions. Keep in mind pertinent standards. Additionally, pay attention to general academic words (called Tier 2 in the CC) that students should learn and highlight or make a list of them. These are the kinds of words that appear across content area texts. Underline words in the text that students will probably not be able to define based on context clues. You will need to signify and provide a definition for these words. (See "How Do Teachers Facilitate Close Reading of Complex Text?")
Examples	<ul><li>allusion</li><li>analogy</li><li>bias</li><li>dialect</li><li>flashbacks</li><li>imagery</li><li>irony</li><li>tone (writer's attitude toward the audience, topic, or character conveyed through words and details)</li></ul> <ul><li>critical visual elements or graphics (e.g., diagrams, maps, tables, graphs, etc.)</li><li>distinctive writing style, such as repetition of sentence structure, phrases, particular words</li><li>passages replete with concepts that are hard to decipher</li><li>passages ripe for making inferences</li><li>passages that are difficult to read because of syntax</li><li>passages that make a significant point or need interpretation</li><li>passages with complicated use of figurative language</li></ul>

◆ ◆ ◆ ◆ ◆

STEP 3: Create a Final Assessment

Explanation	Another important tenet of backward design (mentioned previously in this book) besides identifying standards and key understandings is to determine a form of evidence prior to planning learning experiences and instruction. Therefore, determine now how students can demonstrate their understanding of the text. If the text is part of a greater unit of study, then you can also create a culminating or summative assessment for the whole unit. For now, create an assessment that asks students to use textual evidence to show what they have gleaned from a text selection. Design such an assessment with consideration of the essential understandings (Step 1) and targeted Common Core Standards. After creating all of your text-dependent questions, you might return to your final assessment and revise it, as needed.
Examples	• **Grade 3, 4, or 5:** Hiroki Sugihara's account of his father emphasizes the fact that Mr. Sugihara showed great courage when dealing with the Jewish refugees in Lithuania. Using specific details and quotes from the text [*Passage to Freedom*], explain how Mr. Sugihara's actions are a display of bravery and courage.*

FIGURE 3.6 *(Continued)*

FIGURE 3.6 (Continued)

- **Grade 7:** For homework, choose one of the following prompts to complete: (1) Construct a narrative that teaches the same lesson(s) that Tom [Sawyer] learns at the end of the passage. Incorporate both the voice of a narrator, as well as dialogue in your story. (2) Write a parody of the scene by changing the characters and work being done to reflect a modern dilemma.**
- **Grade 8:** Students use their research and their identification of patterns [emotion word *families*] to help them answer the following prompt: How do [Frederick] Douglass's feelings change over the course of this piece? What is Douglass trying to show about how slavery makes people feel? Write a paragraph in which you show how his feelings change and what you believe he is trying to show the reader.**
- **Middle school:** Use information from the text to create a comic strip that includes living organisms in a wetland as characters. Base the storyline in response to this guiding question—*How do living organisms in a wetland depend on one another and on their environment for survival?*
- **Middle school:** Write an informative piece to be displayed at a zoo describing adaptations that allow animals (and plants) to survive in the harsh desert climate. Incorporate textual evidence from your reading about hot deserts in your writing.
- **Grades 11–12:** Students should write an adequately planned and well-constructed informative essay regarding the meaning of the essay's title—"Living Like Weasels." Why has the author [Annie Dillard] chosen this title? Why is it significant? Students should include at least three pieces of evidence from the text to support their thoughts.**

◆ ◆ ◆ ◆ ◆

STEP 4: Target Vocabulary, Sentence Syntax, and Text Structure

Explanation	Provide opportunities for students to experience strong academic vocabulary through text-dependent questions and tasks. These words, referred to as Tier 2 words in the CC, are pervasive across disciplines so students need to master them to build comprehension. Additionally, address questions pertaining to sentence syntax and text structure. Highlight sentences that are difficult to decode so students have practice in deciphering meaning. Focus not only on teaching students how to figure out what a challenging, complex sentence means, but also the reason an author constructs such a sentence. Target text structure, as well, specifically the overall organization of the piece (e.g., enumeration, chronological order, cause and effect, comparison and contrast, etc.) and how it supports understanding. As always, make sure you have reviewed your grade-level standards and continue to formulate questions that address those that apply to your targeted text.	
	• These words are used in the text: _____ and _____. How do they reinforce *(support, reflect, explain, show)* _____? • Where in the text are words repeated? How does the meaning change in each context or reinforce other usages?	• What mood does the author evoke? What words or phrases support your impression? • Find places in the text that show description. What words or phrases are used to create this description?

	• Why are these words __________ used to describe ________? How do they further support *(explain, illuminate)* a part of the text? • Find some places in the text where stronger or more specific words could have been used. • How does changing key words alter the meaning? • What do these words mean: ________? Does the text help you to determine their meanings? • In what other contexts have you seen these words? Is the meaning different in these other texts? • What tone does the author establish? What words and phrases does the author use to support his/her attitude?	• Are there places in the text where text features are used for effect? How do these features facilitate comprehension? • How does punctuation inside a sentence help you to understand it better? • What is the organizational structure of the text (e.g., enumeration, problem-solution, compare-contrast, cause-effect, sequential)? Give examples from the text to show this structure. • How does the structure of the text facilitate meaning? • How do sentence beginnings enhance or deter from reading fluidly? • How do the sentence beginnings or sentence structures impact the text? Reflect the author's style? • Parse or diagram a long sentence to ascertain its core. • Divide a long sentence into simpler parts. What does each part mean?
Examples	**Examples—Various Grades*** • Reread the last two paragraphs on page 170. Using specific language from the text, what is a refugee? (*Passage to Freedom* by Ken Mochizuki, Grades 3–5) • In the stanza it reads, "A glimmer, and then a gleam of light!" Using context clues, what does "glimmer" mean? ("Midnight Ride of Paul Revere" by Longfellow, Grades 6–8) **Frederick Douglass, *Narrative of the Life of Frederick Douglass an American Slave, Written by Himself*—Grade 8**** **(Q5)** Which of these meanings of "trouble" is Douglass using? Why did he choose this word? How would the meaning have changed if he had chosen the word "anger"? **(Q6)** Why does Douglass describe the master's response as both "desired" and "unexpected"? Why the contrast between these two words? **Assignment:** Ask students to parse the syntax of the final sentence in the passage, paying careful attention to how the constituent parts of the sentence add up to create the unique meaning of Douglass's words. **(Q7)** When Douglass says, "They gave tongue to interesting thoughts," how is he using the word "tongue"? **(Q9)** How does the word "enable" change the meaning of the line it appears in? How can documents "enable" him to "utter [his] thoughts" or write? **(Q10)** In what ways is Douglass saying slaveholders are like robbers? Find and explore the structure of the sentence that gives voice to this idea most clearly.	

FIGURE 3.6 *(Continued)*

FIGURE 3.6 (Continued)

Annie Dillard, "Living Like Weasels"—Grades 11–12**

(Q13) In paragraph 15, Dillard imagines going "out of your ever-loving mind and back to your careless senses." What does she mean by "careless" in that sentence, and how is that reflected in the rest of the paragraph?

(Q14) Dillard urges her readers to "stalk your calling" by "plug[ging] into" your purpose—yet she describes this process as "yielding, not fighting." What message is she trying to convey with these words?

(Q17) Dillard also employs reflexive structures such as, "I startled a weasel who startled me." Identify an additional instance of this. What is the purpose of these sentences?

◆ ◆ ◆ ◆ ◆

STEP 5: Recognize Key Details

Explanation	Help orient students to what they are reading and draw their attention to key details in the text. These are a combination of foundational questions that support students in responding to more challenging questions that will follow and also questions that are typically literal. These answers can be found in the text or call for readers to connect ideas or information from the text. Think about what important information or ideas readers need to know and fashion questions around this. Use the basic question words to assist you: *who, what, where, when?* You might use *why, how?* In Step 6, you will tackle more sophisticated questions that require students to go to the next level of analysis. As mentioned, do not forget to review your grade-level standards and devise questions that fit accordingly. Here are the kinds of questions you can ask; customize them to your targeted text:

• What is the topic, idea, or major premise? Who are key individuals (or characters, historical figures, etc.)? • What does the introduction state about the information readers will learn? • What claim is the author making? What reasons support this claim? • How does the writer prove his/her hypothesis, position, or idea? • What does the text reveal about the subjects (e.g., individuals, animals, characters)? Physical appearance or attributes? Personality? Action or behavior? • What do you learn about this topic, idea, individuals, or characters? Given this information, what can you predict or hypothesize based on evidence in the text?	• What event is the basis for this text? What time period does the event take place? Where does it occur? What clues from the text help readers to recognize the time period and location? • What are significant dates and places reflected in the text? Which dates or places are most relevant? Why? • How does the text reveal information about geographical location or historical time period? • Who is the writer? From whose point of view is the text told? How do you know this? What is the author's purpose in writing? • What main idea or theme begins to emerge? What evidence supports your assertion? • Do you see a pattern begin to take shape? • What causes _____ (*a particular action, reaction, or event*) to happen?

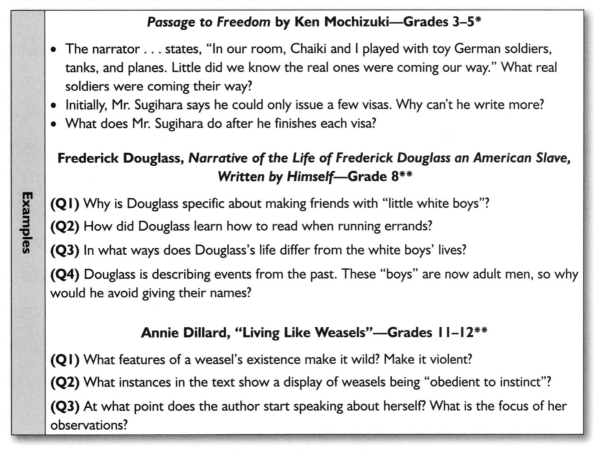

Examples

Passage to Freedom by Ken Mochizuki—Grades 3–5*

- The narrator . . . states, "In our room, Chaiki and I played with toy German soldiers, tanks, and planes. Little did we know the real ones were coming our way." What real soldiers were coming their way?
- Initially, Mr. Sugihara says he could only issue a few visas. Why can't he write more?
- What does Mr. Sugihara do after he finishes each visa?

Frederick Douglass, *Narrative of the Life of Frederick Douglass an American Slave, Written by Himself*—Grade 8**

(Q1) Why is Douglass specific about making friends with "little white boys"?

(Q2) How did Douglass learn how to read when running errands?

(Q3) In what ways does Douglass's life differ from the white boys' lives?

(Q4) Douglass is describing events from the past. These "boys" are now adult men, so why would he avoid giving their names?

Annie Dillard, "Living Like Weasels"—Grades 11–12**

(Q1) What features of a weasel's existence make it wild? Make it violent?

(Q2) What instances in the text show a display of weasels being "obedient to instinct"?

(Q3) At what point does the author start speaking about herself? What is the focus of her observations?

♦ ♦ ♦ ♦ ♦

STEP 6: Delve Into Challenging Areas of the Text

Explanation

Design questions that help students to understand particularly difficult sections of the text. These might be passages that contain dense material or inferential opportunities that make meaning hard to discern. It could be that certain literary devices are hard to interpret, there is complicated figurative language, or the author's writing style interferes with grasping the meaning. There might be overlap with Step 4 if passages with challenging sentence structures include sophisticated content. Use your notations from Step 2 to help formulate these text-dependent questions. Once again, remember to review your standards and craft text-dependent questions that address those expectations that apply to your text. Use these generic questions as a springboard for creating your own text-specific questions.

- What does this passage mean: _____? What is the message in it? What would the text mean without it?
- Where in the text can you make inferences? How does your inference help you understand the text more deeply?

- Why does the text include this information: _____? What makes it noteworthy?
- What images come to mind as you read a particular passage? How do these images help you to better understand the text and come to new realizations or deeper understandings?

FIGURE 3.6 (Continued)

FIGURE 3.6 (Continued)

- What inferences or interpretations can you draw from this passage _____?
- How can you rephrase this passage _____?
- Summarize the passage.
- Paraphrase a portion of the text.
- Rewrite a salient passage in your own words.
- How are ideas, conditions, characters, or individuals transformed (*influenced, impacted*) as a result of specific actions or events?
- What literary devices does the author use (e.g., *suspense, flashback, symbolism, dialect, dialogue, allusion*)? Provide an interpretation or rewrite the passage in your own words.
- Why does the author use this literary device (*hyperbole, allusion, dialect,* etc.): _____?
- Why does the writer choose the particular graphic (e.g., diagram, graph, table, etc.) to convey meaning? Is it effective in deepening your understanding of the topic?

- How does each argument build to give a whole sense of the author's claim?
- Is there sufficient evidence to aptly support the claim? What additional information should be included?
- What impact do counterclaims have on the argument?
- How does each idea in informational text build to provide readers with a clear sense of the whole?
- How does each detail about setting and characterization support the plot?
- How does the narrator's point of view impact the story?
- What remains unstated or unclear? Why does the writer choose this tactic?
- How does the title support the work? Would you recommend another title after reading it?

Examples

Examples—Various Grades*

- The poet writes about a spark from the horse's hooves. He says the spark "kindled the land into flames with its heat." What is the author referring to? ("The Midnight Ride of Paul Revere" by Longfellow)
- What do Karana's decisions about building her shelter tell you about her character? (*Island of the Blue Dolphins* by Scott O'Dell)
- On page 359 [of the text], the author says that "from the kitchen comes an endless parade of dishes" during the feast. What is the meaning of this idiom? ("Two Lands, One Heart" by Jeremy Schmidt)
- What does Mr. Sugihara mean when he says, "I may have to disobey my government, but if I don't I will be disobeying my conscience"? (*Passage to Freedom* by Ken Mochizuki)

Mark Twain "The Glorious Whitewasher"—Grade 7**

(Q5) List at least four of the ways Twain has used so far to describe Tom painting the fence. What impact do these descriptions have on Ben's attitude toward painting?

(Q8) Put the "great law of human action" and the difference between "work" and "play" into your own words.

Frederick Douglass, *Narrative of the Life of Frederick Douglass an American Slave, Written by Himself*—Grade 8**

(Q8) What moral did Douglass learn from these books?

(Q11) What prediction did Douglass's owner make about what would happen if he learned to read? Did it come true? Why or why not?

(Q12) What is the horrible pit? Why does Douglass envy someone's stupidity?

(Q13) Why is freedom tormenting Douglass?

Annie Dillard, "Living Like Weasels"—Grades 11–12**

(Q7) Dillard is careful to place these opposing descriptions (of the natural and man-made) side-by-side. How does this juxtaposition fit with or challenge what we have already read? Why might she have chosen this point in the text for these descriptions?

(Q10) When she sees the weasel Dillard says, "I've been in that weasel's brain for sixty seconds." What did she find there?

Homework: In your journal, write an entry describing the effect of seeing the weasel. What experience does Dillard compare it to, and how is this an apt comparison?

(Q18) Paragraphs 12 and 13 contain several questions instead of statements. What is the effect of using questions rather than declarations at this point in the essay?

◆ ◆ ◆ ◆ ◆

STEP 7: Arrange Questions in Appropriate Order for Instruction

Choreograph a logical sequence of questions so you can guide students in building a coherent understanding and analysis of the text. Aim for students to ascertain meaning gradually as you lead this type of planned discussion emanating from close reading of the text.

FIGURE 3.6

---

*Basal Alignment Project, www.edmodo.com.

**Achieve the Core, http://achievethecore.org.

HOW DO TEACHERS FACILITATE CLOSE READING OF COMPLEX TEXT?

Devising strong text-dependent questions is one critical step toward assisting students to independently and proficiently read and comprehend complex text. However, instruction is also a critical piece of the puzzle, and you should strive to conduct rich classroom experiences that allow time for students to examine and analyze such text and engage them in this work.

The designers of the Common Core do not mandate a particular strategy or method of teaching; rather, they allow teachers and curriculum designers to use their professional judgment and expertise to help students meet the goals articulated in the standards. That stated, what I provide here is a lesson outline that you can use to teach complex text. It demonstrates where the discussion around text-dependent questions resides. Note that students should not receive instruction designed around a particular reading strategy (e.g., questioning, clarifying, rereading) in isolation. Rather, as your students grapple with text, you should employ these strategies in a more authentic way and as the need arises. These lesson suggestions are culled and adapted from www.achievethecore.org, a website hosted by the nonprofit organization Student Achievement Partners. It includes cost-free resources for educators to use to implement the CCSS.

1. *PREPARATION: Prepare for close reading (teacher).* Prior to beginning instruction around a text, *divide it into sections* or passages. Students will then focus on one section or passage at a time.

- *Underline words* in the text that students will probably not be able to define based on context clues. Provide definitions of these words in the margin or on a separate sheet of paper.
- Use **bold** to indicate Tier 2 words, or **general academic words**, that students should learn. These are the kinds of words that appear across content area texts and might be defined using context clues (e.g., *determine, vary, abstract, associate, parallel*). During instruction, spend time teaching these words, as they are the pathway to understanding a variety of texts. Also model how to use context clues to determine meanings of these high-value words. Let students know that you expect them to use the same process to master words in other text they read independently. (For more information on vocabulary, see Appendix A, pages 33–35 of the Common Core.)
- Develop *essential understandings* of the whole text and *text-dependent questions* associated with each section of the text. (See Figure 3.6.)

2. *INTRODUCTION: Introduce the passage (teacher).* Consider these options:

- Avoid conducting prereading activities; however, minimal commentary is okay.
- Give brief definitions of words in which context clues do not reveal meanings.
- Set the stage for the lesson by posing an essential guiding question and stating the title and author.
- Tell students that the text is considered challenging. Explain to them that they will need to reread and examine it carefully to discover its deep meaning (which is what they will be doing with your guidance). It is okay to share with students that they might struggle during the first reading, that this is to be expected, and that perseverance is warranted.

3. *INITIAL EXPOSURE: Read, annotate, discuss, and listen to the passage (students).* Expose students to a given text passage two times initially: through independent reading and through asking them to listen to the text as it is spoken. For this initial exposure, you might reverse the order so that students first listen to the text and then read silently. Your decision is dependent upon the difficulty of a passage and the fluency abilities of students.

- *Read silently/record observations.* Students read silently either in class or as a homework assignment. During silent reading, encourage students to take notes in the margin or affix sticky notes to ask questions, clarify thinking, or make observations. Tell them also to circle, highlight, or place a sticky note on words they do not know or on passages that seem confusing or particularly noteworthy.
- *Discuss with a partner and class.* Invite students to discuss and respond to one another's thoughts about the text based on their annotations. Ask partners to share their discussion highlights and constantly remind them to refer to evidence from the text when offering their insights. Have students make a list of words that are unknown; discuss and model how they can use context clues to determine meanings.
- *Listen to text.* Students follow along or listen as the teacher or a skilled student reader reads aloud, or teachers can play a recording of the text section. Hearing the text allows students to internalize the rhythm and syntax that they might not have considered when reading silently. Also, it gives students the opportunity to hear the proper pronunciations of unknown words.

4. *IN-DEPTH EXAMINATION: Answer text-dependent questions and perform tasks (students).* Students work in various grouping configurations as you employ strategies to lead instruction around text-dependent questions and tasks. Students ultimately transfer what they learn to future interactions with challenging text. The following suggestions will help you orchestrate learning experiences around complex text:

- Present a series of text-dependent questions and tasks that prompt students to reread carefully to delve deeply into the author's surface and hidden meanings. At this point, students have already encountered the text by reading it independently and also listening as the text is read aloud (see number 3 above). Students are now prompted to reread the text frequently and independently to address text-dependent questions and tasks that teachers pose. Remind them to consistently refer to evidence from the text when responding.
- Some questions and tasks involve deciphering meaning from particularly difficult sentences that require decoding skills. Be prepared to engage in instruction around helping students ascertain meaning from syntactically complex sentences in targeted and future texts.
- Tasks can be varied and might include a combination of formal and informal responses, such as summarizing, paraphrasing, responding to prompts, completing a graphic organizer, and so forth.
- Use a variety of teaching methods when leading discussions, such as think aloud, think-pair-share, reciprocal teaching, cubing, and modeling.
- Use a variety of grouping configurations as students respond to questions: partner responses, small group interaction, and whole class discussion.

5. *FORMAL ASSESSMENT: Complete formal assessment (students).* Prepare and administer a final assessment that calls on students to demonstrate their understanding of the targeted text. This is not a culminating or summative assessment of perhaps an entire novel or chapter book, but rather a final assignment for the passages that are the focus of your text-dependent questions. See Step 3 in Figure 3.6.

EXAMPLES OF ESSENTIAL UNIT AND LESSON GUIDING QUESTIONS FOR GRAMMAR AND CONVENTIONS

This section provides examples of guiding questions that are related to grammar and conventions and that complement and extend the language strand of the Common Core Standards. There is widespread evidence to support teaching these skills in context. Isolated grammar and conventions lessons alone will not yield student achievement and will typically end in disappointment for both the student and teacher. However, if you provide a context for teaching these writing skills by featuring published and student work—in addition to conducting compelling, engaging language lessons around a text—then you will be more successful.

Such was the mindset when I worked with California sixth-grade teachers at Corte Madera School in Portola Valley. We had been working diligently on incorporating the research around using guiding questions across disciplines, and we wanted to expand the work to grammar and conventions. Even though this content is largely skill based, we were determined to devise relevant essential unit guiding questions that were overarching and could span the year. The following list is what we crafted. These unit questions were posted on the wall all year so students could understand the purpose for their work in this area any time language standards were taught:

- How does proper use of grammar and conventions help writers communicate ideas clearly?
- How can strong word choice make writing more colorful and powerful?
- How does dialogue impact writing?
- How can sentence fluency improve written communication?

We tied specific, standards-based lesson guiding questions to these essential unit questions. Then we chose reading selections that had examples of a targeted skill so teachers could teach grammar and conventions in context. Students produced a culminating assessment that not only demonstrated their understanding of the unit's content, but also showed how they grasped specific language standards that complemented the unit. For example, in September–October the unit focus was narrative; therefore, the summative assessment was a historical fiction writing piece linking language arts and social studies. In creating this story, students applied what they learned about elements of literature, included historically significant details (e.g., historically accurate clothing, food, events, etc.), and also demonstrated their understanding of language skills (e.g., punctuating and capitalizing dialogue, using adjectives for character descriptions, varying sentence beginnings, etc.). See Figure 3.7 to show you a sample of what we created. Note that those standards without a Common Core notation, such as L.6.1a, are expectations we added.

Grammar and Conventions Map

Timing: September/October	
Writing Focus: Narrative (W.6.3) **District Prompt:** October **Social Studies:** Early Man (California 6.1)	**Literature:** Summer Reading and *Dar and the Spear-Thrower* by Marjorie Cowley **Nonfiction:** social studies text and resources

Skills/Standards	Unit Guiding Questions	Lesson Guiding Questions
GRAMMAR/WORD CHOICE: Nouns, Verbs, and Adjectives • Distinguish among the connotations of words with similar denotations (L.6.5c). • Use verb tense to convey various times, sequences, states, and conditions (L.5.1c).	**How does proper use of grammar and conventions help writers communicate ideas clearly?** **How can strong word choice make writing more colorful and powerful?**	**NOUNS** • What is a noun? • What is a subject? • How do I identify the subject of a sentence?

Skills/Standards	Unit Guiding Questions	Lesson Guiding Questions
• Recognize and correct inappropriate shifts in verb tense (L.5.1d). • Consult reference materials (e.g., dictionaries, glossaries, thesauruses), both print and digital, to find the pronunciation of a word or determine or clarify its precise meaning or its part of speech (L.6.4c). • Use precise words and phrases, relevant descriptive details, and sensory language to convey experiences and events (W.6.3d).	(see previous row)	**VERBS** • What are verbs? What are the different types and functions of verbs? • What is verb tense? How do tenses help readers understand when events happen in a story? • What are action verbs? What action verbs does Marjorie Cowley use? Are there other action verbs she could have used? • What is subject-verb agreement? How do writers create subject-verb agreement? • How can action verbs contribute to a strong plot and engaging dialogue tags? • *My story:* What verb tense should I use for my story? What action verbs can I use in my story to make it stronger? **ADJECTIVES** • What is the function of adjectives? What strong adjectives does Marjorie Cowley use? What other adjectives could she have used? • What descriptive adjectives can writers use to help readers visualize what they write? • *My story:* What adjectives can I use in my story to make it stronger?
GRAMMAR: Pronouns • Ensure that pronouns are in the proper case (subjective, objective, possessive) (L.6.1a). • Recognize and correct inappropriate shifts in pronoun number and person (L.6.1c).	**How does proper use of grammar and conventions help writers communicate ideas clearly?**	**PRONOUNS** • What is point of view? What are first-, second-, and third-person point of view pronouns? How are pronouns used to indicate point of view? • What is the function of pronouns? How can authors use pronouns correctly and clearly?

FIGURE 3.7 (Continued)

FIGURE 3.7 (Continued)

Skills/Standards	Unit Guiding Questions	Lesson Guiding Questions
• Recognize and correct vague pronouns (i.e., ones with unclear or ambiguous antecedents) (L.6.1d).	(see previous row)	• What point of view does Cowley use in the novel? How would the story be different if told from another point of view? • **My story:** What point of view will I use for my story? How do I maintain a consistent point of view in my writing?
CONVENTIONS/WORD CHOICE: Dialogue • Demonstrate command of the conventions of standard English capitalization, punctuation, [and spelling] when writing (L.6.2). (Punctuate and capitalize dialogue correctly.) • Use narrative techniques, such as dialogue, pacing, and description, to develop experiences, events, and/or characters (W.6.3b).	**How does dialogue impact writing?** **How can strong word choice make writing more colorful and powerful?** **How does proper use of grammar and conventions help writers communicate ideas clearly?**	**DIALOGUE: Content** • How do readers identify dialogue? • How does dialogue reveal information about the characters or plot? • Can there be too much dialogue in a story? Is the dialogue that Marjorie Cowley uses meaningful? **DIALOGUE TAGS: Action Verbs/Adverbs** • How do writers use action verbs and adverbs to create strong dialogue tags? What are examples of strong and weak dialogue tags in *Dar and the Spear-Thrower*? • How can action verbs and adverbs improve dialogue tags? (Example: She shouted <u>loudly</u>, "I hate peas!") **DIALOGUE: Punctuation** • How do writers punctuate dialogue for beginning, middle, and end tags?
SENTENCE STRUCTURE • Vary sentence patterns for meaning, reader/listener interest, and style (L.6.3a).	**How does proper use of grammar and conventions help writers communicate ideas clearly?**	• **Complete sentences:** What is a complete sentence? • **Fragments:** What is a fragment? How can I turn a fragment into a complete sentence?

Skills/Standards	Unit Guiding Questions	Lesson Guiding Questions
• Identify fragments and write in complete sentences; identify run-ons and write sentences without them. • Identify and write compound and complex sentences. • Identify and use coordinating conjunctions; use commas before the coordinating conjunction to separate independent clauses in a compound sentence. • Identify and use subordinating conjunctions; use a comma after a dependent clause that begins a sentence.	**How can sentence fluency improve written communication?**	• **Run-ons:** What is a run-on? How do writers avoid run-ons? **SENTENCE STRUCTURE** • What are different sentence types? • What is the formula for a compound sentence? How do writers punctuate compound sentences? What are coordinating conjunctions, and how are they used properly in compound sentences? • What are examples of these sentence types in *Dar and the Spear-Thrower*? • *My story:* How can I use varied sentence types in my story?
GRAMMAR/WORD CHOICE: Adverbs • Distinguish among the connotations (association) of words with similar denotations (definitions) (L.6.5c). • Consult reference materials (e.g., dictionaries, glossaries, thesauruses), both print and digital, to find the pronunciation of a word or determine or clarify its precise meaning or its part of speech (L.6.4c).	**How does proper use of grammar and conventions help writers communicate ideas clearly?** **How can strong word choice make writing more colorful and powerful?**	**ADVERBS** • What are adverbs? What are the different types and functions of adverbs? • What are examples of adverbs to show manner in published and student work? • How can adverbs enhance narration, dialogue, and dialogue tags? • What adverbs does Cowley use? How do they enhance meaning? • *My story:* What adverbs can I include in my story that engage readers and enhance meaning?

FIGURE 3.7 (Continued)

FIGURE 3.7 (Continued)

Skills/Standards	Unit Guiding Questions	Lesson Guiding Questions
• Use precise words and phrases, relevant descriptive details, and sensory language to convey experiences and events (W.6.3d).	(see previous row)	(see previous row)
SENTENCE BEGINNINGS: Dependent Clauses, Prepositional Phrases, Adverbs • Use a variety of transition words, phrases, and clauses to convey sequence and signal shifts from one time frame or setting to another (W.6.2c). • Vary sentence patterns for meaning, reader/listener interest, and style (L.6.3a).	**How can transitions improve written communication?**	**SENTENCE BEGINNINGS** • How can sentences begin in different ways? • Why is it important to vary sentence beginnings? • What is the difference between a dependent clause and a prepositional phrase? • What are examples of sentence beginning variety in Cowley's novel and other published and student work? • *My story:* How can I use dependent clauses, prepositional phrases, and adverbs to vary my sentence beginnings?
TRANSITIONS: Sentences and Paragraphs • Use a variety of **transition** words, phrases, and clauses to convey sequence and signal shifts from one time frame or setting to another (W.6.3c).	**How can transitions improve written communication?**	**TRANSITIONS** • What is the function of transitions, and why are they important? What are examples of transitional words and phrases? • How do transitions contribute to effective writing? • What is the difference between a choppy paper and a fluid one? • When are commas needed after a transition? • What are examples of transitions in the novel? • *My story:* Where do I include transitions? Which ones work best to make my story flow?

FIGURE 3.7

CONSTRUCTING YOUR OWN ESSENTIAL UNIT AND LESSON GUIDING QUESTIONS

At this point, the book has guided you through three exercises that mirror the unit template components:

1. What is the best way to group standards?

2. How are standards used to determine what students should know?

3. How do educators create essential understandings?

Now you are ready for Exercise 4:

4. How do educators create essential unit and lesson guiding questions?

Because you will create your own questions, let's look at the two types side by side and analyze them. Ask yourself or discuss with colleagues: *What characterizes each kind of question—the **essential unit** guiding question and the **lesson** guiding question?* You can peruse Figure 3.8 to foster discussion around this prompt. Know that Figure 3.9 answers this question, so cover it up with a sheet of paper now if you earnestly want to respond to my query without peeking.

Essential Unit and Lesson Guiding Question Examples

Essential Unit Guiding Questions	Lesson Guiding Questions
How does setting affect characters?	• What are the major settings in *The Giver?* • How does the community affect different characters' actions, thoughts, or beliefs, such as Jonas, Fiona, and their parents?
How do authors develop characters?	• What is characterization? What are the methods of characterization? • How does Lois Lowry use methods of characterization to develop the character of the Giver, Gabe, and Jonas? • What does "new depth of feeling" mean? How has Jonas changed his view of the world around him?
How does mood influence the plot?	• What is mood? How do authors create mood? • What words describe the mood in this passage by Lois Lowry?: "His hope diminished further when the sharp, cold air began to blur and thicken with swirling white. Gabriel, wrapped in his inadequate blanket, was hunched, shivering, and silent in his little seat."

FIGURE 3.8

Features of Essential Unit and Lesson Guiding Questions

Distinguishing Features	
Essential Unit Guiding Questions	**Lesson Guiding Questions**
• Are written in general terms with no proper nouns. • Include present-tense verbs and no form of the verb *to be*. • Include at least one concept or maybe two that form a relationship. • Begin with *why* or *how*. • Cannot be answered with a list or finite response; these questions are more provocative and engaging than the straightforward, factually based lesson guiding question. • Can foster transference and connections as students relate the questions to other units of study, other text, the world, or personally. • Are featured prominently on poster board or chart paper in the classroom for the entire unit.	• Can be written to elicit factual information specific to a unit of study, so references to characters, historical events or figures, titles of books, or particular places are fair game. • Include at least one skill or concept for each question. • Begin with any type of question: *who, what, where, when, why/how, is, does*. • Are foundational as they serve to support the unit question; when teachers conduct lessons associated with all the lesson guiding questions, students should be prepared to demonstrate understanding of the overarching, associated essential unit question. • Are posted individually as the lesson objective for the day(s) on the whiteboard, SMART Board, or easel.

Common Features

- **Logical order**. Both types of questions are sequential, so write unit questions that are scaffolded; begin with the less complex to the most in-depth. By the same token, write the associated lesson guiding questions for each unit question in an order for teaching. The only caveat is that you might return to unit guiding questions throughout the course of study. For example, *How do characters change throughout time?* could be a unit question revisited frequently throughout a novel or short story as characters show change as a result of different factors. The same idea applies to unit questions around reading strategies, such as *How can readers employ the questioning strategy to gain more meaning from the text?*
- **Appropriate timing**. You must consider how much time you have to teach a unit and plan the number of questions accordingly.
- **Language**. It is important that students for whom you are writing this unit can read and understand the words in your questions. However, if you include a concept term that you will expose them to and use it as the basis for instruction, then by all means add it (e.g., *interdependence, cultural diffusion*).
- **Distinction**. Make sure that there is no overlap among your questions. If there is too much similarity, combine questions or choose the strongest one. Each question—unit or lesson—should stand alone.
- **Visibility**. Whereas the unit questions are posted and remain visible throughout the entire unit, the lesson questions are featured for each lesson to set the stage, so write them on the whiteboard or interactive board. The commonality is that they are both clearly in the students' line of vision.

FIGURE 3.9

EXERCISE 4: HOW DO EDUCATORS CREATE (OR REVISE) ESSENTIAL UNIT AND LESSON GUIDING QUESTIONS?

The following steps will help you create your own questions for your targeted unit of study.

STEP 1: Assemble Materials

If you have adhered to the exercises in this book so far, then you should have your grouped standards and the knowledge list entered on the unit template. In addition, you have created and entered essential understandings. Keep the textbook, materials, and resources for your unit available. And, of course, you'll need the laptop or paper and pencil. Replenish your chocolate, as needed. If you haven't already, peruse the unit template in Chapter 4 to see other examples of unit and lesson guiding questions, in addition to other component entries.

STEP 2: Use Essential Understandings to Create Unit Guiding Questions

- Review your essential understandings and circle the concepts that you included in every statement. Using these concepts, create a unit guiding question for each essential understanding that begins with *why* or *how*. Focus on at least one concept. If you want to include two concepts, form a relationship between them as you did for your essential understandings. To assist, use Figure 2.8, "Verbs That Show Relationships." Stay true to the guidelines you read in this chapter. They are summarized in Figure 3.9, "Features of Essential Unit and Lesson Guiding Questions." You will undoubtedly need to brainstorm a list of possible unit questions for each essential understanding and then wordsmith and combine some to avoid repetition. This should be familiar since you did this in Exercise 3 when you created essential understandings. It is acceptable and sometimes necessary to have two essential unit questions tied to one understanding.
- Remember that you want all students to be able to demonstrate their understanding of all the unit guiding questions at the end of the course of study. To this point, these types of questions should be incorporated in a unit's summative (or culminating) assessment.
- Warning: Essential unit guiding questions are **not** simply the essential understandings with the words *how* or *why* tacked on to the beginning. You also do not want essential unit guiding questions that are too wordy and reveal all that students will come to realize once you engage them in lessons. Remember that guiding questions are pointed, succinct, and provocative; they guide instruction and promote self-discovery.

STEP 3: Create Lesson Guiding Questions

- You might complete this step in tandem with Step 2 as you determine what lesson questions are needed to support students in understanding the overarching essential unit guiding questions. Therefore, either tackle each essential unit question and its corresponding lesson questions together, or you might prefer to go through and create all unit questions and then return to the more specific and detailed lesson questions.

- As you create these lesson questions, again use Figure 3.9, "Features of Essential Unit and Lesson Guiding Questions," and be mindful of the fact that the goal of lesson questions is to get students to answer the bigger conceptual unit questions.
- Enter these unit and lesson guiding questions on the appropriate pages of your unit template to correspond with the essential understandings.

Note: It is not unusual to have to go back to the essential understandings and tweak them after you have completed this exercise.

STEP 4: Consider the Options for Displaying Your Questions

- Feature each *lesson guiding question* on a whiteboard or SMART Board to identify a specific lesson goal for a class segment.
- Conspicuously display all **unit questions** throughout the entire course of the unit so students are mindful of the overarching purpose of their work.
- Format your unit questions on a computer and add graphics or make a poster by hand in preparation for posting. You can take the sheet and have it enlarged to create a poster. Some teachers mention that they will feature their unit questions on a SMART Board or a similar interactive board. I veto this idea because you want the unit guiding questions to be visible throughout the whole unit for easy reference while teaching.

Note: Essential unit guiding questions might not always be shown at the very outset of the unit, as explained in the scenarios below:

- Launch your unit by asking students what they think the upcoming unit will be about, conducting a simulation, showing a video, or featuring a guest speaker. After a debriefing following such a launch, you could then share the questions and post them.
- Ask students to get into groups and brainstorm questions they want addressed in the unit. For example, you might say, *We are beginning a unit on religions of the world. Make a list of questions that you have about this topic that you want to explore together.* You could then invite each group to share and compile a class-generated list. If you conduct this exercise, still prepare your unit and lesson guiding questions so you have unit goals in mind. Because you are the professional, you must be grounded in the standards-based essential understandings so you know the unit outcomes and can be sure that any student-generated questions meet the necessary criteria. When students brainstorm guiding questions, take dedicated time to review and edit them. Assign any pertinent questions as unit or lesson questions, as appropriate. This method helps with student buy-in and involvement while still maintaining the intended purpose of the unit.

LOOKING AHEAD

Now that you have completed the exercise in this chapter, your unit template should include a group of standards, a list of knowledge items, the essential understandings, and the associated unit and lesson guiding questions. In the next chapter, you will have the opportunity to review a comprehensive unit map for argumentation to show you an example of a finished product that might result from completing the exercises in this book.

4

Unit Map Template and Example

This chapter represents a crossroads in this book. It was designed to give you the opportunity to look back and reflect on what you've learned in previous chapters and to give you a glimpse of what is still to come. Now that you've mastered the unit components of standards, knowledge, essential understandings, and guiding questions, you have the foundational capacity you need to continue drafting your own complete unit map. In the section that follows, you will find the unit template (Figure 4.1) that you have probably already downloaded from Exercise 1, plus a completed example of an argumentation unit map for your reference (Figure 4.2). My argumentation map may at first appear daunting in its extensive treatment of a unit of study. However, as you read more about it in this chapter, embark upon the project of getting at the real essence of your unit and its supporting factual information, and prepare for meaningful lesson design, you will come to understand how you can teach with more depth, with more insight, and with more focus than you might have in the past. You will feel empowered as a result, knowing that your students will benefit tremendously from your wise guidance. Additional completed unit map examples can be found in my other book, *Mapping Comprehensive Units to the ELA Common Core, K–5.*

CUSTOMIZING AND ADAPTING THE UNIT MAP TO FIT YOUR NEEDS

There are numerous instruments referenced within the unit map (i.e., argumentation rubric, checklist, revision sheet) that are located in different chapters and on the companion website. They should be adapted based on the grade you teach. Even though

I grouped a combination of ELA Common Core Standards for Grade 8 and broader CCR Anchor Standards in Figure 4.2, you can adapt it for middle and high school since argumentation is taught in all of these grades. In fact, you can compare the essential understandings and guiding questions with those in Figure 3.2 ("Argumentation Writing Standards With Essential Understandings and Guiding Questions"), which is geared for high school and includes fallacies, deduction, and induction. Depending on the grade you teach, you might also consider adding instruction around Aristotle's rhetorical appeals—*ethos, pathos, logos* (with a particular emphasis on *logos* when teaching argumentation).

In the unit map example (Figure 4.2), you might notice that I include columns for unit and lesson guiding questions adjacent to the essential understandings at the beginning of the template. I like to have these components up front to see at a glance what the detailed pages will include.

Another observation you probably made is that the activity column of Figure 4.2 is very detailed, but this doesn't mean that you have to be so extensive in your own explanations. This is addressed in Chapter 6, when you craft your activities. Essentially, you must determine how comprehensive you want to be in your descriptions of the exercises. That has a lot to do with your own style, who will be using and viewing this document besides you, what lessons you already have that satisfy a certain activity, and how accomplished you are at typing! If an activity is already written, you might be brief in the activity column and reference it in the resources. Note that the activities all begin with a verb and are written as if this sentence frame precedes each bullet: *Students will. . . .* Each bullet is directed for students and should be fairly self-explanatory regarding what the teacher needs to say or do to conduct the activity. However, if you feel this treatment is incomplete, by all means, insert what the students and teacher will do. In some instances, you'll find an additional, parenthetical remark with regard to preparations or the order of a particular lesson.

Do not feel you have to pace your unit the exact way that I have it outlined. This is how I might do it; however, you might have a different teaching style and choose to position lessons differently. Also, you might teach an argumentation unit with teachers from other content areas and divvy up certain line items. For example, if students are writing an essay for social studies or science, these content area teachers might tackle lessons on thesis, reasons, and evidences; English language arts teachers might focus on lessons related to conventions, sentence structure, and formal style; and librarians or media specialists might conduct lessons on credibility. Therefore, some lessons can be taught concurrently but others need to be orchestrated so that one follows another. For instance, a lesson on in-text citations would make sense after students have gathered evidence so they use their own source material to implement this skill.

In Chapter 2, I stated that you generally don't want any more than six essential understandings for a unit of study. However, what I include in Figure 4.2 are many *options* for the unit. If teaching this unit, you might choose to delete some understandings and questions based on your goals, what students have already mastered, and your time constraints. You can also merge some of what I have to condense lessons. Alternatively, you might add some lessons if students need a more thorough review of a skill or concept or it is new material that I haven't covered.

ORGANIZING UNIT MAPS AND STUDENT WORK

In terms of the logistics of how completed units are housed, I'll share with you what I do with teachers I collaborate with on writing comprehensive units of study:

- We design and assemble our work in three-ring binders.
- The table of contents is situated at the front, as is customary, followed by a completed unit template that serves to orient readers to the overall contents.
- Each section of the binder is divided and organized by the essential unit guiding questions and consists of specific lessons with accompanying student handouts and pertinent manipulatives to use for an activity. See Chapter 8 for examples of detailed lessons along with support resources.
- The last section of the binder is the culminating assessment and the rubric that is used to score it. I plan for the culminating assessment during the curriculum design phase, just as you will do while reading this book. The teacher presents the assessment to students near the start of the unit so they are clear about goals and expectations.

As students progress through a writing unit, you might have them keep a folder as they advance along the steps of the writing process. In it, they can accumulate all their work from prewriting to publishing along with the resources that support their task. For example, they might include their graphic organizer, works cited handout that shows how to format sources, in-text citation handout that explains proper conventions for giving attribution within the paper, list of transitions, published and student writing samples, rubric (if age appropriate), and so forth. They should staple the student writing checklist to the front cover to be forever mindful of the expectations for their finished paper.

LOOKING AHEAD

In the next chapter, I explain the various types of assessments and focus primarily on summative (or culminating) assessments as well as preassessments. I provide a detailed explanation of these assessments along with examples of various rubrics and checklists that provide the criteria for assessing student work. Formative (or ongoing) assessments are addressed later in the book. As you continue reading and building your map, I hope you will see the beauty in this process and all it entails. It may be frustrating and tedious at times, but in the end, I assure you it will pay off as you see your students rise to new heights and realize that you have grown, as well. Onward we go.

Unit Template

Unit: _____

Subject: _____ **Grade:** _____ **Timing:** _____

Common Core Standards	Knowledge	
Content Area Standards (if applicable)	**Knowledge**	
Essential Understandings	**Essential Unit Guiding Questions**	**Lesson Guiding Questions**
1.		
2.		
3.		
4.		
Culminating Assessment (Summative)		

Essential Understanding #__:				
Essential Unit Guiding Question #__:				
Lesson Guiding Questions	**Skills**	**Activities**	**Resources**	**Formative Assessment Evidence**
Lesson __.__				
Lesson __.__				

FIGURE 4.1

Argument Writing

Argument Unit Map

ELA Common Core Standards	Knowledge
WRITING	• Purposes of argumentation—to change readers' point of view, bring about some action on the readers' part, or ask readers to accept the writer's explanation or evaluation of a concept, issue, or problem
• Write arguments to support claims with clear reasons and relevant evidence (W.8.1).	• Argument—reasoned, logical way to demonstrate the validity of the writer's position, belief, or conclusion
a. Introduce claim(s), acknowledge and distinguish the claim(s) from alternate or opposing claims, and organize the reasons and evidence logically.	• Terms—*argument, counterclaim/counterargument, reasons, evidence, thesis, works cited, argumentation, call to action, credibility, plagiarism,* terms related to topic
b. Support claim(s) with logical reasoning and relevant evidence, using accurate, credible sources and demonstrating an understanding of the topic or text.	• Structure, element, and development of an argument
c. Use words, phrases, and clauses to create cohesion and clarify the relationships among claim(s), counterclaims, reasons, and evidence.	• Introduction—quotes, anecdotes, background information, or definition of key terms; plus thesis statement to stake claim
d. Establish and maintain a formal style.	• Thesis—arguments must have a debatable thesis or claim in the introduction. If the thesis is generally accepted or a mere fact, there is no point to try to persuade people. (Not debatable: *Smoking is bad for people's lungs.*)
e. Provide a concluding statement or section that follows from and supports the argument presented.	• Body paragraphs—reasons (topic sentences), textual evidence, interpretations or explanations, concluding sentence
• Produce clear and coherent writing in which the development, organization, and style are appropriate to task, purpose, and audience (W.8.4).	• Options for textual evidence—facts, data, examples, quotes
• With some guidance and support from peers and adults, develop and strengthen writing as needed by planning, revising, editing, rewriting, or trying a new approach, focusing on how well purpose and audience have been addressed (W.8.5).	• Ways to use evidence—paraphrase, summarize, direct quote
	• Opposing viewpoints—weave in body paragraphs or dedicate to own paragraph; acknowledge and address counterclaims
• Gather relevant information from multiple print and digital sources, using search terms effectively; assess the credibility and accuracy of each source; and quote or paraphrase the data and conclusions of others while avoiding plagiarism and following a standard format for citation (W.8.8).	• Conclusion
	• Transitional words, phrases, clauses
	• Sentence structure variety
• Draw evidence from literary or informational texts to support analysis, reflection, and research (W.8.9).	• Formal style, objective tone; consistent point of view
	• Point of view—first or third person
	• Inference

FIGURE 4.2 (*Continued*)

FIGURE 4.2 (Continued)

ELA Common Core Standards	Knowledge
READING • Read closely to determine what the text says explicitly and to make logical inferences from it; cite specific textual evidence when writing or speaking to support conclusions drawn from the text (R.CCR.1). • Analyze the structure of texts, including how specific sentences, paragraphs, and larger portions of the text (e.g., a section, chapter, scene, or stanza) relate to each other and the whole (R.CCR.5). • Assess how point of view or purpose shapes the content and style of a text (R.CCR.6). • Delineate and evaluate the argument and specific claims in a text, including the validity of the reasoning as well as the relevance and sufficiency of the evidence (R.CCR.8). • Analyze how two or more texts address similar themes or topics in order to build knowledge or to compare the approaches the authors take (R.CCR.9). **LANGUAGE** • Demonstrate command of the conventions of standard English (L.CCR.1-2). **SPEAKING AND LISTENING** • Delineate a speaker's argument and specific claims, evaluating the soundness of the reasoning and relevance and sufficiency of the evidence, and identifying when irrelevant evidence is introduced (SL.8.3). • Present claims and findings, emphasizing salient points in a focused, coherent manner with relevant evidence, sound valid reasoning, and well-chosen details; use appropriate eye contact, adequate volume, and clear pronunciation (SL.8.4).	• Writing process—prewriting, drafting, editing, revising, publishing • Research—search terms, credible sources, citation for sources • Conventions/format—in-text citations, works cited, quotation marks, titles • Formal debate sequence • Appropriate speaking techniques—eye contact, volume, clear pronunciation

Essential Understandings	Essential Unit Guiding Questions	Lesson Guiding Questions
Purpose/Audience/Style: The purpose and audience for writing shape the content, structure, and style of an author's work.	1. How do purpose and audience influence an author's work?	• **Lesson (L) 1.1:** What are the purposes and audiences for different types of writing? How are arguments different from short stories? • **L 1.2:** What are the elements and structure of an argument? • **L 1.3:** What kind of writing style is best for the task, purpose, and audience? How do I maintain a formal style and objective tone in my paper?
Introduction: Introductions provide context for an argument and give writers an opportunity to make a favorable impression on readers.	2. How can I write an effective introduction for my argument?	• **Lesson (L) 2.1:** What are the expectations for a strong argument piece? • **L 2.2:** What is a debatable topic or issue I can use as the basis for my argument? What claim can I make? • **L 2.3:** How can I write a thesis statement to stake a claim? Where should I include my thesis in my introduction? • **L 2.4:** What strategies can I use to begin my argument so I get my reader's attention?
Reasons/Evidence: Writers provide clear reasons and relevant evidence culled from multiple, reliable sources to strengthen an argument. **Organization/Development:** A well-organized and developed argument facilitates the flow of ideas and promotes understanding.	3. How can I organize and develop a logical argument?	• **Lesson (L) 3.1:** How are my reasons relevant to the argument? How do they link to the thesis? • **L 3.2:** What sources can I use to gather relevant evidence? What evidence should I use from these sources to support my reasons? • **L 3.3:** How can I interpret my evidence to explain what it means?

FIGURE 4.2 (*Continued*)

FIGURE 4.2 (Continued)

Essential Understandings	Essential Unit Guiding Questions	Lesson Guiding Questions
Credibility/Attribution: With proper attribution, writers selectively integrate credible and accurate information from multiple sources to construct a sound argument.	4. How can I evaluate the credibility of my sources and give proper citation?	• **Lesson (L) 4.1:** How do I evaluate the credibility of sources and determine which ones to use for my argument? • **L 4.2:** How might the tone or style of the writing impact its credibility? • **L 4.3:** What is plagiarism? How do I properly reference sources I use? What form is needed for in-text citations and works cited?
Counterclaims: Writers who anticipate and address opposing viewpoints exhibit deep understanding of an issue, which strengthens the overall argument.	5. How do I anticipate and address counterarguments?	• **Lesson (L) 5.1:** Why do arguments include opposing viewpoints? How do they impact an argument? • **L 5.2:** How do counterclaims, along with reasons and evidence, strength a whole argument? • **L 5.3:** What are the opposing viewpoints to my claim? How do I acknowledge and address them? Where do I insert counterarguments in my paper?
Conclusion: Writers create conclusions for an argument to leave a lasting impression on readers and compel them to act or change their views.	6. How can I effectively conclude my argument paper?	• **Lesson (L) 6.1:** How do writers create a strong conclusion? • **L 6.2:** How can I summarize the main points of my argument? What strategies that I used for writing my introduction would work for my conclusion?
Transitions: To assist readers in following a coherent argument, writers use transitions to form logical connections among ideas and clarify relationships among sections.	7. How do transitions help readers follow the logic of my argument?	• **Lesson (L) 7.1:** Why do writers use transitions? What are some examples of transitions? • **L 7.2:** How can I use transitions to form logical connections among ideas?
Writing Process: Employing the writing process enables writers to challenge their own ideas and make necessary edits, which can lead to an improved and stronger argument.	8. How do writers use the writing process to help produce optimal results?	• **Lesson (L) 8.1:** How do I use each step in the writing process to develop and strengthen my argument?

Culminating Assessment (Summative)

Argumentation essay on a student-selected topic or issue; accompanying assessment pieces (some adaptation might be needed based on the targeted grade): "Argument Writing Checklist" (Figure 8.11) and "Argument Writing Rubric" (Figure 5.14)

◆

◆

◆

◆

◆

Essential Understanding 1

The purpose and audience for writing shape the content, structure, and style of an author's work.

Essential Unit Guiding Question 1

How do purpose and audience influence an author's work?

Lesson Guiding Questions	Skills	Activities (Students will . . .)	Resources	Formative Assessment Evidence
Lesson (L) 1.1: What are the purposes and audiences for different types of writing? How are arguments different from short stories?	• Identify purposes and audiences for writing. • Compare and contrast the structure of texts.	• Read different kinds of text and answer: *What are the purposes for each writing type? Use examples from the text to prove you know the purpose. Who are the audiences? What is the name of each kind of writing?* (**Teacher:** Feature a short story, research report, and argument; allow students time to read and determine the type and the purpose of each writing type.) • Focus on the short story and argument; discuss the differences between them. • Identify the organizational structure of a story versus an argument; answer: *What are the elements of a plot? What are the elements of an argument?*	• Writing samples: research report, short story, and argument	• Participation during discussion

FIGURE 4.2 *(Continued)*

FIGURE 4.2 (Continued)

Lesson Guiding Questions	Skills	Activities (Students will . . .)	Resources	Formative Assessment Evidence
L 1.2: What are the elements and structure of an argument?	• Identify elements of genre. • Analyze the structure of texts.	• Read and discuss "How Are Arguments Structured?" handout. • Read and examine writing samples in small groups; using the handout as a guide, match each argument element card (e.g., thesis, reason, evidence, etc.) with the appropriate sentences on the samples. (To **differentiate by readiness**, group homogeneously; distribute appropriately challenging samples; provide adult support, as needed.) • Determine missing argument elements in specific writing samples; suggest ways authors could improve. • Share observations with whole class. • Using a new argument writing sample, complete a graphic organizer to demonstrate identification of argument elements in text. (To **differentiate by learning style,** provide various organizers to allow for student choice; to **differentiate by readiness,** distribute appropriately challenging argument writing samples to students.)	• "How Are Arguments Structured?" handout • Argument writing samples—published and student work (use textbook, Internet, and Appendix C of Common Core) (**differentiated** by **readiness**) • "Argument Identification Cards" (see Figure 7.7) • Various graphic organizers (**differentiated** by **learning style**)	• Participation during discussion • Participation in matching activity • Graphic organizer (**differentiated** by **learning style** and **readiness**)
L 1.3: What kind of writing style is best for the task, purpose, and audience? How do I maintain a formal style and objective tone in my paper?	• Assess how point of view or purpose shapes the content and style of a text. • Cite specific textual evidence to support conclusions drawn from the text.	• Recall the various argument papers; discuss these questions for each: *How do purpose and audience influence the author's work? What kind of style do the writers use? How do you know? How does the style match the purpose and audience, or doesn't it?* • Select a paper written in formal style; circle or highlight evidence from the text that indicates formal style and objective tone; share impressions. (To **differentiate by readiness,** allow students to choose an appropriately challenging paper within a targeted selection.)	• Argument writing samples with formal style—published and student work (use textbook, Internet, and Appendix C of Common Core) (**differentiated** by **readiness**)	• Participation in discussion • Annotated argument paper (**differentiated** by **readiness**)

Essential Understanding 2

Introductions provide context for an argument and give writers an opportunity to make a favorable impression on readers.

Essential Unit Guiding Question 2

How can I write an effective introduction for my argument?

Lesson Guiding Questions	Skills	Activities (Students will . . .)	Resources	Formative Assessment Evidence
Lesson (L) 2.1 What are the expectations for a strong argument piece?	• Assess writing against criteria using specific textual evidence.	• Brainstorm criteria for an argument; compare list with the teacher-generated "Argument Writing Checklist" to be clear on writing expectations. (Conduct Lesson 4 in Chapter 8.) • Read argument paper samples in small groups and assess them against the checklist using specific examples from text. (For **differentiation** by **readiness**, prepare tiered checklists based on student readiness; distribute different argument paper samples to match students' levels.)	• "Argument Writing Checklist" (Figure 8.11) • Chapter 8, Lesson 4 of this book: "What Are the Expectations for My Finished Argument?" • Argument writing samples (**differentiated by readiness**)	• Participation in discussion • Scoring results
L 2.2: What is a debatable topic or issue I can use as the basis for my argument? What claim can I make?	• Choose a debatable topic.	• Review previously read argument papers; make a class list of the topics or issues. • Review class list and answer questions for each: *Can people have differing opinions on this topic or issue? What claim (position) does each author stake?* Note that papers without a debatable claim contain issues that are generally agreed upon or accepted as fact,	• Argument writing samples previously used	• Participation in discussion • Debatable topic for argument paper (**differentiated by interest**)

FIGURE 4.2 *(Continued)*

FIGURE 4.2 (Continued)

Lesson Guiding Questions	Skills	Activities (Students will . . .)	Resources	Formative Assessment Evidence
		which gives writers no reason to persuade others (e.g., *Smoking is bad for the lungs*). • Consider a topic or issue for your argument paper; verify that it is a debatable issue. (To **differentiate** by **interest**, allow students to choose their argumentation topic.)		
L 2.3: How can I write a thesis statement to stake a claim? Where should I include my thesis in my introduction?	• Write thesis statement to introduce claim.	• Critique various introductions; identify introductory elements of argument focusing on thesis statements. • Sort various cards into two piles: thesis and non-thesis statements; analyze thesis cards to create a definition of thesis with teacher's support. • Find thesis examples from various argument samples; in groups, rewrite weak ones and critique them with class. (To **differentiate** by **readiness**, provide samples at varying degrees of sophistication in writing and topic.)	• "Thesis and Non-Thesis Activity" cards • Introductions from various argument writing samples (**differentiated** by **readiness**)	• Participation during discussion and card sort activity • Rewritten thesis statements (**differentiated** by **readiness**) • Original thesis statements for argument paper (**differentiated** by **interest**)

Lesson Guiding Questions	Skills	Activities (Students will . . .)	Resources	Formative Assessment Evidence
		• Draft thesis statements for your chosen topic using thesis definition and strong examples. (To **differentiate by interest**, students choose topic for thesis.) • (**Teacher:** You may want to conduct lessons around reasons and evidence under Essential Guiding Question 3 before students write their introductions.)		
L 2.4: What strategies can I use to begin my argument so I get my reader's attention? For example, what quotes, anecdotes, background information, or definitions of key terms should I use?	• Evaluate strength of introduction according to criteria.	• Review "Options for Beginning and Concluding Your Paper" handout. • In pairs, identify which options each writer uses in various argument samples; evaluate the effectiveness of each beginning to draw in the reader and establish context; use "Argument Writing Checklist" (Figure 8.11) as a guide. • Write introductions to precede thesis statement for your argument paper after conducting preliminary research.	• "Options for Beginning and Concluding Your Paper" handout • Introductions from various argument writing samples (used in previous lessons) • "Argument Writing Checklist" (Figure 8.11) • Internet access	• Participation in peer discussions and conducting research • Written introductions for argument paper (**differentiated by interest**)

FIGURE 4.2 *(Continued)*

Essential Understanding 3

Writers provide clear reasons and relevant evidence culled from multiple, reliable sources to strengthen an argument.

A well-organized and developed argument facilitates the flow of ideas and promotes understanding.

Essential Unit Guiding Question 3

How can I organize and develop a logical argument?

Lesson Guiding Questions	Skills	Activities (Students will . . .)	Resources	Formative Assessment Evidence
Lesson (L) 3.1: How are my reasons relevant to the argument? How do they link to the thesis?	• Evaluate and determine the validity and logic of the reasoning. • Link the reasoning to the thesis.	• Match sentence strips of possible reasoning to various thesis statements; put aside strips that do not apply to any thesis. (To **differentiate**, distribute appropriately challenging sentence strips to groups based on **readiness**.) **(Teacher:** Prepare sentences that include reasons that support thesis statements and nonreasons that are random.) • Write this sentence in journals or binder: *Arguments are claims backed by logical reasons that are supported by evidence.* • Verify that strips associated with thesis statements are all logical reasons; reasons answer the question about the thesis/claim: *Why do you think that?* • In groups, read argument papers; circle the thesis and highlight topic sentences (reasons); discuss with a partner if the reasons support the thesis and are logical. (To **differentiate by readiness,** distribute appropriately challenging papers.)	• Teacher-prepared sentence strips of various thesis statements, reasons, and random sentences (nonreasons) (**differentiated** by **readiness**) • Student journals • Argument writing samples previously used (**differentiated** by **readiness**) • Graphic organizer in Figure 5.2 or another organizer with same	• Participation in matching activity (**differentiated** by **readiness**) • Participation in discussions • Marked-up argument papers • Student journals • Graphic organizer—work-in-progress (**differentiated** by **learning style**)

FIGURE 4.2 (Continued)

Lesson Guiding Questions	Skills	Activities (Students will . . .)	Resources	Formative Assessment Evidence
		• Individually, begin completing a graphic organizer with the thesis and reasons for your argument. (To **differentiate by learning style**, allow students to use the Figure 5.2 organizer or another one they create.) • (**Teacher:** Expect incomplete graphic organizers at this point. As students conduct research, they will refine their organizers. You might first conduct Lesson L 3.2 and then ask students to use their organizers.)	argumentation elements—work-in-progress for students' own papers (**differentiated by learning style**)	
L 3.2: What sources can I use to gather relevant evidence? What evidence should I use from these sources to support my reasons?	• Read closely to identify elements of a genre. • Critique the validity of reasons and relevancy of evidence.	• Read assigned argument writing sample; identify the evidence associated with each reason and how it relates to the argument. (To **differentiate by readiness**, assign appropriately challenging argument papers.) • In groups, discuss and then complete an argument graphic organizer based on this paper; discuss strengths and weaknesses of paper; particularly focus on the logic of the reasoning and relevancy of evidence to support claim. (To **differentiate by readiness**, arrange students in homogeneous groups based on the papers they read.)	• Argument writing samples (**differentiated by readiness**) • Graphic organizer (Figure 5.2)	• Participation in discussions • Group graphic organizer
	• Gather relevant information from multiple print and digital sources, using search terms effectively.	• Create search terms for your argument to gather resources. • Begin researching for evidence to support each reason; keep in mind this question as you search for sources: *How do you know this reason is true?* • (**Teacher:** Conduct pertinent lessons on credibility now under Essential Unit Guiding Question 4.)	• Internet access • Graphic organizer— work-in-progress for students' own papers (**differentiated by learning style**)	• Search terms • Participation in collecting research • Graphic organizer— work-in-progress

FIGURE 4.2 (*Continued*)

FIGURE 4.2 (Continued)

Lesson Guiding Questions	Skills	Activities (*Students will . . .*)	Resources	Formative Assessment Evidence
	• Quote or paraphrase the data and conclusions of others. • Cite specific textual evidence from the text to support argument. • Cite sources adhering to a standard format.	• Determine which kind of evidence is relevant to use for your argument: facts, examples, data, quotes; see previously read exemplary arguments as samples. (**Differentiation:** Provide support to individual students or small groups, as needed.) • Continue to complete graphic organizer for your argument paper by adding evidence (quotes, data, examples, paraphrasing, etc.); use additional organizer, if needed. • Keep a running list of sources; use format shown on "Works Cited" handout to cite sources properly.	• "Works Cited" handout	(**differentiated by learning style**) • Works cited draft
L 3.3: How can I interpret my evidence to explain what it means?	• Determine sufficiency of evidence. • Interpret and explain evidence to demonstrate understanding and further argument.	• Working with a partner, share each other's evidence and answer these questions in discussion: *Is there sufficient, relevant evidence to support my claim? How can I interpret this piece of evidence and explain what it means to my readers to further my argument?* (To **differentiate by learning style**, allow students to choose a partner to confer with, or allow students to meet in small groups for feedback. Teachers to provide feedback, too.) • Use conversation with others to give you ideas on revising evidence, adding to evidence, and working on the interpretation column of the graphic organizer; conduct additional research, as needed.	• Internet access • Graphic organizer—work-in-progress for students' own papers (**differentiated by learning style**)	• Participation in partner and teacher discussions and collecting research • Graphic organizer—work-in-progress (**differentiated by learning style**)

Essential Understanding 4

With proper attribution, writers selectively integrate credible and accurate information from multiple sources to construct a sound argument.

Essential Unit Guiding Question 4

How can I evaluate the credibility of my sources and give proper citation?

Lesson Guiding Questions	Skills	Activities (Students will . . .)	Resources	Formative Assessment Evidence
Lesson (L) 4.1: How do I evaluate the credibility of sources and determine which ones to use for my argument?	• Assess the credibility and accuracy of each source.	• Investigate the credibility of sources by either engaging in a scavenger hunt or playing a game using teacher preselected websites. (**Teacher:** Conduct Lesson 3 in Chapter 8.) • Debrief with classmates about key findings from website investigation; complete sentence starter using what you learned from the activity: *When we research, it is important to . . . .* • Use "How Do I Identify Credible Sources?" handout as a guide while researching for your argument.	• Chapter 8, Lesson 3 in this book • Internet access • Teacher preselected websites. (**differentiated** by **interest** and **readiness**) • "Scavenger Hunt Record Sheet" (Figure 8.8) or "Source Sleuth Game" gameboard (Figure 8.9) • Game pieces and number cards • "How Do I Identify Credible Sources?" handout (Figure 8.10) • Teacher resource: www.google. com/insidesearch/ searcheducation/lessons.html	• Participation in activity and discussion • "Scavenger Hunt Record Sheet" (Figure 8.8)

FIGURE 4.2 *(Continued)*

FIGURE 4.2 (Continued)

Lesson Guiding Questions	Skills	Activities (Students will . . .)	Resources	Formative Assessment Evidence
L 4.2: How might the tone or style of the writing impact its credibility?	• Assess the credibility and accuracy of each source.	• Listen as peers read prepared cards; record a list of words that depict the tone students use as they read each card. • Define tone as it relates to speech; write definition of tone as it relates to text in student journals or binder: *Tone conveys the author's attitude toward the audience and subject matter.* • Use textual evidence to identify words and phrases that reflect author's tone or style in teacher preselected websites; answer: *How does tone or style impact credibility?* • Evaluate the sources you use for your argument to insure reliability and credibility.	• Teacher-prepared "tone" cards (e.g., *Say in a loving way,* "You can't have that." *Say in a frantic way,* "You can't have that."). • Student journals • Internet access • Teacher preselected websites • Teacher resource—conduct a lesson from "Evaluating Credibility of Sources" in this link: www.google.com/insidesearch/searcheducation/lessons.html	• Participation in activity and discussion • Student journals

Lesson Guiding Questions	Skills	Activities (Students will . . .)	Resources	Formative Assessment Evidence
		• (**Note:** This activity is a summary of a lesson, "Evaluating Credibility of Sources," referenced in the link listed in the Resource column.)		
L 4.3: What is plagiarism? How do I properly reference sources I use? What format is needed for in-text citations and works cited?	• Distinguish plagiarism from paraphrasing. • Reference and cite sources adhering to a standard format for in-text citation.	• Read excerpts of original text from a document with associated writing examples; determine which writing samples are paraphrased with proper attribution versus which are plagiarized. • Discuss ramifications of plagiarizing material and the ethics involved. (Option: Read articles or watch a video about plagiarism and its impact.) • Arrive at a class definition of *plagiarism* and write it in your journal or binder. • Practice paraphrasing material from original sources for your argument paper without plagiarizing; provide attribution using proper conventions shown on "In-text Citation" handout.	• Text excerpts with paraphrased and plagiarized examples • Newspaper articles about plagiarism (option) • Video about plagiarism (option—search Teacher Tube for an appropriate video: www.teachertube.com/) • Student journals • "In-text Citation" handout	• Participation in activity and discussion • Student journals • Paraphrased material with proper attribution

FIGURE 4.2 (*Continued*)

Essential Understanding 5

Writers who anticipate and address opposing viewpoints exhibit deep understanding of an issue, which strengthens the overall argument.

Essential Unit Guiding Question 5

Why and how do I address counterarguments?

Lesson Guiding Questions	Skills	Activities (Students will . . .)	Resources	Formative Assessment Evidence
Lesson (L) 5.1: Why do arguments include opposing viewpoints? How do they impact an argument?	• Critique counterarguments. • Use transitions to create cohesion and clarify the relationships among sections of a paper.	• In small groups, read argument writing samples; find the counterarguments and evaluate whether the treatment of opposing viewpoints furthered or hindered the argument. (To **differentiate** by **readiness,** assign groups appropriately challenging papers.) • Discuss answers to these prompts: *Why do arguments include opposing viewpoints? How do they impact an argument?* • Return to the writing samples and highlight or underline transitional words, phrases, or clauses that are used to acknowledge and address counterclaims; share these with the class to make a collective list of transitions. (**Teacher:** You might conduct this activity with Lesson 7.1 or 7.2.)	• Argument writing samples with counterclaims (**differentiated** by **readiness**)	• Participation during discussion • Marked-up argument samples for transitions • List of transitional words and phrases

Lesson Guiding Questions	Skills	Activities (Students will . . .)	Resources	Formative Assessment Evidence
L 5.2: How do counterclaims, along with reasons and evidence, strengthen a whole argument?	• Present claims and findings coherently, with valid reasoning and relevant evidence. • Use speaking techniques effective for presentations. • Delineate specific claims, evaluate the soundness of the reasoning and relevancy and sufficiency of the evidence, and identify any irrelevant evidence. • Acknowledge and distinguish the claim from opposing claims.	• Conduct debates on various issues using resource material to make your argument and address counterclaims. (To **differentiate** by **interest**, allow students to choose their topics.) • When acknowledging and addressing the opposing view, use class list of transitions or other sentence starters: *While you have shown that . . . , others might say . . . ; Those who disagree with your claim assert that . . . ; Opponents of your view maintain that . . . ; I realize you might feel that . . . but this is weak because . . . ; Contrary to your opinion that . . . , I feel. . . .* • Critique each group's debate by: (1) delineating a group's specific claim, (2) evaluating the soundness of reasoning, (3) determining the relevancy and sufficiency of evidence, (4) identifying any irrelevant evidence, and (5) assessing the strength of addressing counterclaims. (**Teacher:** You may hold this debate earlier; however, be mindful that instruction around counterclaims needs to be conducted prior to this activity.)	• Informal debate topics (**differentiate** by **interest**) • Source material • Internet access • Sentence starters for opposing viewpoints (including class list from Lesson L 5.1) • Criteria sheet	• Participation in debate preparation, debate performance, and discussion • Criteria sheet

FIGURE 4.2 *(Continued)*

FIGURE 4.2 (Continued)

Lesson Guiding Questions	Skills	Activities (Students will . . .)	Resources	Formative Assessment Evidence
L 5.3: What are the opposing viewpoints to my claim? How do I acknowledge and address them? Where do I insert counterarguments in my paper?	• Acknowledge and distinguish the claim from opposing claims.	• Return to student samples; pay attention to the placement of the counterclaims by discussing answers to these questions with a partner: *Are the counterclaims woven into the body paragraphs? Are they dedicated to their own paragraph? Which treatment is most effective?* • Identify opposing views about your issues; complete portion of the graphic organizer that acknowledges and addresses these opposing views; research, as needed. • Determine if you want to devote a paragraph to counterclaim(s) or integrate them into paragraphs; see student samples for support.	• Argument writing samples with counterclaims (use those from Lesson L 5.1) • Sentence starters for opposing viewpoints • Internet access • Graphic organizer—work-in-progress for students' own papers **(differentiated by learning style)**	• Participation during discussion and collecting research • Graphic organizer—work-in-progress **(differentiated by learning style)**

Essential Understanding 6

Writers create conclusions for an argument to leave a lasting impression on readers and compel them to act or change their views.

Essential Unit Guiding Question 6

How can I effectively conclude my argument paper?

Lesson Guiding Questions	Skills	Activities (Students will . . .)	Resources	Formative Assessment Evidence
Lesson (L) 6.1: How do writers create a strong conclusion?	• Critique and rewrite a concluding section that follows from and supports the argument presented.	• In groups, read and compare several conclusions of argument papers; discuss responses to questions related to each conclusion: *How does the conclusion further the argument? What lasting impression does it leave on you? Does it compel you to act or change your views? What main points does it sum up? What could the author have done to improve the conclusion? What ideas does it give you for your own argument paper?* (**Teacher:** You might use the cubing strategy with these questions; see Chapter 7 for an explanation.) • Discuss your impressions with the whole class.	• Argument papers with strong and weak conclusions • Optional: prompts on cubes (see Chapter 7)	• Participation in class activity and discussions • Revised conclusions

FIGURE 4.2 *(Continued)*

FIGURE 4.2 (Continued)

Lesson Guiding Questions	Skills	Activities (Students will . . .)	Resources	Formative Assessment Evidence
		• In groups, rewrite a weak conclusion so it is more effective. • Listen to each group's conclusion; vote as a class on the strongest conclusions and defend your vote using evidence from their writing.		
L 6.2: How can I summarize the main points of my argument? What strategies that I used for writing my introduction would work for my conclusion?	• Write a concluding section that follows from and supports the argument presented.	• Consider options for beginning the paper to determine which might be effective for a conclusion: quotes, anecdotes, background information, or definition of key terms. • Complete the graphic organizer for your argument with notes on how to write a conclusion that will leave an impression on readers. • Share your ideas with peers to get feedback.	• "Options for Beginning and Concluding Your Paper" handout • Graphic organizer—work-in-progress for students' own papers **(differentiated by learning style)**	• Graphic organizer—work-in-progress **(differentiated by learning style)**

Essential Understanding 7

To assist readers in following a coherent argument, writers use transitions to form logical connections among ideas and clarify relationships among sections.

Essential Unit Guiding Question 7

How do transitions help readers follow the logic of my argument?

Lesson Guiding Questions	Skills	Activities (Students will . . .)	Resources	Formative Assessment Evidence
Lesson (L) 7.1: Why do writers use transitions? What are some examples of transitions?	• Use transitions to create cohesion and clarify the relationships among sections of a paper.	• Read papers without transitions; discuss your impressions. (**Teachers:** Steer discussion so that students understand the function and value of transitions.) • Review previous argument papers and highlight transitional words, phrases, and clauses; use textual evidence to illustrate their function in creating cohesion and clarifying relationships among the claims, reasons, evidence, and counterclaims. • View "Transitions" handout; identify any transitions that were highlighted on the argument writing samples. (To **differentiate** by **readiness**, prepare two or three versions of the "Transitions" handout with varying degrees of difficulty and number of items; distribute an appropriately challenging handout to each student.)	• Teacher-prepared papers void of transitions • Argument papers used in previous lessons • "Transitions" handout (**differentiated** by **readiness**)	• Papers with highlighted transitions • Revised body paragraphs with transitions (**differentiated** by **readiness**)

FIGURE 4.2 (*Continued*)

FIGURE 4.2 (Continued)

Lesson Guiding Questions	Skills	Activities (Students will . . .)	Resources	Formative Assessment Evidence
		• Option: Return to original papers without transitions; in groups, use assigned handout to revise these papers to include transitional words, phrases, and clauses; compare revised papers with class. (To **differentiate** by **readiness**, arrange students in homogeneous groups to revise papers based on differentiated transition list.)		
L 7.2: How can I use transitions to form logical connections among ideas?	• Use transitions to create cohesion and clarify the relationships among sections of a paper.	• Select transitions that you could use for your paper; write these transitions on your graphic organizer or highlight them on the "Transitions" handout to use when you write your first draft.	• "Transitions" handout or graphic organizer—work-in-progress	• Graphic organizer or marked-up "Transitions" handout

Essential Understanding 8

Employing the writing process enables writers to challenge their own ideas and make necessary edits, which can lead to an improved and stronger argument.

Essential Unit Guiding Question 8

How do writers use the writing process to help produce optimal results?

Lesson Guiding Questions	Skills	Activities (Students will . . .)	Resources	Formative Assessment Evidence
Lesson 8.1: How do I use each step in the writing process to develop and strengthen my argument?	• Develop and strengthen writing using the writing process.	• Create a first draft using your graphic organizer and the "Argument Writing Checklist" (Figure 8.1) as a guide while writing. (For **differentiation** by **readiness,** create tiered versions of checklist; distribute the appropriate one to match students' **readiness** levels.) • Organize reasons and evidence logically, with the strongest argument as the last. • Share/seek response from peers and teacher (or another adult) one on one or in small groups.	• Graphic organizer—work-in-progress for students' own papers • "Argument Writing Checklist" (**differentiation** by **readiness,** see Figure 8.11) • "Argument Writing Rubric" (see Figure 5.14)	• Graphic organizer • Student drafts • Final argumentation with works cited

FIGURE 4.2 (*Continued*)

FIGURE 4.2 (Continued)

Lesson Guiding Questions	Skills	Activities (*Students will . . .*)	Resources	Formative Assessment Evidence
		• Revise work to include stronger word choice, transitions, sentence fluency, and more relevant or sufficient effective evidence; use appropriate reference and source materials. (For **differentiation** by **readiness,** provide various levels and types of reference and source materials.) • Edit one another's and your own work for grammar and conventions using "Proofreader's Symbols" handout (or poster) after revision; use reference materials, as needed; confer with teacher to ensure accuracy. • Create subsequent drafts focusing on individual growth areas; submit final copy to teacher. • Read final papers in small groups or to the whole class. (**Teacher:** See "Revision Ideas" and "Editing Ideas" that follow as a resource for teaching; these lists are not finite.)	• "Proofreader's Symbols" handout (or poster) • Various differentiated resources • Works cited format • Student papers • "Revision Ideas" (see below) • "Editing Ideas" (see below)	

Revision Ideas	Editing Ideas
• Should I refine my thesis and provide new reasons or evidence to support it? • What information can I delete that is trivial or irrelevant? • What sections do I need to reorder for clarity or to make a stronger argument? • Is there sufficient evidence to make a strong argument, or do I need to add more? • Does my introduction need to be more compelling? • Do I need to rewrite any repetitive sentence beginnings? • Do I need to add or rework my conclusion to leave a stronger impression on readers? • Is my style formal enough, or do I have to rework the paper to reflect a more formal style?	• Can I substitute weaker words for stronger ones? Can I delete some words altogether? • Do I need to replace a transition? • Are my punctuation marks in the right places, especially for referencing sources? • Do I need to correct any awkward sentences that don't sound right? • Are all of my words spelled correctly? • Have I indented where I should? • Do I have a consistent point of view, or do I need to change my pronouns? • Are my verb tenses consistent?

FIGURE 4.2

5

Summative Assessments and Preassessments

> *How will we know if students have achieved the desired results and met the standards? What will we accept as evidence of student understanding and proficiency? The backward design approach encourages us to think about a unit or course in terms of the collected assessment evidence needed to document and validate that the desired learning has been achieved, so that the course is not just content to be covered or a series of learning activities. This backward approach encourages teachers and curriculum planners to first think like an assessor before designing specific units and lessons, and thus to consider up front how they will determine whether students have attained the desired understandings.*
>
> —Grant Wiggins and Jay McTighe (1998, p. 12)

One of the hallmarks of the backward design approach is the practice of identifying assessment evidence and criteria at the genesis of planning a lesson or course of study. The idea behind this is that teachers should plan with the end in mind to be clear-sighted about what they really want students to glean in any unit. Those of you who have developed professional learning communities may also be familiar with assessments as one of the major tenets of that model. In his article "What Is a 'Professional Learning Community'?" Richard DuFour (2004) states that one of the significant questions that educators must address together in their professional learning communities is, "How will we know when each student has learned it?" It is imperative that you use standards, knowledge, essential understandings, and guiding questions to formulate culminating projects because the goal of these projects should be to have students demonstrate their understanding of the key aspects of a unit. Therefore, this chapter focuses primarily on summative assessments; however, it also addresses preassessments, since collecting information about what students know prior to launching into a unit will help teachers target learning more effectively.

TYPES OF ASSESSMENTS

There are three types of assessments to provide teachers and students with necessary information for optimal learning and growth:

1. **preassessments** (or *diagnostic assessments*)

2. **formative** (or *ongoing*) assessments

3. **summative** (or *culminating*) assessments

In my book *Lesson Design for Differentiated Instruction*, I state, "Preassessments are issued before a unit and sometimes even before a lesson to help teachers answer these questions: *What might students want to know or already know about a particular course of study? How do students learn best? What are their particular interests in a targeted area?* . . . A well-written and administered pre-assessment gives you a clear understanding of students' current knowledge base, interests or learning styles" (Glass, 2009). You can issue a readiness-based preassessment by using graphic organizers, pretests, or quick writes. To determine what interests students or identify their preferred learning modality, you might interview them or instruct them to complete a questionnaire or survey. I provide more discussion about preassessments near the end of this chapter.

When you disseminate new information or content to students, the students will not necessarily learn what is presented. It is through a multitude of formative assessments—or enriching learning opportunities that you purposefully design and conduct—that students work with these new ideas to process them. Formative assessments—or assessments *for* learning—allow students to practice and learn material on a daily basis. These ongoing assessments of student performance serve to improve your craft and inform you of students' progress so you can enrich, reteach, reinforce, or modify instruction, as appropriate. A partial list of formative assessments includes audience response systems, homework assignments, quizzes, graphic organizers, journal writes, exit cards, think-pair-shares, games, and discussions. Formative assessments are addressed more thoroughly in Chapter 7, as they align with learning activities; they are also discussed in Chapter 8, with differentiated instruction.

A thorough explanation of summative assessment is featured in the following sections, along with a variety of assessment instruments, such as rubrics, checklists, and assignment sheets. These can be used as written or adapted for the grade and subject you teach or support. At the end of this chapter, you will complete Exercise 5, in which you identify the summative (or culminating) assessment for your targeted unit.

SUMMATIVE (CULMINATING) ASSESSMENTS

After students grapple with and explore new information through a series of learning experiences and formative assessments, teachers then ask them to demonstrate that they have indeed mastered the unit content. This is referred to as the summative assessment or culminating product, which essentially is evidence *of* learning after a considerable unit or coursework. These culminating assessments call upon students to prove they have mastered the intended content goals presented throughout the unit or course of study.

Therefore, they must be designed to incorporate the "big three": what students have come to *know, understand,* and be able to *do* (KUD). To aptly evaluate summative assessments, you should design and use rubrics so there are clear and appropriate criteria for success. Creating these assessments and rubrics in tandem with delineating the KUDs in a curriculum unit map will enable you to have a clear direction for the overarching unit goals.

Summative projects (or products) come in many forms. State or district tests are one type of summative assessment. Teachers can also selectively find or create meaningful and effective assessments to allow students to show what they learned. Whereas a traditional final objective exam can reveal factual information that students have come to know, it will not give students the opportunity to demonstrate deep understanding. Therefore, if you prefer objective tests or need to administer them as a mandate in a course you are teaching, consider issuing them along with another type of culminating assessment to get a comprehensive picture of how well students have mastered all of the unit goals. Here are some examples of summative assessments in different subject areas:

- In language arts, students put on a performance; create a poster project with art and writing; or complete an interview, portfolio, or formal writing assignment (e.g., argument essay, research project, literary critique).
- In science, teachers assign a research report or videotape a student conducting a lab.
- In math, students respond to various prompts or assemble a portfolio with an accompanying reflection/evaluation sheet.

Differentiating products is a powerful and valuable means of allowing students to exhibit what they have learned. (See Chapter 7, "Differentiated Instruction," for other ideas.) You should present the summative assessment to students at or near the beginning of the unit so all students are well aware of your expectations and have specific goals in mind as they work to accomplish their final products.

Since you will create a culminating assessment for your unit during this chapter, I include ideas on the following pages about various ways that you might go about having students demonstrate understanding. Although each example is geared to a grade level or cluster, some can be adapted to accommodate the grade level and subject matter you teach or support.

- *Literacy template tasks.* The Literacy Design Collaborative (LDC) produced a series of twenty-nine template tasks that incorporate College and Career Readiness Anchor Standards for reading and writing. The instructional frameworks that it designed allow teachers to insert targeted texts, writing types, and content customized for a unit of study. They are geared for middle and high school students in language arts, science, and social studies. Suggestions for additions (referenced with "L" for Level) or extension activities are offered. In addition, the organization created rubrics for teachers to use based on Common Core text types. Figure 5.1 features a couple of the many fill-in-the-blank templates along with completed versions to show how they can be used in various subject areas. I suggest capitalizing upon your guiding questions and inserting them, as appropriate, into a pertinent frame. You can access any of the templates, sample prompts, and rubrics at www.literacydesigncollaborative.org. Other options for writing prompts across content areas can be found in Chapter 1 of this book.

Literacy Design Collaborative Sample Template Tasks

Argumentation/Analysis Template Task
Task 2 Template: [Insert question] After reading _____ (literature or informational texts), write a/an _____ (essay or substitute) that addresses the question and support your position with evidence from the text(s). **L2** Be sure to acknowledge competing views. **L3** Give examples from past or current events or issues to illustrate and clarify your position.
Task 2 ELA Example: Would you recommend *A Wrinkle in Time* to a middle school reader? After reading this science fiction novel, write a review that addresses the question and support your position with evidence from the text.
Task 2 Social Studies Example: How did the political views of the signers of the Constitution impact the American political system? After reading *Founding Brothers: The Revolutionary Generation,* write a report that addresses the question and support your position with evidence from the text.
Task 2 Science Example: Does genetic testing have the potential to significantly impact how we treat disease? After reading scientific sources, write a report that addresses the question and support your position with evidence from the texts. **L2** Be sure to acknowledge competing views. **L3** Give examples from past or current events or issues to illustrate and clarify your position.

Informational or Explanatory/Definition Template Task
Task 12 Template: [Insert question] After reading _____ (literature or informational texts), write a/an _____ (essay, report, or substitute) that defines _____ (term or concept) and explains _____ (content). Support your discussion with evidence from the text(s). **L2** What _____ (conclusions or implications) can you draw?
Task 12 ELA Example: What is a "metaphor"? After reading *The House on Mango Street* and drawing from other works you've read this year, write an essay that defines "metaphor" and explains how authors use it to enhance their writing. Support your discussion with evidence from the texts.
Task 12 Social Studies Example: What did the authors of the American Constitution mean by "rights"? After reading the Bill of Rights, write an essay that defines "rights" and explains "rights" as the authors use it in this foundational document. Support your discussion with evidence from the text. **L2** What implications can you draw?
Task 12 Science Example: Can "talent" be learned? After reading scientific sources, write an essay that defines "innate abilities" and explains its relevance to "talent." Support your discussion with evidence from the texts.

FIGURE 5.1

Source: © Literacy Design Collaborative, November 2011, www.literacydesigncollaborative.org.

- *Argument writing brainstorming sheet.* Argumentation is one of the three writing types included in the Common Core. Teachers can have students write logical arguments using textual evidence to support their positions across content areas, such as stake a claim for a theme in a literary work, defend one social justice cause over another, argue for or against a particular environmental issue or one politician versus another, and so forth. Figure 5.2 includes a brainstorming sheet for such a paper. There are different, albeit related, terms used for an argument paper and versions for how to structure it. Therefore, use or adapt Figure 5.2 to reflect how you teach this kind of writing while staying true to the dictates of your grade-level Common Core Standards for this text type. For instance, should the strongest argument be saved for last? Should counterclaims be woven throughout the paper rather than in a paragraph dedicated to this aspect of an argument? Some teachers introduce terms like *grounds, backing, qualifiers, bridge,* or *rebuttal.* Replace my terms for those you use. Additionally, for transitional words and phrases, you might suggest others, such as *While I have shown that . . . others may say . . . ; Those counter to this idea claim that . . . ; While some may disagree with this position . . . ; Contrary to what others might think. . . .* Figure 5.14 features an argumentation rubric that you might want to use.

- *Newspaper assignment.* Figure 5.3, "Causes of the American Revolution Newspaper," is an assignment sheet I created with an exemplary veteran teacher, Nancy Rhodes. Although this assessment is written for a unit on colonial America, you could use the strategy outlined here for another unit on conflict if you teach history. If you don't teach history, alter it accordingly, paying attention to the relationship between the guiding questions and topics, the choice of perspective students are given, and the types of writing students can select.

This group project requires students to choose a perspective—either the Patriot or Loyalist point of view. (You could add the Neutralist viewpoint, too.) Each student in the group writes a feature article, news story, or editorial in response to guiding questions based on selected topics from this agreed-upon group vantage point. Adding the component of guiding questions invites more rigorous thought for students than just focusing on a topic alone. Although students write an article individually, the group works together to produce other aspects of the newspaper (e.g., illustrations, advertisements, etc.), discuss viewpoints, and ensure that collective contributions respond to all guiding questions.

You will notice that students choose two of the five guiding questions to focus their writing; to determine which questions best associate with chosen topics is a critical-thinking exercise in and of itself. Since students need to demonstrate their understanding of all unit guiding questions, follow this activity with a brief writing exercise that addresses those questions individual students did not address in their own articles. The assignment calls for discussion of all guiding questions, and they've been addressed all unit long, so a brief essay might suffice. In addition, students should use the checklist and accompanying graphic organizer for the particular type of article they will write. Figures 5.4 and 5.5 are examples of a checklist and graphic organizer, respectively, for students who choose to write a news article.

- *Character study or societal contributions.* Figure 5.6 includes two related assignments. One is for a character, which would obviously be more applicable for realistic or historical fiction. The other is more global, as it is geared to an individual who has made a significant contribution to society in the past or today, such as a scientist, inventor, leader, artist, or political figure. Whichever project you issue, make sure students respond to pertinent guiding questions. For a summative assessment, have students address all essential unit guiding questions to demonstrate their understanding of all key curricular goals. You can, however, adapt Figure 5.6 to use as a formative assessment by selecting one guiding question to accompany a particular lesson highlighting a targeted concept.

- *Multiple intelligence options.* When using Figure 5.7, "Project Choices," each student has an opportunity to select the project that fits his or her learning style. While it is generic and can work with any unit, it does refer to guiding questions, so there is an assumption that you have written and will incorporate these into your unit. To guide students as they work on their projects and presentation, introduce the Project Checklist in Figure 5.8.

Argument Writing Brainstorming

⇨ **Introduction (First Paragraph)**

Engaging Opening—Introduction attracts and draws in the reader.
Thesis—Writer clearly stakes a claim or states a position on one issue.

⇨ **Body Paragraphs**

Here are my *reasons* and my *evidence* with *interpretations* to support each reason:

	Reasons— topic sentence	*Evidence*—relevant and accurate evidence including facts, quotes, data, examples that are not common knowledge	*Interpretation*— explanation of the evidence
Paragraph 2			
Paragraph 3			
Paragraph 4 (strongest argument)			

Counterclaim (separate paragraph or woven into body paragraphs)	Others might feel . . .	But this is weak because . . .

⇨ **Conclusion (Last Paragraph)**

Restate thesis and sum up main points:
Include a call to action (as appropriate):

FIGURE 5.2

Causes of the American Revolution Newspaper

Final Project. You will work in a group to create a Loyalist *or* Patriot newspaper focusing on the causes of the American Revolution. Each group member will write his or her own newspaper article from the perspective of a Loyalist or Patriot. Together as a group, you will layout the articles to look like an authentic newspaper of the colonial time period.

What type of newspaper article do I write?

You will choose to write a feature article, a news article, or an editorial. However, you must have a group discussion about who is writing which kind of article so that there is a balance among the three types of newspaper articles. In addition, you will make one other contribution to the paper (see "What else do I contribute to the newspaper?"). Use the checklist and graphic organizer for each article type to guide you while writing.

What else do I contribute to the newspaper?

- **Advertisement**—The ad must reflect the time period. Consider what kinds of ads would be appropriate before creating one, such as persuading someone to fight for a side or to buy a certain colonial product.
- **"Flag"**—Create a flag for the newspaper that includes a name, date, and location.
- **Maps with captions**—Include one or more historically accurate maps with captions to accompany articles.
- **Illustrations**—Include one or more illustrations with captions.

What do I write about?

Each of you will select a **topic** for your article. Within your article, you must address at least **two guiding questions** and write from the **perspective** of either a Loyalist or Patriot. As a group, discuss which questions you will each address in your article so that your group newspaper addresses all guiding questions.

Guiding Questions	Topics	
1. How can differences in political and economic beliefs and interests create conflict? 2. How can people who share interests work together to change for the better? 3. How might political independence create risks and rewards? 4. How do government documents reflect key political ideals and a system of government? 5. How can individuals make a difference in creating political change?	A. French and Indian War B. Stamp Act (and Sugar Act) C. Townshend Acts D. Boston Massacre E. Boston Tea Party F. Coercive or Intolerable Acts G. Iroquois Confederacy H. Committees of Correspondence I. First Continental Congress J. Second Continental Congress K. Declaration of Independence L. "Taxation without representation"	M. Paul Revere N. Samuel Adams O. George Washington P. Thomas Paine/ *Common Sense* Q. Thomas Jefferson R. Patrick Henry S. Ben Franklin T. King George III U. John Adams V. Loyalists W. Patriots

How do I get information for my article?

Use multiple sources to get the content you need for your article, such as facts, details, examples, quotes, and definitions. Your textbook can be one source, but use others, such as reliable websites, books, and other resources. Use the school and classroom library, as well as the public library, for resources.

FIGURE 5.3

Source: Glass (2012).

News Story Checklist

Ideas/Content and Organization

- ☐ I write a <u>news story</u> with a lead and supporting paragraphs.
- ☐ I focus my news story on a <u>particular topic</u> and also respond to the <u>guiding questions.</u>
- ☐ I write an attention-grabbing and appropriate <u>headline</u>.
- ☐ I include a <u>byline</u> and <u>dateline.</u>
- ☐ I <u>indent</u> each paragraph appropriately.
- ☐ My news story follows the <u>inverted pyramid</u> format so my most important information is at the beginning in the lead, and the least important is at the end.

➡ Beginning (Lead)

- ☐ My <u>lead paragraph</u> answers the questions <u>who, what, where,</u> and <u>when.</u> The lead includes the most important facts about my topic.

➡ Middle

- ☐ My <u>body paragraphs are clearly structured,</u> with topic sentence, support, and ending sentence.
- ☐ I <u>support each topic sentence</u> by using <u>evidence,</u> such as facts, quotes, data, and/or examples from many credible sources. I answer the <u>why</u> and <u>how</u> questions.
- ☐ I <u>cite my sources</u> so readers know where I got my information.

➡ Ending

- ☐ My <u>ending</u> includes the least important details of the news event.

Word Choice

- ☐ I use specific and accurate <u>vocabulary</u> suited to my topic.
- ☐ My <u>news story does not include unclear language</u> since I use specific verbs and nouns to explain the news event.

Conventions

- ☐ I use correct <u>punctuation and capitalization</u> in my news story and headline, and also for any quotations.
- ☐ I <u>spell</u> all words correctly.
- ☐ I use <u>correct formatting.</u> My news story, title, and any illustrations complement the formatting of the other items in this group newspaper and reflect the colonial period.
- ☐ My sentences make sense and do not have <u>grammar</u> errors.
- ☐ I write using <u>present tense verbs</u> since my news story reflects a current colonial period event.

Sentence Fluency

- ☐ I write <u>complete sentences</u> and do not include fragments or run-ons.
- ☐ I use <u>a variety of sentence structures:</u> simple, compound, and complex.
- ☐ My <u>sentence beginnings vary</u> so that each sentence does not start in the same way.

Voice

- ☐ I write my news story in <u>third-person point of view.</u> I keep this consistent point of view throughout my article.
- ☐ I know to whom (<u>audience</u>) I am writing and why (<u>purpose</u>) I am writing.

FIGURE 5.4

Source: Glass (2012).

News Story Organizer

Perspective: _____ Loyalist _____ Tory

- Headline: _____

- Byline: _____

Event	
What newsworthy event happened that you will cover in your article?	What guiding questions will you address that relate to this event?
Beginning (Lead)	
Who?	What?
Where?	When?
Middle (Why? How?)	
Support—What other information will readers want to know? What is your evidence? Use and cite credible sources to answer *why* and *how*. Consider these types of evidence, although you don't need one from each category. You may have two from the same category.	
FACTS	Source:
QUOTES	Source:
DATA	Source:
EXAMPLES	Source:
Ending (Additional Information)	
Include least important details:	

FIGURE 5.5

Character Study

Directions: Choose a project to highlight a character you select from the story. Respond to pertinent guiding questions in your project: *How and why does this character change? How does a setting impact the character? How do the character's motivations and beliefs shape the plot? How does this character's interaction with another create conflict or reconciliation?*

Speech

Write a speech from a character's point of view about one of the following:

- ☐ a particular event or situation
- ☐ a conflict
- ☐ another character

In the speech, respond to the guiding questions. Then, deliver the speech to the class live or pretaped as if you were this character, so use costumes or props, as appropriate. Submit the typed speech to your teacher after delivering it.

Illustrations

Draw a series of detailed, creative, and accurate illustrations that reflect a character's feelings or decisions about an event or situation, a conflict, or another character. Beneath each drawing, provide an appropriate caption. Make sure to address the guiding questions in your project. Present these pictures in an order that makes sense.

Research

Write eight to ten questions that you would want to pose to a character if you had the chance to meet. Include the guiding questions in your list along with other questions you want answered. Then, answer each question. You can do this activity with a partner in which you each pose questions, and then discuss answers to your partner's questions. Submit typed questions and well-developed answers to your teacher.

Poetry or Prose

Choose a character. Then write prose or poetry using these line starters that address the guiding questions in your work. Create an original title.

- ☐ I wish that . . .
- ☐ I realize that . . .
- ☐ I decide that . . .
- ☐ I wonder about . . .
- ☐ I see that . . .
- ☐ I believe that . . .
- ☐ I feel that . . .
- ☐ I hope that . . .

Societal Contributions

Directions: Select an individual who has made a significant contribution to society. Choose a project to highlight this individual and the impact he or she has made. Respond to these guiding questions in your project: *Why did you make this contribution? How has your contribution impacted individuals and society then and now? How have others hindered or supported you in your achievements? How have you overcome obstacles?*

Speech

Assume the role of your selected individual. Determine an audience who would benefit from hearing a speech from you. Write and deliver the speech from this individual's point of view that addresses the guiding questions. You can deliver the speech to the class live or pretaped as if you were this person, so use costumes and props. Submit the typed speech to your teacher after delivering it.

Illustrations

Create a series of illustrations that feature this individual and the contribution(s) he or she has made. Present these pictures in chronological or thematic order and write a detailed caption for each drawing. Illustrations and captions must address all guiding questions.

Research

Conduct an interview by assuming the role of your chosen person, centering on the contributions he or she has made and responses to the guiding questions. Or, conduct an interview between the person who has made the contributions and another who is impacted by it. Dress the part and use props since you will present the interview live or pretaped. Submit typed questions and well-developed answers to your teacher.

Poetry or Prose

Write prose or poetry using these line starters based on your selected individual's contribution and responses to the guiding questions. Create an original title and add appropriate pictures.

- ☐ I wish that . . .
- ☐ I realize that . . .
- ☐ I decide that . . .
- ☐ I wonder about . . .
- ☐ I see that . . .
- ☐ I believe that . . .
- ☐ I feel that . . .
- ☐ I hope that . . .

FIGURE 5.6

Project Choices

Choose one of these projects to demonstrate your understanding of our unit. Make sure you thoroughly *address responses to all guiding questions* in whichever project you select. You will present your project to the class. Read the "Project Checklist" to guide you as you work.

Game

 Create a game that includes game cards, directions, a game board, and anything else that others would need to actually play the game. The game cards need to address the guiding questions in some format (e.g., true/false, multiple choice, etc.) plus include other questions that pertain to our unit. Provide questions as well as answers. Be creative in the visual appeal of the game and the strategy required to play.

Play

Write a script and perform a play. You may perform your play live or videotape it and show it to the class. Use props and costumes. For the script, include narration and actors'/actresses' lines. Make sure to have a beginning, middle, and end, and include responses to the guiding questions somewhere in your script. Submit your script to your teacher.

Song

Create lyrics to a song that address the guiding questions. You might create a song from scratch by making up the melody and lyrics, or you might create lyrics to a familiar tune. Record the song on audio- or videotape and share it with the class. If you play an instrument, use it as you sing. Include a chorus and at least three verses. Submit your song lyrics to your teacher.

Picture Poster

Create a picture poster consisting of five drawings accompanied by captions that are each at least four sentences long. Address the guiding questions in either the pictures or captions, or a combination of both. First make a poster layout in which you draft the text and sketch drawings before finalizing your project. Remember to provide a title for your poster.

Technology

Choose a project using technology that focuses on the guiding questions. Examples include PowerPoint, iMovie, Comic Life, or other ideas you have. Get approval before beginning your project to discuss expectations.

FIGURE 5.7 (*Continued*)

FIGURE 5.7 (Continued)

Trial

You are a prosecuting attorney putting one of the people (or characters) you learned about on trial for a crime or misdeed he or she has committed. Prepare your case on paper with all your arguments and support each one with facts. Weave the guiding questions somewhere into your trial. You may videotape yourself in a mock trial, using friends or family to play roles in a court scene. Submit the written version of the case to your teacher.

Party

Plan a party for a guest list based on our unit. Complete each of the following to ensure a successful party: (1) design an invitation to the party which would appeal to those coming, (2) describe what each person should wear to the party, (3) explain the menu for the party from appetizers to dessert, and (4) describe the games or entertainment in detail. Respond to the guiding questions somewhere in your party planning. Display this information however you see fit, such as in a poster, technology, book, or other way.

Short Story or Sequel

Write a short story or sequel that incorporates responses to the guiding questions. Your writing should include a *setting, character, plot,* and *point of view.* Also write descriptive details and dialogue to make it interesting. Feel free to include pictures for your story.

Radio or TV Interview

Create a script and then tape an interview of someone related to our unit. Pretend the person (or character) is being interviewed by a magazine or newspaper reporter. Introduce the person at the beginning of the radio or TV program and ask intriguing questions that would interest the listener. Address the guiding questions at some point in the interview. Have a friend or family member ask the interview questions while you assume the role of the figure. If you are videotaping the program, wear a realistic costume. Be creative, for example by including introductory music for the program, any necessary sound effects, pertinent commercials, and so forth. Submit your script to your teacher.

FIGURE 5.7

Source: Glass (2012).

Project Checklist

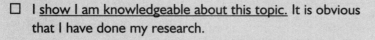

PROJECT

☐ I <u>show I am knowledgeable about this topic.</u> It is obvious that I have done my research.

☐ It is clear that I read the "Project Choices" sheet because I <u>satisfy each point for my chosen project.</u>

☐ I respond to all the <u>unit guiding questions</u> accurately and thoroughly.

☐ I include <u>evidence</u> from the text within my project (e.g., facts, examples, quotes). I check all of my facts to make sure they are correct.

☐ I <u>use accurate terms and descriptive words.</u>

☐ My writing includes <u>proper grammar and conventions</u> (periods, capitalization, punctuation).

☐ I <u>indent</u> as needed.

☐ If my project requires <u>artwork,</u> it is accurate, creative, and detailed.

☐ My writing is <u>organized</u> in a way that makes sense and all of my main points are clearly written.

☐ It is obvious that I have done my <u>personal best.</u>

PRESENTATION

☐ I <u>rehearse</u> several times in preparation for my presentation.

☐ I <u>make note cards</u> for my presentation, if appropriate.

☐ I practice my words so that I do not need to look down at my note cards too frequently. I <u>scan the audience</u> while presenting.

☐ When I speak, I project my voice so it is <u>loud</u> enough for everyone to hear.

☐ I make sure I enunciate my words so that I <u>speak clearly.</u>

☐ My <u>pacing is good</u> – it's not too slow or too fast.

☐ My presentation is <u>organized</u> so it is easy for the listener to understand my main points.

☐ I review all of my notes and am <u>prepared for any questions</u> that the audience may ask me.

☐ Audience members will be able to <u>answer the unit guiding questions</u> from my presentation.

FIGURE 5.8

Source: Glass (2012).

RUBRICS

To assess student performance on a summative assessment, teachers use rubrics—or scoring guides—which represent a set of criteria directly linked to standards and learning objectives. You have undoubtedly seen various types of rubrics. No matter what the format may be, constructive rubrics should have the following two fixed elements: performance factors and levels of quality. However, not all constructive rubrics have the performance factors clearly articulated. These can be general, but they are more effective as a means for providing feedback to students and assessing their work if they are written for a specific assignment and its integral elements (e.g., topic sentence, transitions, academic vocabulary, etc.). Quality levels can be represented numerically, in word form, or in a combination of both forms. For example, the rubric can be written on a 4-, 5-, or 6-point scale or include words like *developing, emergent, capable, advanced,* and *exemplary.* Figure 5.9 illustrates these rubric features and the gradation of quality levels; have yourself a chuckle as you read it.

Sample Rubric

Performance Factors

	Outstanding	Very Effective	Effective	Marginally Effective	Ineffective
Producing Quality Work	Leaps tall buildings at a single bound	Must take a running start to leap over tall buildings	Can only leap over short buildings or medium buildings (no spires)	Crashes into buildings when attempting to jump over them	Cannot recognize buildings at all, let alone jump them
Using Work Time Effectively	Is faster than a speeding bullet	Is as fast as a speeding bullet	Not quite as fast as a speeding bullet	Would you believe a slow bullet?	Wounds self with bullets when attempting to shoot gun
Accepting Responsibility	Is stronger than a locomotive	Is stronger than a tornado	Is stronger than a hurricane	Shoots the breeze	Full of hot air
Job Knowledge	Walks on water consistently	Walks on water in emergencies	Washes with water	Drinks water	Eyes water
Communicating Effectively	Talks with God	Talks with employees	Talks to himself/herself	Argues with himself/herself	Loses arguments with himself/herself

FIGURE 5.9

Source: Kadushin and Harkness (2002).

Rubrics are used to score student work at all grades. However, some teachers present them to students in middle and high school so they are clear about criteria. In this way, they use the rubric as a teaching tool to score student and published samples and to guide their own writing. For students who are unaccustomed to using rubrics, it might be worthwhile to focus on a few line items at a time. Otherwise, students might feel overwhelmed, and it would negate the purpose of sharing the rubric. If you are wary of presenting rubrics to students, then make sure you provide them with a checklist (see the checklist discussion later in this chapter).

The rubric format in Figure 5.9 is probably most familiar to you; indeed, it is the one that I have regularly used in the past. In recent years, however, I have switched to the format shown in Figure 5.10, the narrative rubric excerpt. This alternative format allows for the clear delineation of skills and concepts that represent targeted performance factors (see left column) and indicate what constitutes levels of quality for each skill/concept (see right column with italicized words to indicate these levels). This format also provides more concrete feedback for improvement. You'll see that performance factors include pertinent Common Core Standards that can be referenced in parentheses (e.g., W.7.3a = Writing Strand/Grade 7/Standard 3a). Sometimes I insert other expectations and list them without an identification code so they are not misconstrued as part of the Common Core Standards (e.g., see "Conclusion" cell of Figure 5.10). You might ask: *How can I add criteria?* The designers of the Common Core do welcome teachers to use their professional expertise, and I made sure not to delete Common Core Standards because students will be assessed against them. If you are making significant changes, be mindful to follow proper implementation

Sample Rubric Excerpt

Transitional Words and Phrases Use a variety of transition words, phrases, and clauses to convey sequence and signal shifts from one time frame or setting to another (2010a, W.7.3c).	**4**—*Thoughtful and consistent* use of transitional words, phrases, and clauses to convey sequence and time frame shifts so paper flows; sophisticated beyond grade level **3**—*Usually* uses appropriate and enough transitions to convey sequence and time frame shifts so paper flows **2**—*Weak* use of transitions; more transitions or more appropriate ones needed **1**—*No transitions*
Conclusion Provide a conclusion that follows from and reflects on the narrated experiences or events (W.7.3e); answer questions a reader might have about what happened; make sure it is not abrupt.	**4**—Resolved *completely; all* questions answered; sophisticated beyond grade level **3**—Resolved with *most* questions answered **2**—*Weak* ending; reader left with *many unanswered* questions **1**—*No* ending

FIGURE 5.10

guidelines, especially if rubric design is a districtwide endeavor. (For more information, see the section "Can States Add to the Standards?" in the Resource, "A Brief Primer on the ELA Common Core Standards," for specifics on the 15% guideline. As mentioned in the Introduction to this book, this Resource section is located in the companion website.)

Rubrics that are used to score student writing rely on some subjectivity. Therefore, writing rubrics use adverbs and other words of degree to help differentiate one level from the next. Below are some common adverb groupings that appear on scoring guides. Feel free to mix, match, and add to my list to help you devise a rubric that shows progression. You can surely use them for any level rubric. A score of 3—whether it be on a 4-, 5-, or 6-point rubric—typically denotes at-grade-level work. Scores of 4 or higher represent sophistication beyond the grade level.

- 4—thoroughly; 3—adequately; 2—minimally/weakly/marginally; 1—hardly
- 4—entirely/consistently; 3—mostly/generally; 2—inconsistently; 1—occasionally
- 4—always; 3—sometimes/somewhat; 2—occasionally; 1—rarely
- 4—sophisticated/beyond grade level; 3—appropriately/usually/mostly; 2—somewhat/ marginally; 1—hardly
- 4—minor (errors); 3—some (errors); 2—consistent (errors); 1—serious (errors)
- 4—no (errors); 3—few (errors); 2—many/numerous (errors); 1—replete with (errors)

At times, the use of adverbs is inadequate to convey what is intended. In such cases, I might use different terminology (see the example below).

Presentation Adhere to proper formatting	4—Completely adheres to proper formatting
	3—Mostly adheres to proper formatting
	2—Haphazard formatting
	1—Proper formatting ignored

It is understandable to use *sometimes/some/somewhat* as a 3 (at grade level) for certain line items and *generally/mostly* as a 3 for other line items within the same grade. This would indicate that some line items are clearly expected in certain grades or for particular times of the school year, while others may reflect benchmarks toward which students are still working. You might even create differentiated rubrics and expect high achievers to challenge themselves to the next level and assign indicators to each rubric number accordingly. Figure 5.11 illustrates this scenario, as it provides a Grade 8 rubric excerpt that acknowledges that some students might be practicing a Grade 9 standard. Note that the second row on this figure has more detail, whereas the top row is succinct. Determine with your colleagues how you want to phrase the text in your rubrics.

For grammar and conventions skills, consider two different choices of criteria: quantitative and subjective. Figure 5.12 provides a specific example. Decide with your fellow educators which treatment will provide your students with the best feedback for improvement.

In the same way that many districts identify certain standards as *focus* or *power* or *essential* standards, certain line items of rubrics can be weighted for emphasis. Alternatively, you might merely allot more points to a specific line item that is not only a focus but that constitutes a large part of a student's product. See the example in Figure 5.13. Note that the examples in Figures 5.12 and 5.13 may be construed as generous in issuing a 2 and 1 on the

Grade 8 Rubric Excerpt

Punctuation: Semicolon Use semicolon (and perhaps a conjunctive adverb) to link two or more closely related independent clauses (2010a, L.9–10.2a).	**4**—Always **3**—*Sometimes* **2**—Occasionally **1**—Rarely
Punctuation: Comma and Ellipsis Use punctuation (comma, ellipsis, dash) to indicate a pause or break (L.8.2a).	**4**—Consistently uses commas and ellipses correctly to show a pause or break **3**—*Mostly* uses commas and ellipses correctly to show a pause or break **2**—Occasionally uses commas and ellipses correctly **1**—Rarely uses commas and ellipses; when used, done so incorrectly

FIGURE 5.11

Quantitative Versus Subjective Scoring

	Quantitative	Subjective
Spelling Spell correctly (2010a, L.6–8, 11–12.2b, L.9–10.2c).	**4**—One error **3**—Two to three errors **2**—Four to six errors **1**—Seven or more errors	**4**—No errors **3**—Minimal errors **2**—Several errors **1**—Serious errors; hinders reading

FIGURE 5.12

Sample Weighted Rubric Excerpt

Description/Sensory Language Use narrative techniques, such as dialogue, pacing, and **description**, to develop experiences, events, and/or characters (2010a, W.7.3b); use precise words and phrases, relevant descriptive details, and sensory language to capture the action and convey experiences and events (W.7.3d) and for setting.	**8**—*Consistent, sophisticated* use of precise words and phrases, relevant descriptive details, and sensory language to capture events, character, and setting **6**—*Some* use of precise words and phrases, relevant descriptive details, and sensory language to capture events, character, and setting **4**—*Limited* use of precise words and phrases, relevant descriptive details, and sensory language to capture events, character, and setting **2**—*Rare* or no use of precise words and phrases, relevant descriptive details, and sensory language to capture events, character, and setting

FIGURE 5.13

line items in the last row instead of a 0. I suggest you discuss with your colleagues how to treat papers that have nonexistent elements. Whatever you decide, be consistent so individual teachers don't operate on their own set of criteria for scoring.

I've shown you excerpts of rubrics, so now let's take a look at a completed rubric for an argument writing assignment (Figure 5.14). You'll see it is geared to the eighth-grade Common Core Standards; however, it can easily be adapted for other grades in middle and high school.

Online Resources Included

Argument Writing Rubric

	Components	Points
Ideas/Content and Organization	**Title** Include a unique title to support topic.	**4**—Excellent **3**—Good **2**—Weak **1**—No title
	Introduction Introduce claim(s) (2010a, W.8.1a) through thesis statement; create a hook to draw in reader.	**4**—Attractive opening provides context for argument and entirely draws in readers; thoughtful thesis introduces claim clearly; sophisticated **3**—Opening somewhat provides context and draws in readers; thesis states claim **2**—Weak opening does not provide context or grab readers' attention; weakly stated thesis **1**—No opening to provide context or thesis; introduction clearly incomplete; claim unclear
	Body Paragraphs: Reasons/Evidence and Organization Support claim(s) with logical reasoning and relevant evidence, using accurate, credible sources and demonstrating an understanding of the topic or text (W.8.1b); organize the reasons and evidence logically (W.8.1a); produce clear and coherent writing in which the development, organization, and style are appropriate to task, purpose, and audience (W.8.4); quote or paraphrase the data and conclusions of others while avoiding plagiarism (W.8.8).	**8**—Each body paragraph *very* clearly structured; *very* clear and logical reasons expressed as topic sentences link to thesis; *very* relevant, accurate, and developed evidence (facts, data, examples) support position; *sophisticated* **6**—Each body paragraph *mostly* clearly structured; *mostly* clear and logical reasons expressed as topic sentences link to thesis; *mostly* relevant, accurate, and developed evidence (facts, data, examples) support position **4**—Each body paragraph *weakly* structured; *weak* reasons; reasons do not altogether link to thesis; not completely relevant or accurate evidence; weakly developed evidence to support position **1**—*Any of these apply:* missing *most* of the body paragraph requirements; *mostly* incorrect or plagiarized; *little, if any,* evidence to support position; *no* development

	Components	Points
	Counterclaims Acknowledge and distinguish the claim(s) from alternate or opposing claims (W.8.1a).	**4**—Clearly and thoughtfully acknowledges and addresses opposing claim(s); sophisticated **3**—Acknowledges opposing claim(s); somewhat addresses opposing claim **2**—Weakly acknowledges and addresses opposing claim(s) **1**—No mention of opposing claim(s) or acknowledges there is an opposing claim without addressing it
	Conclusion Provide a concluding statement or section that follows from and supports the argument presented (W.8.1e).	**4**—Clearly sums up thesis and important points without repeating verbatim; call to action (if needed) very clearly motivating; sophisticated **3**—Mostly sums up thesis and important points; little or no repetition of thesis; call to action (if needed) somewhat motivating **2**—Weakly sums up thesis or important points or repeats thesis almost or entirely verbatim; weak call to action (if needed) **1**—No conclusion or conclusion is incomplete, so it appears nonexistent
	Paragraphing Know when to begin a new paragraph and how to indent paragraphs.	**4**—Paragraphing and indenting completely intact **3**—Most paragraphing and indenting intact **2**—Unclear paragraphing and/or indenting **1**—No paragraphing/indenting
	Transitions Use words, phrases, and clauses to create cohesion and clarify the relationships among claim(s), counterclaims, reasons, and evidence (W.8.1c).	**4**—Thoughtful use of transitions links sections of text and creates cohesion so paper flows; sophisticated **3**—Usually uses appropriate and enough transitions to link sections of text and create cohesion so paper flows **2**—Weak use of transitions; additional transitions or more appropriate ones needed **1**—No transitions
Voice	**Point of View/Style** Establish and maintain a formal style (W.8.1d).	**4**—Maintains consistent point of view and formal style **3**—Might get off-track occasionally **2**—Weak sense of point of view; style inconsistent **1**—No sense of point of view; style altogether informal
	Task/Purpose/Audience Adhere to task, purpose, and audience when writing.	**4**—Clearly aware of task, purpose, and audience **3**—Generally aware of task, purpose, and audience **2**—Little awareness of task, purpose, and audience **1**—Unaware of task, purpose, and audience

FIGURE 5.14 (Continued)

FIGURE 5.14 (Continued)

	Components	Points
Sentence Fluency	**Sentence Beginning Variety** Include a variety of sentence beginnings—subjects, prepositional phrases, adverbs, dependent clauses.	**4**—Thoughtful and consistent use of sentence beginning variety using subjects, prepositional phrases, adverbs, dependent clauses; sophisticated **3**—Sometimes uses sentence beginning variety **2**—Most sentences begin in the same way **1**—All sentences begin in the same way by either the same word or the same type (e.g., all subjects)
	Sentence Structure Variety Vary sentence patterns for meaning, reader/listener interest, and style (L.6.3a).	**4**—Thoughtful and consistent use of sentence variety; sophisticated **3**—Sometimes uses sentence variety **2**—Most sentences have the same sentence structure so there is little cadence **1**—All sentences have the same structure; halted reading (or all sentences are simple and compound)
	Run-ons and Complete Sentences Produce complete sentences; no run-ons.	**4**—No run-ons; all sentences are complete, though there may be a minor error **3**—Minimal sentence structure errors **2**—Many sentence structure errors **1**—Unclear about sentence structure altogether
	Transitions Between Sentences Use transitions to link sentences.	**4**—Thoughtful use of transitional words, phrases, and clauses to link sentences; very fluid reading; sophisticated **3**—Usually uses appropriate and enough transitions to connect sentences **2**—Weak use of transitions from sentence to sentence; more needed **1**—No transitions within paragraph
Word Choice	**Word Choice** Use accurately grade-appropriate general academic and domain-specific words and phrases (L.8.6).	**4**—Consistently accurate and strong choice and usage of words and phrases; sophisticated language; no repetition **3**—Mostly accurate and strong choice and usage of words and phrases; some repetition, but minor **2**—Weak choice and usage of words and phrases; fair amount of repetition **1**—Rarely uses appropriate or strong words and phrases
	Presentation Adhere to proper formatting.	**4**—Complete adherence to proper formatting **3**—Mostly adheres to proper formatting **2**—Haphazard formatting **1**—Proper formatting ignored

Components	Points	
Presentation/Conventions		
Grammar Form and use verbs in the active and passive voice (L.8.1b); correct inappropriate shifts in verb voice (L.8.1d).	4—One error 3—Two to three errors 2—Four to six errors **OR** 1—More than seven errors	4—Minor errors 3—Some errors 2—Many errors 1—Serious errors; hinders reading
Capitalization Use correct capitalization.	4—One error 3—Two to three errors 2—Four to six errors **OR** 1—More than seven errors	4—Minor errors 3—Some errors 2—Many errors 1—Serious errors; hinders reading
Punctuation Follow standard format for citation (W.8.8) within the text and works cited; punctuate correctly.	4—One error 3—Two to three errors 2—Four to six errors **OR** 1—More than seven errors	4—Minor errors 3—Some errors 2—Many errors 1—Serious errors; hinders reading
Spelling Spell correctly (L.8.2c).	4—One error 3—Two to three errors 2—Four to six errors **OR** 1—More than seven errors	4—Minor errors 3—Some errors 2—Many errors 1—Serious errors; hinders reading

Student: _____   Highest Possible Points: _____

Total Points Attained: _____   Converted Letter Grade: _____

FIGURE 5.14

In Figure 5.15, "Final Project," I have coupled a student assignment sheet with a straightforward rubric. It includes the guiding questions for both the content, which is based on a literary selection, and for the presentation. Students use this sheet to plan for their differentiated project. As they present to the class, students will receive this same sheet and critique one another as they present. Since the goal of producing a summative project is to demonstrate understanding, I have audience members take an active role in determining if classmates have indeed addressed guiding questions. Therefore, as students present, the others pay careful attention to find answers to the guiding questions and critique peers accordingly. This can also serve as a reinforcement of the unit goals as students actively listen for responses. If you don't teach language arts, use this rubric as a model and adapt it for an assignment in your content area.

Final Project

Literature Guiding Questions	Project Choices	Presentation Guiding Questions
Address *all* of these guiding questions in a project of your choice. See "Project Choices." 1. How do authors develop characters? 2. How does the protagonist interact with other characters and advance the plot? 3. How does the theme of this novel emerge and develop? 4. How does figurative language impact meaning and tone?	Choose one project to demonstrate your understanding of the four literature guiding questions. You may work alone, with a partner, or in a small group. You will present to the class either live or prerecorded, so address "Presentation Guiding Questions," as well. • talk show • skit • technology • song	1. How can I present my information clearly, concisely, and logically? 2. How can I use digital media and props to enhance my presentation? 3. How can I use verbal techniques effectively?

Criteria

Use the content and presentation criteria below to guide you as you create and present your project. You will be scored based on how well the audience can answer the literature guiding questions, so make sure you have addressed them. In addition, the audience will critique you on your presentation skills according to the criteria listed in this scoring guide.

CONTENT	5	4	3	2	1
The presenter(s) clearly addresses these guiding questions:					
How do authors develop *characters*? Analyze how complex characters develop over the course of a text, interact with other characters, and advance the plot or develop the theme (RL.9–10.3).					
How does the *protagonist* interact with other characters and advance the *plot*? Analyze how complex characters develop over the course of a text, interact with other characters, and advance the plot or develop the theme (RL.9–10.3).					
How does the *theme* of this novel emerge and develop? Determine a theme of a text and analyze in detail its development over the course of the text, including how it emerges and is shaped and refined by specific details; provide an objective summary of the text (RL.9–10.2).					
How does *figurative language* impact *meaning* and *tone*? Determine the meaning of words and phrases as they are used in the text, including figurative and connotative meanings; analyze the cumulative impact of specific word choices on meaning and tone (e.g., how the language evokes a sense of time and place; how it sets a formal or informal tone) (RL.9–10.4).					

PRESENTATION	5	4	3	2	1
How can I present my information effectively? Present information, findings, and supporting evidence clearly, concisely, and logically such that listeners can follow the line of reasoning and the organization, development, substance, and style are appropriate to purpose, audience, and task (SL.9–10.4).					
How can I use digital media and props to enhance my presentation? Make strategic use of digital media (e.g., textual, graphical, audio, visual, and interactive elements) in presentations to enhance understanding of findings, reasoning, and evidence and to add interest (SL.9–10.5).					
How can I use verbal techniques to keep my audience interested? Use appropriate eye contact, adequate volume, and clear pronunciation (SL.8.4).					
Additional comments on presentation:					

FIGURE 5.15

Earlier in the chapter I mentioned the Literacy Design Collaborative, which produced twenty-nine template tasks. In addition, this organization created rubrics aligned to the Common Core Standards' text types. You'll see an argumentation rubric in Figure 5.16. This scoring guide and rubrics for narrative and informational/explanatory can also be accessed through LDC's website: www.literacydesigncollaborative.org. I suggest comparing Figures 5.16 with 5.14 to determine which best aligns with a given argumentation assignment.

A significant issue raised around the topic of rubrics is how to translate number scores to letter grades. Typically, when teachers translate a number score to a letter grade, they discover that the percentage is usually lower than a holistic grade that they would issue. I am frequently asked about this dilemma. I suggest that if you or your teachers issue letter grades, use the simple formula shown in Figure 5.17 ("The 4–6–8–10 Rule") to convert the rubric score to a letter. It was devised by Vicki Spandel (2001) and featured in her book *Creating Writers: Through 6-Trait Writing Assessment and Instruction.* Essentially, it is a mathematical conversion. You would first score papers using the rubric and arrive at a percentage. Then you would use the mathematical formula explained on the 4–6–8–10 rule to arrive at a grade. This formula, in essence, accounts for the mismatch between number and letter grades. In using this conversion consistently with teachers who assign letter grades, I have found that it is pretty miraculous how the conversion nets out to a letter grade that coincides with what a teacher would have initially granted. In her most recent edition of *Creating*

Teaching Task Rubric (Argumentation)

Scoring Elements	Not Yet		Approaches Expectations		Meets Expectations		Advanced
	1	1.5	2	2.5	3	3.5	4
Focus	Attempts to address prompt, but lacks focus or is off-task.		Addresses prompt appropriately and establishes a position, but focus is uneven.		Addresses prompt appropriately and maintains a clear, steady focus. Provides a generally convincing position.		Addresses all aspects of prompt appropriately with a consistently strong focus and convincing position.
Controlling Idea	Attempts to establish a claim, but lacks a clear purpose. (L2) Makes no mention of counter claims.		Establishes a claim. (L2) Makes note of counter claims.		Establishes a credible claim. (L2) Develops claim and counter claims fairly.		Establishes and maintains a substantive and credible claim or proposal. (L2) Develops claims and counter claims fairly and thoroughly.
Reading/ Research	Attempts to reference reading materials to develop response, but lacks connections or relevance to the purpose of the prompt.		Presents information from reading materials relevant to the purpose of the prompt with minor lapses in accuracy or completeness.		Accurately presents details from reading materials relevant to the purpose of the prompt to develop argument or claim.		Accurately and effectively presents important details from reading materials to develop argument or claim.
Development	Attempts to provide details in response to the prompt, but lacks sufficient development or relevance to the purpose of the prompt. (L3) Makes no connections or a connection that is irrelevant to argument or claim.		Presents appropriate details to support and develop the focus, controlling idea, or claim, with minor lapses in the reasoning, examples, or explanations. (L3) Makes a connection with a weak or unclear relationship to argument or claim.		Presents appropriate and sufficient details to support and develop the focus, controlling idea, or claim. (L3) Makes a relevant connection to clarify argument or claim.		Presents thorough and detailed information to effectively support and develop the focus, controlling idea, or claim. (L3) Makes a clarifying connection(s) that illuminates argument and adds depth to reasoning.

Online Resources Included

Scoring Elements	Not Yet		Approaches Expectations		Meets Expectations		Advanced
	1	1.5	2	2.5	3	3.5	4
Organization	Attempts to organize ideas, but lacks control of structure.		Uses an appropriate organizational structure for development of reasoning and logic, with minor lapses in structure and/or coherence.		Maintains an appropriate organizational structure to address specific requirements of the prompt. Structure reveals the reasoning and logic of the argument.		Maintains an organizational structure that intentionally and effectively enhances the presentation of information as required by the specific prompt. Structure enhances development of the reasoning and logic of the argument.
Conventions	Attempts to demonstrate standard English conventions, but lacks cohesion and control of grammar, usage, and mechanics. Sources are used without citation.		Demonstrates an uneven command of standard English conventions and cohesion. Uses language and tone with some inaccurate, inappropriate, or uneven features. Inconsistently cites sources.		Demonstrates a command of standard English conventions and cohesion, with few errors. Response includes language and tone appropriate to the audience, purpose, and specific requirements of the prompt. Cites sources using appropriate format with only minor errors.		Demonstrates and maintains a well-developed command of standard English conventions and cohesion, with few errors. Response includes language and tone consistently appropriate to the audience, purpose, and specific requirements of the prompt. Consistently cites sources using appropriate format.
Content Understanding	Attempts to include disciplinary content in argument, but understanding of content is weak; content is irrelevant, inappropriate, or inaccurate.		Briefly notes disciplinary content relevant to the prompt; shows basic or uneven understanding of content; minor errors in explanation.		Accurately presents disciplinary content relevant to the prompt with sufficient explanations that demonstrate understanding.		Integrates relevant and accurate disciplinary content with thorough explanations that demonstrate in-depth understanding.

FIGURE 5.16

Source: © Literacy Design Collaborative, November 2011, www.literacydesigncollaborative.org/.

Writers, Spandel (2012) raises an excellent point about using several samples of a student's writing as the basis for formulating a grade. She does not advocate scoring one individual piece, arguing instead that reviewing strengths and weaknesses across a compilation of work offers the most meaningful picture of the student as a writer.

To record and determine the scores, some teachers merely highlight line items on the rubric and enter the score at the bottom of the sheet or on the reverse side, where there is room to enter additional comments. However, since the line items of the rubric are quite specific, comments tend to be brief and emphasize a particular strength as well as one area on which students might focus for the next assignment. At the bottom of the rubric in Figure 5.14, you will see spaces to record what a student earned using this method.

The 4-6-8-10 Rule

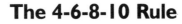

Vicki Spandel (2001), in her book *Creating Writers: Through 6-Trait Writing Assessment and Instruction,* created a mathematical conversion for arriving at letter grades from number scores. She states about this conversion: ". . . you are *not* giving the student extra points by adding in these percentages; you are not *giving* the student *anything.* You are simply making up for the fact that measurement on a continuum is by nature slightly imprecise, so we have to adjust it to make it fit our grading system" (p. 379). Her system could be adapted for use with the rubrics in this book. Here is how it works:

First, figure out the basic percentage for a student's paper. For example, if the paper is worth 80 points and a student scores a 68, the basic percentage is 85%. Now, add the conversion as shown below. For the 85% paper, the conversion would be 91%.

Conversion

- For scores over 90%, add 4 percentage points to the total. Example—92 original percent + 4 = 96% conversion
- For scores over 80%, add 6 percentage points to the total. Example—85 original percent + 6 = 91% conversion
- For scores over 70%, add 8 percentage points to the total. Example—73 original percent + 8 = 81% conversion
- For scores over 60%, add 10 percentage points to the total. Example—69 original percent + 10 = 79% conversion

Note: For scores right on the edge (60, 70, 80, 90), add one additional percentage point. For example, if the percentage is 80%, then add 80 + 6 + 1 to arrive at 87%.

FIGURE 5.17

Source: Creating Writers Through 6-Traits Writing Assessment and Instruction, 3rd edition (Addison Wesley Longman, Inc., 2001).

CHECKLISTS

I'm a pretty good baker. I should be: I've dabbled in the kitchen since age ten making all sorts of desserts that I have no business eating now, since I complain about unwanted pounds. The point is that I'm experienced. But no matter how proficient I am, I will never be able to measure and combine all the ingredients in just the right way and put a cake in the oven, and then *afterward* take a look at the recipe hoping I got it right. Rather, I prop that tattered Betty Crocker recipe next to me on the kitchen counter and follow each step as I go—only today I wear glasses to read it. In the same way, even if students have written arguments or short stories or procedural papers before, the finished product will still be stronger if they follow a criteria sheet, or a checklist, along the way to guide them. They need not be surprised by what you expect, so communicate clearly what that is so they are empowered from the get-go.

Checklists complement the rubrics; both are an expression of the guiding questions. For example, if a guiding question reads: *How do writers use sensory details to describe characters?* then the line items on the checklist and rubric must also refer to sensory details, characters, and descriptions. The purpose of a checklist is twofold: (1) to guide students as they work on a project so they are clear about teacher expectations prior to beginning the task, and (2) to provide you with a guide for planning and conducting lessons. When students are made aware of what a successful project includes through a student checklist or a rubric that states expectations, they will have the opportunity to be more successful. Because you expect students to include these skills and concepts in their work, be prepared to teach lessons that are on the checklist and rubric. Furthermore, it is powerful also to show students samples of work and discuss how you would score these papers or projects using the checklist or rubric. It gives more substance to these assessment instruments—and ensures a higher degree of student success—if there are authentic pieces that have identifiable strengths and weaknesses in terms of the criteria set forth. Use these samples within your instructional program so students engage in activities that make them aware of what to emulate and what not to repeat.

Encourage students to have their checklists (and even rubrics) in front of them as they write so they are crystal clear about expectations. Whereas not all teachers introduce rubrics directly to students, checklists should be front and center for all students so they are clear about expectations. To this point, I encourage you to appropriately present a checklist to all students rather than merely handing it to them. If the checklist is distributed without thoroughly engaging students in what is on the page, you will be disappointed when students do not use it as a tool for success. Be proactive, then, and present it formally to allow students to see clear expectations so they complete their tasks with these criteria top of mind. See Sample Lesson 4 in Chapter 8 for a detailed, step-by-step lesson on how to introduce students to a checklist for argumentation. You can adapt this lesson to any writing type since the important takeaway is to share what you expect before students write. If they are completing a project other than writing, alter the lesson accordingly. Aren't you better at performing a task when it is clear at the outset what is expected of you? Students will be, too.

Following is a list of checklists in this book. Read each checklist to determine the nature of each assignment. Many can be modified or extended to meet the needs of your particular students if the topic is suitable. The criteria on the checklists are categorized according to the six traits, which is a model for instruction and assessment in writing (e.g., ideas/content, word choice, conventions, etc.). The rubrics are similarly grouped. However, there are other subheadings you can use to cluster line items, such as sentence structure, style, mechanics, development, and so forth.

- *Figure 5.4 News Story Checklist.* Although this checklist supports the Revolutionary War assignment sheet (Figure 5.3), it is intentionally void of references to the war so teachers can use it for other units of study where a newspaper assignment might be appropriate.
- *Figure 5.8 Project Checklist.* As stated earlier, this checklist accompanies the multiple intelligence project choices in Figure 5.7. It is fairly generic and can work with many assignments a teacher might create.
- *Figure 5.18 Short Story Checklist.* This is geared to high school students; however, it can be modified for middle school. Also, if you choose to have your students write a particular kind of genre—historical fiction, science fiction, fantasy—or even a memoir or autobiography, alter it accordingly.
- *Figure 8.11 Argument Writing Checklist.* This checklist is embedded in a lesson that introduces students to this writing instrument to engender ownership. By formally presenting the checklist, the likelihood of students using it during the writing process is higher. They will be more successful when writing using this tool to guide them as it delineates clear criteria of expectations.

PREASSESSMENTS

Preassessments—also referred to as diagnostic assessments—allow teachers to determine students' starting points prior to beginning a unit so they can plan accordingly for the following:

- student grouping
- accommodating individual students' strengths and weaknesses
- facilitating acceleration or reteaching
- attending to other learning characteristics

It is prudent to conduct a unit preassessment aligned to the unit goals to gauge students' readiness, interest, or learning style. Preassessments can also alert teachers to misconceptions and incorrect information students might have so they can step in and address the issue.

I've introduced this topic after discussing summative assessments because I find it easier to devise a preassessment once I have determined the goals of my unit and how students will demonstrate understanding of them all. For example, if I want students to produce an argumentation essay, I might issue a preassessment in which they write an argument that is based on a topic of their choice or selected from a teacher-provided list. I will use the checklist or rubric I devise for the culminating assessment as the basis for scoring the preassessment, so I can collect valuable information about my students and plan instruction accordingly.

It is not within the scope of this book to go into great detail on preassessments; however, I do provide some suggestions in this chapter. Using graphic organizers is one way to preassess. I'll explain what I've used for language arts and then share how to adapt the strategy to other subject areas, so keep reading even if you don't teach ELA. I created Figure 5.19 ("Make a Web Preassessment") when I taught language arts and issued it before beginning a short story unit to determine what students knew about the elements of literature. The directions are clearly stated in this figure: Students take the provided words and phrases and arrange them in a way that makes sense in a graphic organizer they fashion. I also

Short Story Checklist

Directions: Use this checklist to guide you in writing a story about a real or imagined event.

Ideas/Content and Organization

☐ I include an original **title.**
☐ I correctly **indent** for each new paragraph.
☐ I use **narrative techniques** (e.g., dialogue, dialect, pacing, suspense, multiple plot lines) to enhance my story.
☐ I sequence events so that they build on one another through a well-structured and developed **plot**.

➔ Beginning

☐ I engage and orient the reader by setting out a **problem** or **situation.**
☐ I introduce a **narrator** and/or **characters**.
☐ I describe the **setting** to establish where the story takes place.

➔ Middle

☐ I thoroughly explain the events of my story in a **logical order.** The reader can follow my story even if I use multiple plotlines or flashbacks.
☐ I include **transitional words and phrases** to connect paragraphs and show sequence (e.g., *After an uncomfortable dinner, Sally stomped away angrily.*).

➔ Ending

☐ My ending **resolves the central conflict.** It answers questions a reader might have about what happened.
☐ My ending is **not abrupt.**

Voice

☐ I establish a **point of view** (first- or third-person limited or omniscient).
☐ I have a clear sense of **task, audience,** and **purpose.**

Sentence Fluency

☐ I **avoid fragments** and **run-ons.**
☐ I use a variety of **sentence patterns** and include **parallel structures** as appropriate.

Word Choice

☐ I use precise words and phrases, details, and sensory language to convey a **vivid picture** of events, setting, and/or characters.
☐ My **dialogue tags** include strong verbs and narration.
☐ I use **dialect**, as appropriate, to signify geographical regions.

Conventions

☐ I **spell** all words correctly.
☐ I use **punctuation** correctly, paying particular attention to dialogue.
☐ I **capitalize** appropriately.
☐ My sentences are void of **grammar** errors.
☐ I properly **format** my paper.

FIGURE 5.18

Source: Glass (2012).

wanted text to support their web, outline, or other organizer, so I asked them to explain their reasoning in a paragraph.

The organizer—coupled with your students' rationale—will give you a clear idea of what factual knowledge they have of the elements and will provide you with any evidence of their higher-order thinking skills. Here are some additional points to consider:

- Some kids may not know the terms and associations among the elements, but you can gain a clear sense of what they do or do not know from the combination of the organizer and their writing.

- Make sure to circulate around the room to observe student behavior during the exercise—this simple observation is another means of preassessment.
- Once students finish their organizers, collect their work and use the exercise as a springboard for discussion.
- As a class, you can fashion a web of the elements of literature and ask students to volunteer examples of each element based on a specific text. Or you can show Figure 5.20, which is a simple web, and have students add to it so they arrive at Figure 5.21. Depending on the level of your students, you can modify your expectations in Figure 5.21. For example, under characters you might add dynamic, static, round, and so forth.

The strategy I've just shared—that of providing students with terms to arrange in a graphic organizer and then articulate through a paragraph—can be adapted to many other subject areas. In math, you might ask students to arrange terms related to the location of a vertex in a graphic organizer and explain their associations. For science, students can categorize terms related to the states of matter. In social studies, they can sequentially display events in history or associate terms or people with particular ancient civilizations. Graphic organizers can take many forms (e.g., compare and contrast, cause and effect, story map, webbing, etc.), so allow students to organize content in a way that makes sense to them and demonstrates to you what they might know. After students fashion their own organizers, reveal the organizer you have prepared that shows the relationships among the terms. Explain to students that the graphic organizer forms the basis for your upcoming unit, so it is incumbent upon you as their teacher to teach them the content within it.

Make a Web Preassessment

1. On a separate sheet of paper, create a web or other graphic organizer of your choice that uses the following words and phrases in a way that you think makes sense. If you want to add your own words or phrases to your organizer, please do.

third person	plot	central conflict
when	character	introduction
first person	rising action	time
where	theme	place
point of view	falling action	elements
central message	antagonist	climax
setting	resolution	protagonist

2. Write a paragraph that explains your graphic organizer.

FIGURE 5.19

Source: Glass (2009), p. 128.

Elements of Literature Web I

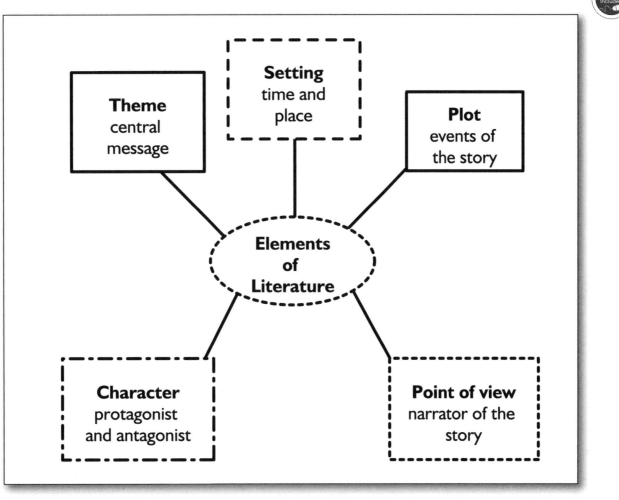

FIGURE 5.20

Although you might conduct either formal or informal preassessments for lessons throughout your unit of study, it is worthwhile to issue formal *unit* preassessments to gather as much information as possible on each student. In addition to the graphic organizer strategy, other formal unit preassessments include asking students to complete a K-W-L chart, respond in writing to a prompt, take a pretest, answer questions, annotate a prepared writing sample, create a drawing with accompanying writing, interpret a poem, make a list and provide a rationale, complete a cloze procedure and explain the entries, write a brief summary, and so forth. When asking students to respond to a writing prompt, you might consider more than just assessing the content of their writing. For example, you might want to know if they are familiar with how to write a comparison/contrast paper. In this case, your goal can be twofold: (1) to determine if students can write in accordance with the structure of a particular writing type, and (2) to ascertain what they might know about the content you are about to teach. Some of the aforementioned suggestions will allow you to glean the readiness levels of your learners. You can also issue multiple intelligence and interest surveys to obtain information about students' learning profiles and interests.

Elements of Literature Web 2

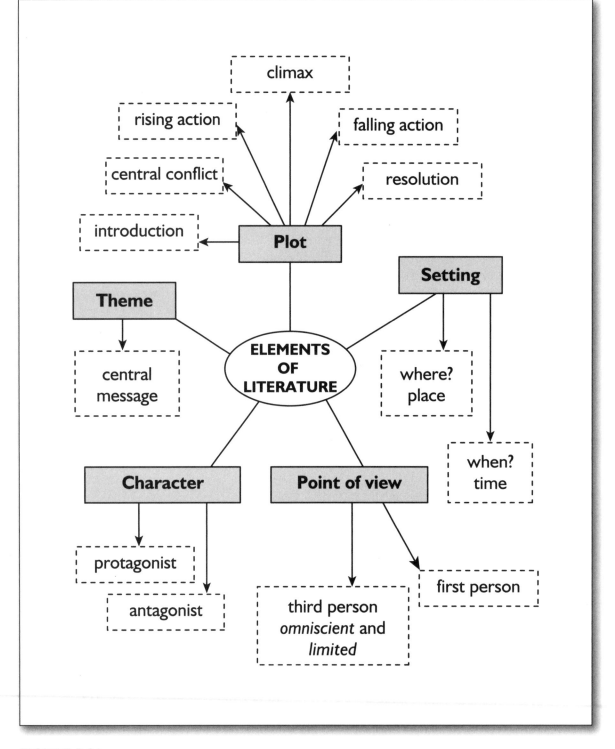

FIGURE 5.21

Preassessments for individual lessons or groups of lessons might include an informal question-and-answer session, games, demonstrations (have students show you what they know), observations, predictions, or entrance slips. Other ideas include *yes/no* cards where students respond to prompts and feature which side of the card they feel represents the correct answer. You can also have students respond on individual whiteboards, handheld electronic gadgets, or the SMART Board. The Common Core stresses vocabulary acquisition, so preassess for words individual students might already know since it is not prudent to devote time to academic and domain-specific words they have previously mastered. Rather, focus attention on increasing their word inventory and usage. Preassessments can double as formative assessments, so feel free to use them throughout your unit of study to check for understanding.

Be aware that preassessments are not graded but that they provide a means for collecting useful information so you can better plan for students' learning. Let students know this, as well. Note, though, that you need to respond to the results of a preassessment if you bother to create and issue one. If you don't, students will wonder why they went through the trouble of responding to the task. The time you commit for conducting a preassessment allows you to learn useful information about your students, so you can plan your lessons with a clear vision of what instruction they need.

CONSTRUCTING YOUR OWN SUMMATIVE ASSESSMENT

By now, you have grouped standards, identified what you want students to know, created (or refined) essential understandings, and fashioned essential unit and lesson guiding questions. To determine what culminating assessment you want students to produce to demonstrate their understanding of what you have worked on so far, review all the hard work you have accomplished. What is in front of you on the unit map represents your unit goals. Using that as a starting point, this exercise will give you the opportunity to find or create a culminating assessment that will enable your students to show you the proof that they have grasped this essential material.

EXERCISE 5: HOW DO EDUCATORS DETERMINE AN APPROPRIATE SUMMATIVE ASSESSMENT?

Use the guidance from this chapter and what you have entered thus far on the unit map to identify and craft your culminating assessment. Remember to create or find a checklist and an accompanying rubric to score students' work. Enter the assessment onto your unit map template; the following are some examples of what you might record:

- Scientific or historical research report on a topic using primary and secondary sources
- Comparative analysis of two ancient cultures or influential historical figures
- Argument essay defending your interpretation or judgment about the theme of a literary work using textual evidence to support assertions

- Short story narrative based on historically accurate characters and settings from a particular social studies unit (historical fiction)
- Personal narrative from the point of view of an organism about its journey through the life cycle
- Demonstration that teaches others how forces make things move, along with an informative brochure
- Virtual museum of a collection of artistic works that share commonalities, along with an explanatory paper of historical context and rationale for grouping
- Live skit or iMovie based on the life of an influential person in history or today

LOOKING AHEAD

Once you have created a meaningful culminating assessment and rubric, you are ready to continue marching forward. Next, you will delve into the other template components, including the final part of the KUD model of know, understand, and *do*—the skills. You will then address activities and formative assessments, since there are myriad engaging ways to design and teach lessons for students to grasp, use, and apply targeted skills. Finally, you will determine evidence of student learning plus find and record varied resources so your unit map will be complete and comprehensive.

6

Skills, Activities, Formative Assessments, and Resources

> *Skills are the actions students should be able to perform or demonstrate as the result of a lesson, a series of lessons, or a unit of study.*
>
> —Carol Ann Tomlinson and Caroline Eidson (2003, p. 239)
>
> *Learning activities are tasks for students designed to develop the knowledge, understanding, and skills specified in the content goals. They should help students perceive, process, rehearse, store, and transfer new information and skill.*
>
> —Carol Ann Tomlinson et al. (2002, p. 56)

Congratulations—you're in the home stretch. The hard part is over, so if you've made it this far, the rest will be a breeze. At this point, you have accomplished a great deal on your unit map. Based on the exercises you've already completed for a targeted unit, you have grouped standards, identified the factual knowledge, created essential understandings and guiding questions, and identified a culminating assessment. To complete the KUD model of know, understand, and do, this chapter focuses on what students will *do*—the skills. In addition, it explains how to teach these skills. Specifically, it describes ways to deliver engaging and rigorous learning experiences based on sound teaching methods within the context of a given unit's overarching goals. These learning experiences should draw from relevant and enriching resources, while providing students with the opportunity to demonstrate content proficiency through ongoing assessments. As you continue to fill in your unit map with details about skills, activities, resources, and evidence of understanding, you'll read about how to make all of these ideals a reality in your classroom.

SKILLS

What is the difference between a skill and an activity? Skills and activities are both written in verbal phrases and seem to indicate what students should do; however, there is a clear distinction between the two. Specifically, learning activities are concrete tasks that serve as *the vehicle* for students to learn a skill, to acquire knowledge, and to understand key concepts (see Figure 6.1 for examples of skills). As you select teaching methods and instructional strategies to engage students in targeted learning opportunities, you set the stage for them to learn particular skills and acquire the knowledge and understanding set forth in the unit outcomes. As educators, it is imperative that you teach pertinent skills and design opportunities for students to demonstrate understanding of these skills through assessments.

When crafting skills, it is important to keep the following considerations in mind:

- *Verbs.* Skills should be written using observable action verbs—none should be nebulous and general (e.g., *understand, learn, know, comprehend*).
- *Transference.* Skills should be written in such a way that they are transferable. That is, they should be general in scope and applicable to a range of situations. Avoid writing words and phrases that are specific to the content of a unit.

  Skills allow for transference of knowledge to different situations. If you write verbal phrases such as *compare and contrast the points of view of the Socs and Greasers in* The Outsiders, you have expressly tied what you want students to do to a particular

Skills	
• Support reasons with factual evidence. • Summarize current events. • Collect and analyze data. • Create a timeline. • Predict outcomes. • Formulate a hypothesis. • Compare perspectives. • Distinguish between fact and opinion. • Critique a play. • Tally results. • Construct a model. • Use context clues to define unknown words.	• Work collaboratively. • Arrive at consensus. • Group objects according to shape. • Revise written work. • Find and write examples of imagery. • Identify parts of speech. • Make connections between types of literature. • Distinguish examples of literal and nonliteral language. • Ask and answer questions about key details. • Paraphrase text.

FIGURE 6.1

novel—the notion of transferability is lost. On the other hand, the phrase *identify examples of imagery* is a skill that can be applied to many novels, poems, and speeches; *compare and contrast points of view* could conceivably apply to newspaper commentators, historical figures, characters in stories, politicians, and so forth.

- *Grade level.* Skills should be appropriate for the intended grade level. Not all statements that are written in verbal phrases and general language and indicate transference are necessarily grade-level-appropriate skills. For example, *brainstorm a list* would qualify as a skill for primary-grade students who need to master it. However, if a teacher in sixth grade asks students to brainstorm a list, he or she would hopefully not feel the need to expressly teach and assess this skill in middle school. The teacher might ask students to brainstorm a list as a springboard activity for a targeted lesson, but it is not an appropriate grade-level skill. So be careful to choose skills that are suited for the grade level of the students you teach.

The Common Core Standards (2010a) are expressed as skills. Take a look at the following examples and notice how they are all transferrable and represent what you might expect students to actually do:

- Cite textual evidence to support analysis of what the text says explicitly as well as inferences drawn from the text (RI.6.1).
- Compare and contrast the structure of two or more texts and analyze how the differing structure of each text contributes to its meaning and style (RL.8.5).
- Provide a concluding statement or section that follows from and supports the argument presented (W.9–12.1e).
- Use precise language and domain-specific vocabulary to manage the complexity of the topic (W.9–10.2d).
- Form and use verbs in the active and passive voice (L.8.1b).

As always, keep in mind that to create context for these grade-level skill expectations, you will need to identify the key concepts within these standards and fashion essential understandings and guiding questions around them.

TEACHING STRATEGIES AND LEARNING ACTIVITIES

Students need guidance in order to acquire skills. It is through a series of learning activities, coupled with teaching strategies (or methods), that students learn pertinent skills. Teaching strategies are what teachers design to orchestrate what students do in a learning activity. Consider teaching strategies, then, as the role of the teacher and learning activities as the role of the student:

Teaching strategies refer to the structure, system, methods, techniques, procedures, and processes that a teacher uses during instruction. These are the strategies the teacher employs to assist student learning. **Learning activities** refer to the teacher-guided instructional tasks or assignment for students. These are student activities. (Wandberg & Rohwer, 2010, p. 164)

You should select both teaching strategies and learning (or instructional) activities based on the learning goals and designated skill areas you have identified as priorities for your students. They should complement and address students' needs for differentiation purposes, be varied instead of repetitive, and allow for student engagement. Sometimes there is an overlap between teaching strategies and learning activities. For example, you might feature a graphic organizer on a document camera and use it as a teaching method while demonstrating or modeling for students how to complete one. Then you might ask students to create their own graphic organizers independently or in pairs as an instructional activity to hone a targeted skill. Do not get too tripped up on terminology. *Just remember that in lesson planning, you need to discern and account for the teaching methods you design, orchestrate, and lead, along with the instructional activities that students perform to ultimately learn a skill.*

In Figure 6.2, you will find samples of teaching strategies and learning activities aligned to skills. You will notice some overlap between the teaching methods and instructional activities, which is reflected and explained within both columns of the chart. In addition, there are separate columns for Common Core Standards and for skills. While the Common Core Standards are indeed expressed as skills, the additional column dedicated to skills represents a targeted portion of a particular standard that relates to the featured teaching strategy and learning activity. Finally, note that I have included suggestions about how to differentiate learning or instructional activities—a topic that is addressed at greater length in the next chapter.

To add even more strategies and activities to your repertoire, explore the additional options in the following list. Each item can be categorized as either a teaching method, instructional activity, or a combination—depending on whether you set it up as being teacher-led or student-run. And still, there are other ways to impart learning I've not included; however, you will have a wide professional inventory of choices with Figure 6.2 and this list.

- *Case studies.* Case studies have been used in business, law, and medical schools for actively engaging students in problem solving, and they can apply to K–12 schools, as well. In this setup, groups of students are presented with a problem to solve that is directly or indirectly based on a real-life scenario. Students work to solve the problem by engaging in discussion and inquiry. Some instructors provide the result of the actual case beforehand as the basis for discussion. Others present the problem and allow students to decide how to solve it, and then present the result of the case as the basis for comparison.
- *Debate.* Students focus on different sides of an issue, identify and address counterarguments, and determine the strongest points in order to arrive at a decision. Teachers and/or students can collect various differentiated resources to use for researching evidence for their arguments and counterclaims. Formal debate terms and rules can apply if teachers choose to introduce them (e.g., *affirmative and negative constructives and rebuttals, adjudicators—or judges*).
- *Jigsaw.* Groups of students read different but conceptually and topically related material based on readiness or their interests. Together, they prepare notes or graphic organizers that highlight the major points. Students then redivide into a second group configuration, where one member from the original group is grouped with others. Students take turns teaching their new group members the reading material from the

initial group, and together they create an assignment that compiles the key points from the collective reading material (Aronson, Blaney, Stephan, Silkes, & Snapp, 1978).

- *Lecture.* Lectures are an age-old, familiar strategy in which an instructor delivers an oral presentation that sometimes contains visuals. Even PowerPoint presentations can be classified as a type of lecture tool because they provide the means for instructors to disseminate information orally to a small or large group. Some lecturers provide opportunities for interaction with the audience; others do not.

- *Literature circles.* Teachers present a collection of books covering a range of student reading levels as well as topics of interest, themes, genres, and so forth. In groups, students read the same book and are each assigned a specific role that rotates among students, such as *discussion director, illuminator, illustrator, summarizer,* and so forth. The roles are intended to elucidate the reading by providing a structured way for students to delve into the complexities of a work of literature or nonfiction. Once students are well versed in the roles, the structured aspect of each job is suspended with the aim of allowing spontaneity to emerge (Daniels, 1994).

- *Museum or gallery walk.* Students create various projects, such as posters, PowerPoint presentations, timelines, project cubes, and so forth that are based on defined criteria. They then display them throughout the classroom on walls and tables. Teachers devise several guiding questions or prompts and students respond to them using the museum pieces as the vehicle for gathering this information. Students can view the "museum" (or "gallery") individually, in pairs, or in small groups, as the teacher dictates. After viewing the projects and responding to the questions and prompts, the class reconvenes and holds a discussion based on student findings and impressions.

- *Project-based learning (PBL).* Students work in groups to explore real-world problems and challenges. This instructional method involves an interdisciplinary approach and is designed to empower students to make decisions, think critically, and collaborate with peers while designing and completing a project.

- *Role playing.* Role playing can be used to explore issues or to better understand a historical event or figure, literary text, or individual. Students act out the historical, literary, or present-day situation assuming the roles of historical figures, literary characters, or individuals who are involved. Some students might observe the role playing; all students offer insights, impressions, and reactions.

- *Simulation.* Students mirror a real-world, complex situation by assuming the roles of those involved in order to gain better insight and understanding. In simulations, participants make decisions and see the results of their actions so they can apply what they learned to life. For example, teachers can ask students to conduct the following: *simulate a trial; assume the role of delegates in the Electoral College; create a business plan and simulate running a business to learn about entrepreneurship; operate a store by selling "goods" and exchanging "money"; or play videogames like SimCity to simulate building cities and solving problems associated with city planning.*

- *Visualization.* Students listen while a teacher reads a poem or passage aloud or while music or another audio recording is playing. While listening, students can draw a picture, produce an abstract representation, or create or complete a graphic organizer to record an observation or demonstrate comprehension. Or students can merely listen—with eyes open or shut—to a situation or a passage. To debrief in a visualization exercise, teachers can pose these questions for students to answer orally, in writing, or in a combination of both forms.

How do images help you to . . .

- o *draw conclusions?*
- o *make connections?*
- o *create interpretations?*
- o *recall significant details?*
- o *better comprehend?*

- **Graphic organizers.** Organizers allow students to use visual diagrams to brainstorm and structure writing projects; help problem solve and make decisions; summarize key ideas in reading, audio, or video; assist with studying; plan research; and more. If you lead a session in which students complete a graphic organizer based on a text, a video, or perhaps a guest lecturer, then it is a *teaching strategy.* If students create the organizers on their own, it would qualify as an *instructional strategy.* Technically speaking, if you model how to complete the organizer and talk through your thinking as you do so, then three strategies are in play: demonstration, think-aloud, and graphic organizer. I don't think you need to be so precise, but for those of you who were wondering, there you have it.

FORMATIVE ASSESSMENTS

In contrast to the preassessments and culminating assessments you learned about in Chapter 5, formative assessments are assessments *for* learning. Specifically, you would conduct *formative* (or *ongoing*) *assessments* consistently throughout a unit to collect information about how to modify, extend, enrich, compact, reteach, redirect, or do whatever is necessary to help students make meaning and capitalize upon unit goals. Since these assessments are used as a vehicle to check for understanding, they will aid you in determining when intervention and enrichment are necessary and in designing differentiated instructional strategies accordingly. Effective teachers use formative assessments often, and they pay attention to the results they collect in order to serve students optimally. For those of you who appreciate analogies, here are a couple: Just as doctors take the vital signs of patients to inform them of adjustment to a health regimen or gardeners routinely assess their plants and administer more or less fertilizer or water to ensure growth, so too do teachers check for understanding regularly to further the progress of their students.

Formative assessments also serve as a means for students to self-assess and self-monitor so they have a sense of how they are faring and can be advocates for their own learning. Paul Black and Dylan William (1998), two British researchers who are experts on the topic of assessments, state, "the term 'assessment' refers to all those activities undertaken by teachers, and by the students in assessing themselves, which provide information to be used as feedback to modify the teaching and learning activities in which they are engaged. Such assessment becomes 'formative assessment' when the evidence is actually used to adapt the teaching work to meet the needs."

So what types of formative assessments can you use in the classroom, and how might they inform your teaching practice? Formative assessments are an integral part of a differentiated classroom (you'll read more about differentiation in Chapter 7) and can be informal or formal activities. You read about many learning activities in the previous section. These instructional practices can be formative assessments when teachers utilize the information

Samples of Teaching Strategies and Learning Activities Aligned to Skills

Common Core Standards	Skills	Teaching Strategies	Learning or Instructional Activities (Students will . . .)
• Use words, phrases, and clauses to clarify the relationships among claim(s) and reasons (2010a, W.6.1c). • Use words, phrases, and clauses to create cohesion and clarify the relationships among claim(s), reasons, and evidence (W.7.1c).	• Identify and use transitional words, phrases, and clauses.	**Demonstration/Modeling** Demonstration and modeling are two strategies that are akin to one another. Whereas demonstration involves watching someone perform a task—which can appear more passive—modeling takes it a step further by requiring more active mental engagement. Demonstrations allow students to view new learning tasks or ideas from others, such as a teacher, expert in a particular field, or a professional in the workforce. In a demonstration, teachers or another individual can perform a lab experiment, prepare a meal, make a geometric quilt, operate machinery, write a paragraph on the overhead or document camera, or complete steps to solve a math problem. In modeling, teachers can facilitate instructional interaction during the demonstration to involve students.	• Listen to a paragraph from an argument essay that doesn't have transitional words and phrases. Discuss what makes the writing choppy. (**Teacher:** Do not mention what is missing; let the students discover it.) • Listen to a more fluid piece of writing and identify the transitions that make it easier to follow. Circle the transitional words and phrases used in the writing. • Review a list of transitional words and phrases that your teacher distributes. Compare what you circled with the teacher's list. • Watch the teacher model how to revise a paragraph by inserting appropriate transitions using the list as a guide. • Listen to the teacher share his or her thinking as the teacher completes this task. Answer the teacher's questions as he or she works, such as the following: *How do I know where to put a transition? What transition will work best in this spot? How do transitions improve writing?* • Use the list of transitions to revise another piece of writing. (For **differentiation** by **readiness**, give individual students

FIGURE 6.2 (*Continued*)

173

FIGURE 6.2 (Continued)

Common Core Standards	Skills	Teaching Strategies	Learning or Instructional Activities (*Students will . . .*)
		For example, teachers can model what they demonstrate by using the think-aloud strategy, whereby they talk through their thinking as they complete a task. Or they might conduct a think-pair-share in which students think individually about an answer, partner with another to discuss, and then share discussion highlights with the class. The activity described in the column to the right involves a combination of direct instruction, demonstration, and modeling.	appropriately challenging paragraphs or multiparagraphs to revise to include transitions. In addition, differentiate the list of transitional words and phrases and distribute based on readiness levels.)
• Present claims and findings, emphasizing salient points in a focused, coherent manner with relevant evidence, sound and valid reasoning, and well-chosen details; use appropriate eye contact, adequate volume, and clear pronunciation (SL.8.4).	• Critique debate. • Present claim(s) and relevant evidence in a focused and coherent manner. • Address and acknowledge counterclaim(s). • Use presentation skills.	**Demonstration/Modeling Through Video** In this demonstration example, teachers show a video of a debate team in action to demonstrate how to present claim(s) and support them with reliable evidence in a focused and coherent manner. To involve modeling so the demonstration is not passive, teachers stop the recording at intervals for students to take notes, make observations, and discuss what they hear and observe about content and presentation skills.	• Watch and then critique a video of a debate using a graphic organizer to record content about claim(s) and evidence. Make notations about the presentation skills and manner in which the argument is presented. • In groups, informally debate on different topics of interest using prearranged resources from the teacher. (For **differentiation** by **readiness** and **learning style**, provide a host of resources at varying readability levels and modalities for accessing information: informational texts, audio centers, videos, software, etc.) • Complete the following steps in your debating team:

Common Core Standards	Skills	Teaching Strategies	Learning or Instructional Activities (*Students will . . .*)
• Acknowledge new information expressed by others, and, when warranted, qualify or justify their own views in light of the evidence presented (SL.8.1d).		To practice the targeted skills, students engage in a debate to emulate what they observed in the demonstration video.	○ Select a topic. (To **differentiate**, students choose a topic of **interest** to debate.) ○ Research information about your topic; complete a graphic organizer with key points. (To **differentiate**, students choose graphic organizer for note-taking that appeals to their **learning style**.) ○ Stake a claim and support this point of view with reasons and evidence. ○ Address and acknowledge the opposing viewpoints. • Serve as an audience member when your team is not debating to summarize and critique arguments of both sides to arrive at a decision. • Compare the skills each debate team in class exhibited with those from the students in the video.
• Cite specific textual evidence when writing or speaking to support conclusions drawn from the text (R.CCR.1).	• Cite textual evidence to support conclusions. • Determine the main idea. • Summarize key details and ideas.	**Reciprocal Teaching** This reading strategy is designed to allow students to work collaboratively with peers to assist one another in understanding a text. It relies on activating four different comprehension strategies: (1) *predicting*, (2) *questioning*,	• In groups, assign different roles to one another in preparation for responding to a lecture your teacher gives. One person provides a summary of the lecture, another poses questions, a third makes connections between the lecture and another topic or idea, and a fourth makes predictions based on the content of the lecture.

FIGURE 6.2 (*Continued*)

FIGURE 6.2 (Continued)

Common Core Standards	Skills	Teaching Strategies	Learning or Instructional Activities (*Students will . . .*)
• Determine central ideas or themes of a text and analyze their development; summarize the key supporting details and ideas (R.CCR.2). • Analyze the main ideas and supporting details presented in diverse media and formats (e.g., visually, quantitatively, orally) and explain how the ideas clarify a topic, text, or issue under study (SL.6.2).		(3) *clarifying*, and (4) *summarizing*. (Note: Teachers should model reciprocal teaching and allow students to practice before they work in groups. Older students might have had instruction in lower grades; if that is the case, they can launch into this strategy without an introduction as detailed in the instructional activity to the right.)	• Listen to a PowerPoint lecture your teacher presents and take notes. (**Differentiate** by allowing students to choose a note-taking device that appeals to their individual learning styles.) If your teacher supplies a handout, add notes to it to help process the content. • Complete your assigned task; draw on evidence from the lecture to support your work. Then lead a group discussion based on this task as you solicit input and answer questions from group members. • Share the highlights of your group discussion with the whole class to gain clarity about the lecture and to share new ideas. • Complete an individual assignment your teacher issues that requires you to use evidence from the lecture to respond.
• Write narratives to develop real or imagined experiences or events using effective technique, relevant descriptive details, and well-structured event sequences (W.6–8.3).	• Identify criteria for narrative writing.	**Roundtable** This strategy is used for students to preview or review material, and also for teachers to check for understanding. Teachers pose a prompt or topic. In groups, students rotate one piece of paper around in a circle as each student inputs a response to the prompt in list form. The paper continues to move	• Review features of narrative writing after reading several stories and studying about the elements of literature. • Participate in the roundtable activity by entering one word or phrase on a group sheet when it is passed to you in answer to the prompt: "What does a strong short story include?" Avoid duplications with other group members.

Common Core Standards	Skills	Teaching Strategies	Learning or Instructional Activities (Students will . . .)
		around the circle, with each student contributing one item per turn. The exercise is over when students have exhausted the list of entries. Each group reports out its list to the whole class, avoiding duplications.	• Remember to include not only elements of literature, but also what all good writing involves. • Keep passing the paper around the group until everyone has finished contributing. (Examples of contributions are *setting, descriptive words, central conflict/problem, sentence variety, correct spelling, sensory details,* etc.) • In groups, report out to compile a comprehensive class list in response to the prompt. • Read the teacher-generated short story checklist of expectations for a writing assignment. (To **differentiate,** create tiered checklists to appeal to **readiness** levels. For this exercise, which introduces writing expectations, use the at-grade-level version.) • Compare each line item on the checklist with the posted class list. Discuss commonalities and differences; make justified changes to the prepared checklist if there is consensus.
• Read closely to determine what the text says explicitly and to make logical inferences from it; cite	• Make logical inferences from text. • Cite textual evidence to support responses.	**Direct Instruction** This is a methodology that involves explicitly and carefully organized lessons taught directly by the	• Review a definition of *inference* that your teacher provides. Listen to examples of inferential reasoning based on sample text excerpts.

FIGURE 6.2 *(Continued)*

FIGURE 6.2 (Continued)

Common Core Standards	Skills	Teaching Strategies	Learning or Instructional Activities (Students will . . .)
specific textual evidence when writing or speaking to support conclusions drawn from the text (R.CCR.1). • Engage effectively in a range of collaborative discussions (one-on-one, in groups, and teacher-led) with diverse partners on grade [6–8] topics, texts, and issues, building on others' ideas and expressing their own clearly (SL.6–8.1).	• Build on others' ideas and express own ideas clearly during group and teacher-led discussions.	teacher in a prescribed way through explanation, teacher-student interaction, and practice. **Cooperative Learning** In this teacher-led strategy, students work together in a small group to solve a problem or complete a project. Teammates are responsible for their own learning as well as assisting other group members to learn and improve understanding of a topic, so there is collective achievement. (Note: With more teacher support and guidance, as is necessary for certain groups of students and grade levels, cooperative learning can be a *teaching strategy*. With more student group autonomy, it can serve as an *instructional strategy*.)	• Articulate the difference between citing what a text states explicitly and making logical inferences from it to prepare for the upcoming task. • Read a new passage of text silently and listen to it again as the teacher reads it aloud. • Listen to the teacher's instruction for conferring with your group and answering questions about the text. • In groups, tackle text-dependent questions that rely on explicit and inferential meaning. Arrive at a group consensus for responses. • Share your answers with the class and engage in discussion by building on others' comments. Use teacher-provided sentence starters to bridge your comments with those of others (e.g., *I agree with Wendy; however, I also think that . . . ; What Carlos made me think of is . . .*) • After group and class discussions, complete a written exercise your teacher assigns involving textual evidence to make inferences.
• Determine the meaning of words and phrases as they are used in the text, including figurative and connotative meanings (RL.6–12.4).	• Identify and define examples of figurative language. • Interpret figurative language.	**Concept Attainment** Students compare and contrast teacher-prepared examples and nonexamples of a concept (e.g., rhetorical device, metaphor, sentence pattern, etc.). After sorting these examples and nonexamples, students identify the common	• In groups, sort several paragraphs mounted on individual index cards into two piles according to the style of the writing and the language used. You will have to read all the paragraphs to determine how you might group paragraphs that all share common traits and those that do not. (**Teacher:** Provide paragraphs that contain imagery, simile, and metaphor and paragraphs that lack figurative language. Leave the instructions

Common Core Standards	Skills	Teaching Strategies	Learning or Instructional Activities (*Students will . . .*)
	• Use figurative language in writing.	attributes of items that qualify as examples and arrive at a definition. Through discussion and inquiry, teachers work with students to verify that the examples comply with the correct definition of the concept. Students then add their own examples to show that they have grasped the concept (Bruner, Goodnow, & Austin, 1956).	open for interpretation so students look carefully at the writing for sorting purposes. For **differentiation**, group students homogeneously. Give different paragraphs to sort based on **readiness** levels so the material is appropriately challenging for students in each group.) • Identify the group of paragraphs that share attributes and articulate a reason for grouping them. Focusing on this set, discuss and list characteristics that are common among these paragraphs. Cite specific examples in the text that support the group of commonalities. • Define figurative language (i.e., imagery, simile, metaphor); verify examples of figurative language in the grouped paragraphs. Discuss the meaning of the passages with figurative language and its impact on the text. • Select and rewrite a paragraph from the set of nondescriptive paragraphs to include figurative language. (For **differentiation** by **interest**, students select the paragraph that is of interest to them to rewrite.)

FIGURE 6.2

they gather about student learning in a productive way to boost student achievement. Additional ideas for formative assessments are as follows:

- Cubes and manipulatives can be used during an instructional activity as formative assessments to check for student understanding. If students roll a die or sort sentence strips and discuss responses and reasoning, it becomes a more informal method to gauge their understanding. If, however, students respond to the activity orally and then write in their journals or create a graphic organizer to submit to teachers, their responses can be studied more carefully, thereby making it a formal assessment. See a detailed explanation and examples of these two strategies in Chapter 7, "Differentiated Instruction."
- Quizzes, portfolio reviews, written responses, homework assignments, brainstorming sheets, graphic organizers, annotated text, outlines, pictures with captions, responses to exit cards, dialectical journal entries, and literature circle sheets are some of the many examples of formal ongoing assessments.
- Listening to students' responses during a discussion or a think-pair-share; watching students participate in a group activity; observing responses to yes/no cards, finger symbols (thumbs up or thumbs down), or entries on mini-whiteboards or electronic devices—these can be used as informal formative assessments when you carefully observe students engaged in the task and use it for teaching purposes. As students work, you might also record comments on a recordkeeping sheet or sticky notes about the progress of individual students to help inform your instruction.

Another formative assessment is RAFT, which is an acronym: R for role, A for audience, F for format, and T for topic. This popular differentiated assessment can be used for virtually any unit of instruction across the content areas. It's enticing for students because it has endless possibilities in terms of what they can create, and it's fruitful for teachers because it can show depth of understanding in a nontraditional way. See Figures 6.3 and 6.4 for examples; study them alongside this detailed explanation:

- *Role* involves the following: *What role should the student assume? From whose point of view is the piece written?* For example, are students assuming the role of a character in a novel, a historical figure, a scientist, a personified object (e.g., a water drop, an infectious disease, a carbohydrate, a bill waiting to become a law, etc.), or themselves?
- *Audience* answers the following: *Who will read, see, or use what I have written or created?*
- *Format* responds to the following: *What is the most effective and meaningful product format to show understanding of content?* This could be an advertisement, document, speech, skit, essay, PowerPoint presentation, clay model, or myriad other possibilities. Use "Assessments A–Z" in Figure 6.5, located in the companion website, to see an extensive list of other format choices (visit http://www.corwin.com/mappingela6-12).
- *Topic* refers to the focus of the project: *What is the basis for this project, such as feelings about the war, explanation about the periodic table, or demonstration of a procedure?*

In this type of assignment, you or your students would make decisions about the role, audience, format, and topic based on the content in your unit of study. Make sure you communicate to students that no matter which project they choose (or are assigned), they must use textual evidence to support their answers.

Figure 6.3 shows a typical RAFT format where students choose an assignment across a particular row. Look at the top row. Here is how it reads: The student assumes the role of a lord or lady who writes a persuasive letter to a monarch. The lord or lady complains about the rise of charters that results in the peasants' removal from their rule. Let's try another example. See the third row: Write a journal entry as if you were a beggar and use imagery to describe your life in the city. Whereas Figure 6.3 would be an assignment given at one point in a unit because it addresses the content covered in a particular lesson, Figure 6.4 can be revisited throughout the unit since it includes unit guiding questions. In this figure, students can select any audience or format choice, but they must address different unit guiding questions throughout the duration of the unit.

RAFT can be differentiated by learning style if teachers or students create a variety of format choices that appeal to how students like to learn. For example, a photo essay, newspaper article, interview, or three-dimensional model will appeal to different types of learners. (See Figure 6.5 for more options.) RAFT can also become a readiness-based assessment if the choices for role, format, and topic are written at varying levels of difficulty. For example, a journal entry is less involved than an editorial. The RAFT choices can also be made more or less challenging based on the resources students use as the basis for completing the assignment. Consider creating three different tables that represent differentiation by learner readiness. Then you can distribute the appropriate RAFT version to students based on their readiness. If needed, you can also set up this formative assessment so that some students are working together in pairs. See Chapter 7 for a thorough explanation of learning style, interest, and readiness.

Another example of a formative assessment that is less formal than RAFT but that can still serve as an excellent barometer for gauging student understanding involves using the "Elements of Literature Bookmarks" in Figure 6.6. This figure is a template for bookmarks,

RAFT I

What Was Daily Life Like in Medieval Society?			
Role	**Audience**	**Format**	**Topic**
lord or lady	monarch	persuasive letter	complaining about the rise of charters that removes peasants from their rule
merchant	trader from the East	advertisement with illustrations and text	persuading traders to purchase his goods
beggar	self	journal entry	using imagery to describe his life in the city
member of the clergy	God	prayer	explaining how he serves the townspeople
monarch	other monarchs	formal letter	justifying his position and what he and other monarchs do or don't do for their subjects

FIGURE 6.3 (Continued)

FIGURE 6.3 (Continued)

Literary Analysis			
Role	**Audience**	**Format**	**Topic**
dynamic character	static character	dialogue	explanation about how their interaction affects the plot
dynamic character	himself/herself	personal journal entries	self-reflection about personal traits and its impact on other characters
literary device (e.g., foreshadowing, tone, dialect)	author	thank-you letter	how the literary device is significant to the work and adds to its appeal
author of the literary word	author of another literary work that shares the same theme	article in a literary magazine	how the two works share common themes

FIGURE 6.3

RAFT 2

History			
Role	**Audience**	**Format**	**Topic**
HISTORICAL FIGURE	• another historical figure in this same time period • a citizen who lived during the time of this historical figure • a historical figure in any time period • a citizen of any time period (even today)	• formal letter • historical diary entry or entries • political document • set of laws • propaganda	Answer one or more of these guiding questions in your writing: • How do political and religious ideas bring about change? • How does conflict affect others socially and economically? • How do leaders affect the outcome of conflict? • How do leaders support or fail their citizens?

Literature			
Role	**Audience**	**Format**	**Topic**
CHARACTER	• another character in the *same* literary work • a character in *another* literary work • a famous person today or a historical figure • the reader	• informal letter • picture portfolio of drawings and detailed captions • persuasive letter • play script	Answer one or more of these guiding questions in your writing and/or pictures: • How does the setting affect you? • How have you changed, and why? • What internal conflicts do you face, and how can you overcome them?

FIGURE 6.4

which need to be prepared before you conduct the assessment. Here are the directions for setting up and conducting this activity:

✓ Copy the page on 100 lb. cardstock, laminate, and cut out these bookmark strips.
✓ Give two or more sets to each student.
✓ As students read core novels, independent books, or literature circle texts, ask them to insert the appropriate bookmark to indicate the place where an element of literature appears.
✓ Walk around the room quietly and approach one student at a time; ask the student to explain why the bookmark is in the spot where it is.
✓ Have students confer with one another to discuss the placement of their bookmarks, too. Conducting these brief conversations with students, or listening in on their conversations with peers, can provide you with valuable information about their knowledge of character, setting, and plot.

Even though informal or formal instructional activities engage learners in a task based on unit goals, remember that the task only translates into formative assessment if you gather the results and respond to the information you've gleaned about your students' learning. Additionally, to capitalize on student achievement through ongoing assessments, you should offer continual feedback to students in a timely manner so that they can learn from your comments, apply them, and make improvements. As McTighe and O'Connor state, "To serve

Elements of Literature Bookmarks

FIGURE 6.6

Source: Glass (2012).

learning, feedback must meet four criteria: It must be timely, specific, understandable to the receiver, and formed to allow for self-adjustment on the student's part" (McTighe & O'Connor, 2005).

RESOURCES

Resources are the books, handouts, videos, teacher guides, manipulatives, websites, and so forth that are needed for a particular activity. Figures 6.7 and 6.8 provide ample examples. Cross-reference the columns in these figures, as you might find some items on one that you would not see on the other. Of course, you can add to these lists as new resources become available, but the information provided here should be comprehensive enough to get you started and to help you generate more ideas.

You may utilize these figures in different ways. The obvious way would be to record what resources you would need for a lesson on your unit template, which I suggest you to do in the exercise at the end of this chapter. There is a column for such purposes that you have already probably spotted on the template. Record what you, a substitute, colleagues, or others who would teach the lesson would need—include everything that makes sense to teach a particular activity. Another way you might use Figures 6.7 and 6.8 is to carefully read the items as you are thinking of the activities you want to conduct in order to teach a particular skill. The resource lists might generate ideas that you might not have previously considered. For example, you

Resource Ideas for Any Classroom

General Resources	
• biography • autobiography • memoir • folklore (e.g., myth, legend, fable) • short story • novel/novella • diary • student journal • published journal • drama/play • reader's theater • graphic organizer • literary review and critique • speeches (audio and text) • poem • textbook • video/audio • librarian • media specialist • PowerPoint or Keynote presentation • magazine article • newspaper article • poster • pamphlet/brochure • flyer/handout	• encyclopedia • dictionary/thesaurus • website • classroom or individual student blog • computer/software • LCD projector • interactive whiteboard (Promethean or SMART Board) • electronic student response device • document camera • flip video camera • iPod touch/iMovie • artwork • calendar with pictures • photograph • music (CDs, cassettes) • primary source document • guest speaker • student handout (e.g., for homework, in-class assignments, journal prompts, etc.) • published and student examples • quiz and test • student checklist • scoring rubric • teacher resources (e.g., websites, college textbooks, literature guides, etc.) • content area standards (e.g., national, state, district)

Digital and Online Resources

- Bubbl.us (a tool that allows students to visually web/map understanding of words and concepts; free alternative to Kidspiration) https://bubbl.us
- CAST UDL (Universal Design for Learning) Exchange (online site to browse and build resources, lessons, and collections to support instruction guided by UDL principles; UDL is a set of principles to develop learning environments that give all individuals equal opportunities to learn and proposes a set of flexible scaffolds and supports to meet individual needs) udlexchange.cast.org/home
- Google Docs (online word processor for creating and formatting text documents and collaborating with others in real time) www.docs.google.com
- Google search lessons (complete lessons for research projects; e.g., finding the right search terms, evaluating credibility of sources, etc.) www.google.com/insidesearch/searcheducation/lessons.html
- graphic organizers

FIGURE 6.7 *(Continued)*

FIGURE 6.7 (Continued)

- o www.edhelper.com/teachers/graphic_organizers.htm
- o www.edselect.com/worksheets-lesson-plans#Graphic%20Organizers
- o www.educationoasis.com/curriculum/graphic_organizers.htm
- o www.eduplace.com/graphicorganizer
- o www.freeology.com/graphicorgs
- o www.teachervision.fen.com/graphic-organizers/printable/6293.html

- Learning Ally (collection of more than 75,000 digitally recorded textbooks and literature titles that can be accessed and downloaded on mainstream and specialized assistive technology devices) www.learningally.org
- LibriVox (free audiobooks from the public domain) www.librivox.org
- Many Books (more than 29,000 free Ebooks) www.manybooks.net
- Poem Hunter (database of poems) www.poemhunter.com
- Purdue Online Writing Lab (writing resources to use across content areas; especially helpful for research projects) http://owl.english.purdue.edu/owl
- Reading Like a Historian (curriculum project from Stanford University; includes a series of lessons that engages students in historical inquiry by investigating essential questions through careful analysis of primary source documents) http://sheg.stanford.edu/node/45
- ReadWriteThink (compilation of lesson plans, activities, and other ideas) www.readwritethink.org/classroom-resources
- Scholastic (teacher and parent resources across content areas) www.scholastic.com/home/
- Storynory (free audiobooks of original stories, fairy tales, myths and histories, poems) http://storynory.com
- Teacher Tube (online community site for educators and students to share instructional videos) http://teachertube.com
- VoiceThread (digital tool for sharing stories or conversations with people around the world via voice, text, audio file, or video) http://voicethread.com
- WebQuests (web-based software for creating WebQuests in a short time without writing any HTML codes; see other educators' Webquests, as well) www.zunal.com
- Wordle (tool to generate "word clouds" from text that students provide) www.wordle.net

FIGURE 6.7

might see the entry *guest speaker* and realize that inviting someone to speak to your class would be an excellent way for students to learn and experience content. Seeing this item on the list might encourage you to build an activity around it—to have a guest come to speak and create an accompanying graphic organizer for students to use as they capture key points from the talk. In short, instead of perusing these figures *after* you've finished designing your activities, consult them early on as a source of new ideas and inspiration.

Appropriate and rich resources and materials can enhance any lesson. With regard to text, remember to align your reading materials to the Common Core and incorporate

Core Curriculum Resources

Language Arts	Science
<ul><li>biography</li><li>autobiography</li><li>short story</li><li>novel/novella</li><li>diary</li><li>student journal</li><li>play</li><li>prop/costume</li><li>reader's theater</li><li>literary analysis</li><li>speech (written and recorded)</li><li>poem</li><li>literature and grammar textbook</li><li>literature guide (e.g., Novel-Ties teacher guides, Scholastic, etc.)</li><li>video</li><li>grammar textbook</li><li>book on tape</li><li>music</li><li>artwork</li><li>genre-specific writing rubric (e.g., argumentation, informative, etc.)</li><li>field trip (e.g., play, symphony, etc.)</li><li>Storykit (iPod app for creating, editing, and reading stories)</li><li>Common Core Standards for ELA, Appendix B: Text Exemplars and Sample Performance Tasks (2010c)</li><li>Common Core Standards for ELA, Appendix C: Samples of Student Writing (2010d)</li></ul>	<ul><li>newspaper and magazine article (e.g., *American Science Journal*)</li><li>science journal article</li><li>photograph</li><li>field guide</li><li>documentary (e.g., *An Inconvenient Truth, Super Size Me*, etc.)</li><li>website (e.g., www.fossweb.com/ and www.topscience.org/ for interactive activities; http://songsforteaching.com/ for music; www.khanacademy.org for students, parents, teachers)</li><li>perishable lab materials (e.g., pig's intestine, frog, cow's eye, mealworms, crayfish, etc.)</li><li>specimens (e.g., rocks and minerals)</li><li>aquarium/terrarium</li><li>microscope</li><li>thermometer</li><li>telescope</li><li>magnifying lens</li><li>balances and scales</li><li>chart (e.g., periodic table, blood cells, mitosis/meiosis)</li><li>models (e.g., anatomy, torso, plant and animal cells, etc.)</li><li>test tube, beaker, plastic slide, petri dish</li><li>pH supplies (e.g., meter, papers, indicators, test set)</li><li>safety equipment (e.g., safety goggles, apron, plastic covers, etc.)</li><li>dissecting set</li><li>video (e.g., http://teachertube.com/videos.php) and documentary</li><li>field trip (e.g., weather station, nature preserve, wetlands, planetarium, greenhouse, etc.)</li><li>science and technology school resource supplier (e.g., AIMS Educational Foundation, Fisher Science Education, etc.)</li></ul>

FIGURE 6.8 *(Continued)*

FIGURE 6.8 (Continued)

Math	Social Studies
• math textbook • math manipulatives • individual whiteboard, markers, erasers • math journal • math software programs • protractor • ruler • geometric shapes • calculator • two- and three-dimensional figures • bank statement/checkbook • stock report • data display • chart, graph, table, diagram • guest speaker (e.g., architect, engineer, dietician) • graphing paper • scales with weights • abacus • math literature (e.g., *King's Chessboard*, etc.) • websites (e.g., http://songsforteaching.com/, www.khanacademy.org for students, parents, teachers; www.math.org—Algebra and Calculus videos; www.brightstorm .com/)	• documentary (e.g., *The Times of Harvey Milk, Why We Fight, Triumph of the Will*, etc.) • recorded and written speech (e.g., Martin Luther King's "I Have a Dream"; see www .history.com/speeches) • video (e.g., excerpt from *Roots*) • simulation (e.g., Interact materials at www .interact-simulations.com/) • primary source document (e.g., Declaration of Independence, historical journal entries, Reading Like a Historian—see Figure 6.7) • guest speaker (e.g., Holocaust survivor, history professor, historian, local politician, etc.) • field trip (e.g., courthouse, Museum of Tolerance, history museum, factory, etc.) • historical fiction (e.g., *Killer Angels, The President's Lady, The Avengers*, etc.) • WebQuest • graphic organizer (e.g., Venn diagram, outlines, T-chart, etc.; see websites in Figure 6.7) • magazine and newspapers • map, globe, atlas • Google Earth, www.google.com/earth/ index.html

FIGURE 6.8

complex text into your curriculum, as appropriate. Make sure to carefully find and enter all resources on your unit template as you complete the exercise at the end of this chapter. Then take advantage of what your colleagues have and work together to find and share resources that meet unit goals and support differentiation. I am baffled by a recurring complaint I hear all too often from teachers: Their colleagues refuse or hesitate to share resources. I cannot understand why some teachers do not want to share valuable resources, lessons, and other instructional materials so that students can benefit from the collaboration. Hopefully that is not an issue at your school and you welcome collegial support.

IDENTIFYING SKILLS AND CONSTRUCTING ACTIVITIES, EVIDENCE OF ASSESSMENT, AND RESOURCES FOR YOUR TARGETED UNIT

Before you begin the exercise below, you first need to identify targeted skills that are based on the standards and associated with your essential understandings and guiding questions. Remember that these skills must be addressed in context, taught directly, and assessed to demonstrate understanding. Therefore, you will need to sketch appropriate learning activities to teach each skill along with the appropriate resources and corresponding evidence of assessment.

If you haven't already, peruse the examples of the complete unit map in Chapter 4 to help you. What follows are some suggestions and reminders for what to record. The steps for this particular exercise are not numbered because, as mentioned in the previous section on resources, each of you will have your own style in recording entries and it might not be altogether linear from skill through to evidence for each lesson question. Some of you will toggle back and forth between columns as your creative juices flow, you think of resources you already have, or perhaps you stop to sketch a graphic organizer or draft a writing prompt to use. So read the remainder of this chapter and then work on the rest of the template in a fashion that naturally flows. In fact, some of you might want to read ahead to Chapter 7, on differentiation, and then begin this chapter's exercise so you can incorporate differentiation as you complete the map. Others may want to finish the map as explained in this exercise and then return to insert differentiation. That's a personal choice for you to make.

> **EXERCISE 6: WHAT TARGETED SKILLS WITH ASSOCIATED ACTIVITIES, EVIDENCE OF ASSESSMENT, AND RESOURCES CAN EDUCATORS DESIGN (AND FIND) FOR A TARGETED UNIT?**

For this exercise, you will complete the remaining components of your unit template that are circled in Figure 6.9.

What Should You Enter in the Skills and Activities Columns?

Refer to the beginning of this chapter for explanations and examples of skills and activities so you can record this information on your unit template. Skills and activities both begin with verbs. Skills are succinctly stated and emanate from standards. Review the unit map in Chapter 4 for examples of skills along with those in this chapter.

You will notice that the entries for activities on the unit template are extremely detailed. You need to decide how comprehensive you want to be with this component, as the level of specificity might overwhelm some readers. As you enter the information related to activities, consider who is reading your unit map. If others are reading it to develop lessons, then it would be helpful for them if you were to expand upon your activities as I have done in my examples. If it is for your eyes only or for a small group of colleagues, you can be brief on the unit template and save the detail for developing the actual lessons. Just be careful at least to record enough steps in the activities section to satisfy teaching each skill.

Unit Template Excerpt 3

Essential Understanding #__:				
Essential Unit Guiding Question #__:				
Lesson Guiding Questions	**Skills**	**Activities**	**Resources**	**Formative Assessment Evidence**
Lesson __.__				
Lesson __.__				

FIGURE 6.9

Note that in Figure 6.2 earlier in the chapter, I included a column for teaching strategies; however, on your unit templates you can embed these within the activities column. Also, pay attention to how I write the bullets. They are in verbal phrases and written for students (i.e., *Students will . . .*) in a logical progression for how an activity will be conducted. Use parentheses to enclose comments to teachers and differentiation ideas so it isn't confusing. See Figure 6.10 for what you might enter in an activity cell.

Figure 6.11, "Verbs Based on the Revised Bloom's Taxonomy," can also assist you with generating skills and activities. As you might know, Benjamin Bloom and his colleagues developed Bloom's taxonomy, a method of classification on differing levels of intellectual behavior as it relates to learning (Bloom & Krathwohl, 1956). It has since been updated by Lorin Anderson, a former student of Bloom's, and David Krathwohl to have more relevance to twenty-first-century work (Anderson, Krathwohl, et al., 2001).

Keep true to the tenets of the Common Core by ensuring that all levels of students are appropriately challenged. Use Bloom's work or the updated version from Anderson and Krathwohl (2001) as intended and not as a vehicle for differentiation. Bloom and his colleagues meant for all students to enjoy a rich education by experiencing all levels of intellectual behavior. To relegate struggling learners to the lower levels of remembering and understanding would only do these students a disservice—they should ultimately be evaluating and creating, as well. You surely can differentiate the text or an activity for students, because those who have difficulty with access to a text will not be able to analyze or synthesize it if they can't even comprehend it. Tomlinson and McTighe (2006) emphatically make

Sample of Activities Column

Activities

(Students will . . .)

- Critique various introductions for argumentation essays; identify introductory elements of this writing type, focusing on thesis statements.
- Sort various teacher-prepared cards into two piles: thesis and non-thesis statements.
- Examine the thesis cards and arrive at a definition of *thesis* with teacher's support; find thesis examples from various argumentation essay samples; together rewrite weak ones. (For **differentiation** by **readiness**, provide samples at varying degrees of sophistication in writing and topic.)
- Use thesis definition and strong examples to practice writing thesis statements for a debatable topic. (For **differentiation** by **interest**, students choose topic for thesis.)

FIGURE 6.10

Source: Glass (2012).

this point: "[M]any teachers over the years have used the taxonomy as a framework for a misguided approach to differentiating instruction—that is, higher-order thinking for gifted students and basic skills for lower achievers. *Using Bloom's taxonomy as a framework for differentiation is indefensible* [emphasis in original]" (p. 120). To aptly differentiate, refer to Chapter 7, Figure 7.8, "Ideas for Differentiating Instruction," along with other resources you might have to assist you in accommodating the characteristics of the wide variety of students you serve.

Another tool that will help you generate activity ideas that align with targeted skills is Appendix B of the Common Core State Standards, which includes sample performance tasks that you might review (2010c). This appendix is organized by grade clusters (i.e., 6–8, 9–10, 11–CCR), and the performance tasks are tied to their suggested texts that are also included in the same Appendix B.

What Should You Enter in the Resources Column?

Record all materials and resources you will need to conduct your activity. You might choose to input resources on your unit map as you enter skills and activities for each lesson. This method might be fairly natural because as you draft these components, you might automatically think about student and teacher resources and materials necessary to make the activity come to life. However, as mentioned earlier, you can also look at Figures 6.7 and 6.8 to stimulate your ideas for resources and materials. This might also mean returning to the activities and revising or adding, as needed. For example, if your initial activity does not include a video, but as you review the resources it seems like it would be a great vehicle for teaching a particular lesson, then you could add an activity to incorporate that resource.

Additionally, as you consider resources, access support from grade-level colleagues, media specialists, librarians, practitioners in the field, and others, since you will need a wide variety of resources to differentiate instruction.

Verbs Based on the Revised Bloom's Taxonomy

Remembering	Understanding	Applying
alphabetize	account for	adopt
check	advance	apply
count	alter	calculate
define	annotate	capitalize
draw	associate	chart
duplicate	calculate	choose
fill in the blank	classify	complete
find	construe	compute
hold	contrive	conclude
identify	convert	conduct
label	describe	consume
list	discuss	demonstrate
locate	estimate	determine
match	expand	dramatize
memorize	explain	draw
name	expound	employ
offer	express	exercise
omit	identify	exert
pick	infer	exploit
point to	interpret	generate
quote	locate	handle
recall	moderate	illustrate
recite	offer	implement
recognize	order	interpret
record	outline	make
repeat	paraphrase	manipulate
reproduce	predict	map
reset	project	mobilize
say	propose	operate
show	qualify	practice
site	recognize	put in
sort	rephrase	put to use
spell	report	relate
state	restate	schedule
tabulate	retell	show
tally	review	sketch
tell	reword	solve
touch	rewrite	teach
transfer	select	use
underline	spell out	utilize
	submit	wield
	substitute	write
	summarize	
	transform	
	translate	
	vary	

Analyzing		Evaluating		Creating	
analyze	examine	arbitrate	judge	arrange	invent
appraise	experiment	appraise	justify	assemble	manage
audit	explain	argue	measure	build	organize
break down	group	assess	prioritize	change	originate
categorize	identify	choose	rank	combine	plan
check	infer	compare	rate	compile	predict
classify	inspect	conclude	recommend	compose	prepare
compare	investigate	critique	resolve	conceive	prescribe
contrast	order	decide	score	conceptualize	pretend
criticize	question	defend	select	construct	produce
debate	reason	determine	support	create	propose
deduct	relate	editorialize	value	design	rearrange
detect	screen	evaluate	verify	develop	reconstruct
diagnose	search	give opinion	weigh alternatives	devise	reorder
diagram	separate	grade		forecast	reorganize
differentiate	sequence			formulate	role play
discriminate	simplify			generalize	structure
dissect	specify			generate	suppose
distinguish	survey			hypothesize	synthesize
divide	test			imagine	visualize
	uncover			integrate	write

FIGURE 6.11

Source: Glass (2012).

Recording generic resources is fine if it makes sense. For example, those listed in this chapter's figures include *various graphic organizers, photographs of national landmarks,* or *picture calendars.* Where you can, though, be specific in recording your resources for each activity, such as the exact name of a guest speaker (and even contact information), the title of a movie or song, the name of a handout, or the title of a book or newspaper article. See the Chapter 4 unit template for other examples. Oftentimes the resource and the evidence for assessment are identical entries. For instance, if students create a graphic organizer as an activity, then *graphic organizer* will be in the resource and also the evidence columns, because students need it to satisfy an assignment and you will assess it. Or, if you enter *"Sonnet 73" journal prompt* under resources, the companion evidence is naturally *"Sonnet 73" journal response.* The following section will give you more ideas for entering line items for the column about formative assessment evidence.

When a teacher begins to teach a lesson, all pertinent resources and materials need to be available. In a previous book I wrote about lesson design for differentiated instruction, I mention this regarding the importance of preparation: "It is like a baker who reads a recipe and looks at the ingredients. The ingredients listed are what the baker needs to be successful during the baking project" (Glass, 2009, p. 154). If you have been in the middle of cooking or baking only to find you are out of sugar or some other essential ingredient, you know just how important this preparation is. So be proactive and plan in advance for all that you need in a given unit by entering a list on your unit template. In fact, sometimes gathering resources can be a challenge and might even drive decisions about the timing of teaching particular units. For example, when I taught language arts there was not enough inventory to teach the same novel in more than two classes concurrently. Therefore, I collaborated with colleagues to determine when we would each teach a particular text. It is critical to consider the availability of resources and materials as you create a yearlong curriculum map.

What Should You Enter in the Column for Evidence of Formative Assessment?

While you list the steps of an activity and its resources, or after you do so, record the assessments that you will assign, conduct, observe, or collect that will show tangible evidence of understanding:

- If students are completing a graphic organizer, the natural piece of evidence that you will review to check for understanding is the *graphic organizer.*
- If you have students write a *summary,* then naturally the summary is the piece of evidence. The same applies to a *quiz, poem,* or *journal entry.*
- If, however, the formative assessment is informal, like a game, finger symbols, or mini-whiteboard responses, then what do you record? In these instances, it is important to observe students as they participate in these activities and jot down notes, as needed. On your template, record *observation of participation in group activity,* or something similar to that, based on what you will be having students do that you will assess.

When recording information on your unit template, remember to do the following:

- Include evidence of informal and formal formative assessments.
- Be specific and name the actual handout or assignment (e.g., "Phases of the Moon" graphic organizer, "Transitional Words and Phrases" handout, etc.).

- Use nouns or noun phrases, such as *observation during cubing activity; observation during group discussion; "I Am" poem; summary about the physics of roller coasters;* and so forth.

Just remember that whatever students do becomes an opportunity that can inform how you instruct and also help students self-assess. With that in mind, record it all in the unit map to remind you and your students to be keen observers and assessors.

LOOKING AHEAD

Now that you have mastered the concepts of skills, formative assessments, and resources and your unit map is nearly complete, we're ready to move on to the subject of the next chapter: differentiation. In the pages ahead, you'll learn more about differentiated instruction and walk away equipped with specific differentiated instructional strategies to put to the test in your classroom.

7

Differentiated Instruction

> *The key principles of high-quality differentiation include establishing a welcoming and safe classroom, ensuring that what is taught (the curriculum) is of the highest quality, maintaining a commitment to ongoing assessment, offering respectful differentiated tasks, and incorporating flexible grouping practices over time.*
>
> —Cindy A. Strickland (2009, p. 5)

The reality in any classroom is that you will be faced with students who have a range of characteristics. This pervasive diversity should serve as a call to action for you, as you strive to address all students' needs—whether it be through responding to their readiness levels, interests, or learning profiles. This is no easy task, of course, but a necessary part of teaching. So what exactly is differentiation? How can you differentiate judiciously so that all students' characteristics are considered and addressed? The answers to these questions will be discussed in this chapter, so you can identify effective ways to meet the needs of your students.

A leading author in the field of differentiation, Carol Tomlinson (2001), provides this oft-quoted explanation of what a differentiated classroom looks like: "In a differentiated classroom, the teacher proactively plans and carries out varied approaches to content, process, and product in anticipation of and response to student differences in readiness, interest, and learning needs" (p. 7). As you continue reading, we'll expand upon this definition and look at some examples of differentiation that you can use in your classroom. Additional suggestions for differentiation are also woven throughout this book, specifically in the Chapter 4 curriculum unit map example, Chapter 5 suggestions for summative assessments, Chapter 6 activities aligned with skills and resources, and Chapter 8 lesson samples.

Given the importance of differentiation in the classroom, it should be taken into account as a significant component of your lesson design. This is why the overall unit map, which serves as the guidepost for creating comprehensive lessons, includes references to it.

Differentiation is a necessary consideration when choosing teaching strategies and instructional activities, as students are individuals who need different types of opportunities to grapple with and practice learning outcomes. So, too, differentiated resources provide students with a range of options for gaining access to content and understanding. Differentiated assessments provide students with a means of demonstrating their understanding in multiple ways. Thus, within each of these components of the unit map, I recommend you build in appropriate ways to differentiate.

Teachers are constantly reminded of the rigorous expectations of the Common Core Standards. Keep in mind that *all students* are expected to meet the standards, plus grasp the essential understandings, essential unit guiding questions, and skills of any given unit. Therefore, these components—what students should know, understand, and be able to do—are non-negotiable when it comes to differentiation (except in cases when you are working with individuals who have extreme needs). What *can* be differentiated are the instructional and teaching strategies, activities, resources, and assessments that help students meet these ends.

Since students—like all of us—have individual differences, differentiation should be a priority item on your unit map. Figure 7.1 features a unit map excerpt to illustrate how differentiation can be noted.

CONTENT, PROCESS, AND PRODUCT

Those invested in differentiation must be intimate with these key terms, as they form the basis for this type of instruction: *content, process,* and *product.*

Content. The *content* refers to what we want students to actually learn as the result of a unit of study. Content is determined by reviewing the state, district, or Common Core Standards and represents what students should understand, know, and be able to do. There are essentially two aspects of differentiating instruction for content: "First . . . we can adapt *what* we teach. Second, we can adapt or modify *how we give students access* to what we want them to learn" (Tomlinson, 2001, p. 72).

If you conduct literature circles in which students read different books, for instance, you are adapting *what* you teach. If you have some students work on decimals while others focus on percentages, you are adapting *what* you teach. If you assign different vocabulary lists, you are adapting *what* you teach. Let's consider the access piece of content. When you want to get information, where do you turn? For example, when a bloody confrontation erupts in some part of the world, you might seek more information about it by reading the newspaper, listening to radio broadcasts, and going online. *How,* then, do you make information available to students when introducing new content? The typical vehicle is through textbooks, but there are multiple other ways for students to access content, such as through watching a demonstration or video, listening to a guest speaker, viewing a PowerPoint presentation, or reading magazine or newspaper articles. Another way to differentiate is by providing all students with the same type of text, such as an article or textbook, and matching the difficulty level of each reading assignment to individual students' current abilities. When I taught, I had several versions of textbooks in my classroom and would copy appropriate textbook sections to students based on their readiness levels.

To also differentiate *how* students access content, consider student support systems. Some students can grasp content working individually, others might work best in partnerships or groups, and some might need more adult assistance. These various ways of modifying

Unit Template Excerpt Including Differentiation

Essential Understanding
Introductions provide context for an argument and give writers an opportunity to make a favorable impression on readers.

Essential Unit Guiding Question
How can I write an effective introduction for my argument?

Lesson Guiding Questions	Skills	Activities	Resources	Formative Assessment Evidence
How can I write a thesis statement to stake a claim?	Write thesis statement for an argument.	• Critique various introductions for argumentation essays; identify introductory elements of this writing type, focusing on thesis statements. • Sort various teacher-prepared cards into two piles: thesis and non-thesis statements. • Examine the thesis cards and arrive at a definition of thesis with teacher's support. • Find thesis examples from various argumentation essay samples; rewrite weak ones. (To **differentiate** by **readiness,** provide writing samples at varying degrees of sophistication in writing and topic.) • Use thesis definition and strong examples to practice writing thesis statements for your debatable topic. (To **differentiate** by **interest,** students choose topic for thesis.)	• "Thesis and Non-Thesis Activity" cards • Argumentation writing samples **(differentiated by readiness)**	• Participation during discussion and card sort activity • Rewritten thesis statements **(differentiated by readiness)** • Original thesis statements **(differentiated by interest)**

FIGURE 7.1

what you teach and *how* students gain access to the material can be used as rich opportunities for differentiation. These examples of *how* to differentiate are further explained in the "Readiness, Interest, and Learning Profile" section and in Figure 7.8.

Process. Once students are exposed to content, they need to do something to make sense of it and learn the material. Hence, the process can be referred to as sense-making. I can read all night about the history of a Middle Eastern country and its crisis situation or watch repeated news reports, but it probably won't stick unless I actually process the information to make it comprehensible to me. That might mean making a graphic representation of what I've learned (e.g., outline or web); having a discussion with my husband, friends, or colleagues; or conducting an Internet search to find answers to specific, targeted questions I still might have. This *process* piece in teaching involves helping students make sense of the content you have presented or made available to them. It is a significant piece of any unit of study, as it involves many activities and formative assessments—simulations, labs or demonstrations, discussions, games, quizzes, journal writes, homework, and the like. The majority of time in your unit is devoted to this process piece.

Product. When you ask students to demonstrate knowledge at the end of a comprehensive unit of study, you expect them to complete a culminating project or summative assessment, which is addressed in Chapter 5. This assessment is also called a *product* and should not to be misconstrued as a formative or ongoing assessment. A final exam or state-mandated test are examples of summative assessments. However, you might provide students with an additional opportunity that would allow them to provide a more authentic demonstration of what they have learned. Alternatively, in lieu of an exam you could assign one comprehensive and meaningful product that would call upon students to incorporate their understanding of the unit guiding questions. Essays, reports, portfolios, demonstrations, and so forth are all examples of summative or culminating projects. These can be presented at the beginning of the unit so students are aware of unit expectations, but collected at the end of the long period of study that represents the duration of the unit.

As you can see, you can differentiate content, process, or product in a differentiated classroom. It would not behoove you to regularly differentiate all three because the goals of a particular unit may not warrant such an intensive approach. For example, there are times when whole-class instruction is prudent, such as when a guest comes to speak to the class and you know that all students will benefit from the message. Other examples include presenting a video clip to all students, modeling how to perform a task, or delivering a PowerPoint presentation. So be conscious of differentiating when it is appropriate. Creating a unit curriculum map will allow you to look at a given unit in its entirety and help you determine when differentiation makes sense and when whole-class instruction is a better option.

READINESS, LEARNING PROFILE, AND INTEREST

In a differentiated classroom, you should aim to appeal to students' readiness, interests, and/or learning profiles, as well. Students have varying degrees of **readiness** in approaching specific content. Their capacity or scarcity regarding certain subject matter is contingent upon many variables. Some students lack background knowledge because they might have moved schools and missed a segment of learning, have a language barrier, have been disengaged from school, or have struggled with a learning issue that precluded them from fully grasping the material at the pace of their grade-level peers.

Conversely, some students might possess more readiness because they grasp knowledge quickly and retain it, are voracious readers of a particular subject, independently seek knowledge beyond the classroom expectations, or have adults in their lives who engage them outside of school in an area of interest. When you take into account students' readiness by using their current level of understanding as a departure point and then plan accordingly, you will be more apt to get the most learning out of them. Be aware that when differentiating curriculum by readiness, the goal is to challenge students to a level that is about 10 percent higher than what they are able to do. If students are constantly challenged far above their readiness levels, they are acutely frustrated. But if they are repeatedly asked to work way below their capabilities, they are bored and psychologically turned off. As you might have observed, these situations can lead to behavior problems.

The concept of *learning profile* refers to the way in which people process and internalize information, plus the elements that affect individual learning. Put simply, it refers to an individual's preferred way to learn. When you allow students to demonstrate knowledge or work in a classroom environment that supports individual learning styles, student motivation tends to increase. Howard Gardner (1993) popularized this idea with his theory of multiple intelligences: *verbal/linguistic, logical/mathematical, visual/spatial,* and so forth. Robert Sternberg (1996), who is also known for his work in the area of intelligence, identified these three skill areas: *analytical, creative,* and *practical.* You may also be familiar with Rita Dunn and Ken Dunn's (1978) work on the learning styles they identified: *auditory, visual, tactile, kinesthetic,* and *tactile/kinesthetic.* Although there are some criticisms and questions about learning styles and their direct correlation to student achievement, there has been wide support for their existence and their importance in the classroom. As Carol Tomlinson so eloquently stated, "There is neither economy nor efficiency in teaching in ways that are awkward for learners when we can teach in ways that make learning more natural. The goal of learning profile differentiation is to help students learn in the ways they learn best—and to extend ways in which they can learn effectively" (2003, p. 4).

There are also other factors to take into account when striving to appeal to students' learning profiles. Keep in mind the following additional considerations when addressing differentiation based on students' learning profiles:

- *Ambient noise.* Some students might not be bothered by ambient noise, whereas others are mildly or even severely distracted by it. For those students who are adversely affected by the noise, allow them to sit in the periphery of a classroom configuration. You can even provide noise-cancelling headphones or earplugs during times of particular distraction.
- *Light.* There are also students who prefer daylight to fluorescent light. If you have a classroom with windows, invite those who prefer natural light to sit near them.
- *Grouping.* Students' learning profiles might also take into account their preferences for working individually or in pairs or small groups. Sometimes you may wish to introduce opportunities for students to choose their own grouping. If so, allow for this flexibility.
- *Other factors.* The physical temperature of a classroom, optimal energy levels based on a certain time of day, and mobility preferences are some of the other areas that teachers might consider when addressing differentiation to appeal to learning profile.

The concepts of learning profile and *interest* are linked closely together. Students who prefer to demonstrate their knowledge through a technology project are also likely to be more interested in this type of modality than, say, a short story. While students' learning profiles have to do with the manner in which they prefer to work, their interests are more closely related to what fuels their curiosity or passion. For example, if content standards require students to write an argument or informative paper, you need to teach and expect them to produce writing within these genres. To implement differentiation by interest, though, you might allow students to choose their own preferred topics as the subject for their papers. Allowing students to select a book for a literature circle is also an example of interest-based differentiation. For math, you might ask students to record various geometric shapes from a visual of their choice that most appeals to them.

Combining Student Readiness, Learning Profile, and Interest in Your Teaching

You can easily combine two or three of these aspects of differentiation. Look at the assessment example in Figure 7.2 and consider how it appeals to differentiation by readiness, learning profile, and interest.

When I issue this assignment, I briefly give students a snapshot of each individual on the list. Of course, you will make your own list of individuals associated with the subject and grade you teach. I typically have as many figures on my list as there are students in my classroom—plus a couple extra. Then I ask students to put their names on a slip of paper and write down their top three choices in rank order to submit to me to appeal to students' varied interests. However, that night, I review their preferences and assign them one of their three choices based on what I know about their readiness. Specifically, I avoid giving a student who struggles with content a topic where the resources are scarce and hard to read and decipher. When conducting this type of exercise, note that it is perfectly fine to give more than one student the same topic. In fact, students might glean more as

Differentiated Assessment Ideas

Choose a historical figure from the list below. Then create and present one of the following: interview, poem, song, or art with writing. In your project, address the guiding questions: *How did this individual contribute to societal change in his or her lifetime? What are implications of his or her actions on life then and now? Who is an individual today who is like this person, and in what way?*	
Benjamin Franklin	Frederick Douglass
Thomas Jefferson	Harriet Tubman
Abraham Lincoln	Martin Luther King, Jr.

FIGURE 7.2

they collaborate to find and discuss resources and content in preparation for their individual projects.

The assignment in Figure 7.2 also takes into account students' learning profiles since students choose from the list of specified project choices (interview, poem, song, or art with writing). It is important to note that all students are held accountable for responding to the essential unit guiding questions since they represent key conceptual understandings. Consider using this same strategy of intertwining differentiation for student readiness, interest, and learning profile as you have students work in literature circles or investigate a topic in a unit of study with many subtopics.

Differentiation and the Common Core Standards

Even though the designers of the Common Core do not rely heavily on the word *differentiation,* they certainly address it. Consider these introductory comments to the document, which clearly recognize diverse learners: "The Standards set grade-specific standards but do not define the intervention methods or materials necessary to support students who are well below or well above grade-level expectations. No set of grade-specific standards can fully reflect the great variety in abilities, needs, learning rates, and achievement levels of students in any given classroom. . . . It is also beyond the scope of the Standards to define the full range of supports appropriate for English language learners and for students with special needs" (2010a, p. 6). However, the designers clearly expect that all students are given the "opportunity to learn and meet the same high standards if they are to access the knowledge and skills necessary in their post–high school lives" (2010a, p. 6). On the Common Core main website, there are two documents that are pertinent to these diverse populations that warrant further reading: "Application of Common Core State Standards for English Language Learners" and "Application to Students with Disabilities."

Much attention is given to the area of text complexity. In the "Revised Publishers' Criteria for the Common Core Standards in English Language Arts and Literacy, 3–12," coauthors Coleman and Pimentel go into detail. To help provide guidance with regard to differentiating for high achievers, they state the following: "Instructional materials should also offer advanced texts to provide students at every grade with the opportunity to read texts beyond their current grade level to prepare them for the challenges of more complex text" (2012, p. 3). This is in complete alignment with the notion of differentiation, as each student should be challenged at his or her readiness level. Oftentimes, those who are above grade level might get short shrift, as some teachers tend either to teach to the middle or focus on those who struggle. It is imperative that teachers enrich those students who are at the high end of the spectrum and make sure that their needs are met, too. It is faulty logic to assume that these advanced students do not need our support and are fine on their own. They, like all students, need guidance and direction to meet new challenges.

Coleman and Pimentel also make sure to consider struggling students and provide suggestions for this population:

Far too often, students who have fallen behind are only given less complex texts rather than the support they need to read texts at the appropriate level of complexity. Complex text is a rich repository of ideas, information, and experience which all readers should learn how to access, although some students will need more scaffolding to do so. Curriculum developers and teachers have the flexibility to build progressions of texts of increasing complexity within grade-level bands that overlap to a limited degree with earlier bands." (2012, p. 3)

They continue to explain that teachers should employ effective scaffolding to support these students so they can read complex text and satisfy the expectations delineated in the Common Core. At the same time, however, you need to be careful that you don't provide so much support that you supplant the original complex text through extensive translation, summaries, or preview. This would merely prevent students from experiencing the text independently and discovering the content on their own. In essence, "the scaffolding should not become an alternate, simpler source of information that diminishes the need for students to read the text itself carefully" (p. 9).

Douglas Fisher et al. (Fisher & Frey, 2012; Fisher, Frey, & Lapp, 2012) weigh in about text complexity. They assert that students cannot learn information on their own from text they cannot read. This seems like common sense. However, they make the salient point that relegating students who read below their grade level to easier material that they can read independently will not foster growth and allow them to master necessary skills to blossom as readers. Therefore, "[t]he idea is not to either limit a student to a low-level text or allow him or her to struggle without support in a difficult text, but instead to provide texts and couple them with instruction. As students progress, they should be given increasingly challenging materials and taught, encouraged, and supported to use deeper skills of analysis" (p. 8). This seems in concert with the goals of the Common Core authors, as well as these words from Fisher and his colleagues: "The text difficulty is not the real issue. Instruction is. Teachers can scaffold and support students, which will determine the amount of their learning and literacy independence" (p. 7). The challenge will be in how educators teach and instruct so that all students reach their maximum potential.

Overall, the Common Core designers give teachers, curriculum developers, and other key stakeholders the latitude and charge to determine how to reach the goals stated in the document. To this point, the Common Core explicitly states: "Thus, the Standards do not mandate such things as a particular writing process or the full range of metacognitive strategies that students may need to monitor and direct their thinking and learning. Teachers are thus free to provide students with whatever tools and knowledge their professional judgment and experience identify as most helpful for meeting the goals set out in the Standards" (2010a, p. 4).

In the next sections, you will learn about a couple of instructional strategies that can be easily used to meet the needs of the Common Core while differentiating for students' readiness, learning profiles, and interests.

INSTRUCTIONAL STRATEGY: ROLLING DICE OR CUBES

Cubing was originally designed as an instructional strategy for students that would allow them to use their thinking skills to explore a topic or concept. It has since morphed to embrace all sorts of permutations and possibilities. In this strategy, students roll a wooden or paper cube and respond to a prompt featured on the side that lands facing up. Read on for a thorough explanation of two different activity options associated with this strategy.

Option 1: Prompts

What Prompts Can You Feature on a Die or Cube?

I have included a combination of question and task prompts in Figure 7.3 that align mostly to the reading strand of the Common Core Standards. Although text-dependent questions receive major attention in the Common Core materials, not all cubing questions need to be designed solely for complex text. Rather, prompts can pertain to any kind of reading selection, idea, topic, concept, visual, or demonstration, for example. The suggestions for die or cube prompts in Figure 7.3 are more generic in nature, so they are not a substitute for text-dependent questions, which are intended to be used for close reading of a complex text. Some prompts are fine as written for what students explore (e.g., idea, topic, illustration, song, poem, etc.). You could, though, revise pertinent ones to be text-dependent questions to foster keen examination and analysis by tailoring them to a particular reading selection. For example, the cube prompt *What is a personality trait for a character?* can be adapted for Shirley Jackson's "Charles" in this way: *What personality trait can you attribute to Laurie's description of Charles? What does Charles do that supports this trait?* Then you can continue with *How is the story "Charles" an example of irony?*

While the prompts in the figure are categorized (e.g., *character, theme, thinking skills, interest,* etc.), teachers may customize a die or cube by mixing and matching different cells. You can have a die or cube that includes a compilation of elements of literature, such as one character prompt, one setting prompt, one theme prompt, and so forth. Also, some cells in a given row may not all apply to your content, so you might have to adapt some suggested prompts for the activity to be pertinent.

Consider fashioning your own prompts to target the language strand in various grade levels. For example, students would need a text in hand as the basis for responding to these kinds of die or cube prompts:

- Find an example of using commas to set off a **nonrestrictive clause.**
- Find a **dependent clause** in the text.
- Point to two **sentences** that begin in different ways. Explain the way they both begin.
- Find an example of citation used for **quoting text.** Explain how the rules of punctuation apply to this citation.
- Point to an example of a **compound-complex sentence** and a **complex sentence.** Explain the differences in sentence structures between them.
- Write or say the formula for a **complex sentence.**
- Write down one **compound-complex** sentence from the text.
- Find an example of using a comma to separate **coordinate adjectives.**
- Point to three sentences that begin with an **adverb.**
- Find an example of where an author uses **ellipsis.** Explain why the ellipsis is needed.
- Find an instance where the author uses **passive voice.** Rewrite the sentence so it is in the **active voice.**
- Find an example of **parallelism** in the text. Write your own sentence using the author's sentence structure as a model.

How Might Students Respond to Die or Cube Prompts?

This activity is intended to check for understanding. Therefore, students are practicing what you have taught them during some point in the unit, so they need to have some

Die or Cube Prompts

Character 1	What does the character **say** that supports a trait?	What does the character **do** that supports a trait?	What does **another say** about the character?	What is the character **thinking** or **feeling**?	What is a **personality trait** for the character?	What does the character **look like**?
Character 2	How does the character change throughout time?	Why does the character change throughout time?	Is the character static or dynamic? Explain.	How do a character's actions shape the theme?	How does a change in setting affect a character?	How do a character's interactions with another affect the plot?
Setting	Where does the author use climate to portray setting?	What are the settings in this text? Which is most important, and why?	How does the setting impact characters?	What tone does the author create through the setting?	How is a setting in this text similar to the setting in another text?	What sensory phrases does the author use to depict setting?
Theme	What are two or more themes in this text?	What is the definition of *theme*?	What evidence can you cite to support a theme?	What other texts have a similar theme? Explain.	How does the theme of this text connect to the world?	How do two themes interact and build on one another?
Figurative Language	Create your own **simile** for something in the text.	Create a **metaphor** for something in the text.	Find a **metaphor** in the text and explain its meaning.	Find a **simile** in the text and explain its meaning.	Create **imagery** where there is none in the text.	Find **imagery** in the text. How does it impact the text?
General Reading	What is the author's purpose in writing?	Orally summarize the whole text or part of it.	Interpret a part of the text that might confuse others.	Compare and contrast two characters or individuals in the text.	Invent dialogue a character or individual might say. Explain why she or he would say this.	How would the text change if written from a different point of view?
Poetry	What is this type of poem? Does it work for the topic?	What is the purpose of this poem? Does the author accomplish this purpose?	Find a simile or metaphor. What does it mean?	What is this poem's theme? Show evidence.	Find an example of rhythm or rhyme. Is it effective?	What is the tone of this poem? Show evidence.

Online Resources Included

	DESCRIBE	COMPARE	ASSOCIATE	ANALYZE	APPLY	ARGUE FOR or AGAINST
Thinking Skills (Literature)	Describe the setting or a character using sensory detail.	Compare three elements of literature: theme, setting, character.	In what way is this text like another text?	Identify and analyze examples of figurative language.	Interpret a meaningful quote from the story.	Argue for or against a theme. Use textual evidence for support.
Thinking Skills (Issue/ Concept/ Topic)	Describe challenges related to the issue, concept, or topic.	What do two issues, concepts, or topics have in common? How are they different?	Identify individuals associated with this topic, issue, or concept and their roles.	Describe parts of this issue, concept, or topic to explain it to others.	How can this issue, concept, or topic be used or solved?	Agree or disagree with the issue, concept, or topic.
Interest	What do you find interesting about this topic?	What more would you want to learn about this topic?	What questions do you have about this topic?	What is this topic like? What does it remind you of?	Who would benefit from learning about this topic? Why?	What are related topics that you would want to learn more about?
Vocabulary	Create a picture or symbol of the word.	Create an advertisement of the word.	Write a poem or song about the word.	Write a simile or metaphor for the word.	Make a visual collage of the word.	Use technology to teach the word to others.
Word Work	What prefix or affix helps you figure out what this word means?	What is a synonym for this word?	What is an antonym for this word?	Use the word in a sentence to show meaning.	Draw a symbol or picture of the word.	What are nonexamples of this word?

FIGURE 7.3

background knowledge related to the targeted prompts, such as elements of literature, types and purposes of poems, reading strategies, and so forth. Students can respond to this formative assessment informally or formally. Informal responses might entail oral responses to tasks or questions, as appropriate; formal responses might entail writing or completing a project. Or students might respond using a combination: They might first respond orally, gathering input and suggestions to the prompt from peers, and then work independently to complete the task more comprehensively.

Oral Response Ideas

- In a group setting, one student at a time rolls the die or cube and responds to the prompt. Students pass the die or cube so that each has a chance to respond and discuss one prompt at a time. Students in a group can respond to the same prompt in a different way if the die or cube lands on what was previously rolled. For example, *Find imagery that the author uses in the text* can be used repeatedly as students find different examples. The question *How does this theme connect to another work?* will generate various responses from different students, too.
- Each student in a group rolls and is then the first to respond to the prompt shown. After ample time is given for each to respond, all group members are free to participate in the discussion, which can take many forms. For example, students can merely agree with the response given, ask for clarification, provide new insight, or counter the response, in which case more discussion can unfold. It is then the next student's turn to roll and have first dibs at responding to the new prompt before open discussion.
- Teachers can follow up either of the two choices above with whole class sharing and discussion.

Written Response Ideas

- In groups, students each get a turn to roll the die or cube and take note of what they rolled. Once they all roll, students can solicit input from group members, if needed. Individually, students respond to their targeted prompt in writing. If more than one student rolls the same prompt, these students can compare their responses and discuss what they each wrote.
- Independently, students can each roll the die or cube a set number of times from the six options and then complete the rolled prompt(s) in journals or on separate paper to submit.
- Since these prompts are relatively brief, the oral or written responses can be a precursor to a more extensive writing assignment.

For oral or written responses, I suggest you model how to respond and communicate criteria so students are clear about expectations. For oral responses, consider this relevant standard: *Prepare for and participate effectively in a range of conversations and collaborations with diverse partners, building on others' ideas and expressing their own clearly and persuasively* (SL. CCR.1). To support this expectation, you might suggest ways that students can connect their comments to others, such as *Kimberly's comment made me think about . . .*, Or: *I understand Marshall's point; however, my view is. . . .*

How Can Teachers Differentiate Die or Cube Prompts?

1. Arrange students in interest- or readiness-based groups and prepare cubes accordingly so that each group has customized, differentiated cubes. As previously mentioned, you can intentionally cut out different cells from various rows on the prompts provided in Figure 7.3 to correlate with certain content, but also as a means of differentiation.

2. Give all groups the same cubes but use differentiated texts (e.g., textbook excerpts, articles, Internet resources, novels, literature circle books, etc.) as the basis for their responses.

3. Students can also prepare their own cubes to use and play with others who are at the same readiness level or share the same interests. You might choose to color-code the cubes for easy reference to correspond to the way in which you have differentiated.

You can use cubing in conjunction with a summative project that is differentiated by learning profile. For example, let's say students completed one of the project choices listed in Figures 5.6, "Character Study and Societal Contributions," or 5.7, "Project Choices." Once students finish their chosen projects, or while they are working on them, they create die or cube prompts that can be answered by viewing their projects. The prompts have to include the unit guiding questions and others, as well. Then they present their projects to students in small groups along with their prepared dice or cubes and instruct classmates to respond to these prompts using their projects. This would serve many purposes: to reinforce the key ideas in the unit for all students, to provide a vehicle for students to present their work in small groups in a novel way, and to allow students to reflect upon their own projects critically to ensure they are complete and focus on unit goals as they create a single die or cube or a pair. In fact, some students might realize they have to revise their projects if they are struggling with finding die or cube prompts or answers that accompany them—especially if they are having difficulty addressing deeper unit guiding questions.

How Can You Prepare for a Die or Cube Learning Activity?

To prepare for this activity and the one that follows (Option 2: "The Question Designer"), teachers need to be mindful of grouping configurations for either option and arrange students purposefully to work independently or in pairs, trios, or foursomes. Groups larger than four become too chaotic, and students may not be as engaged or invested in the activity if they are distracted by too many peers. To determine the grouping, consider your purpose in assigning the targeted activity and differentiate by interest, readiness, or learning profile. Furthermore, determine and communicate to students how to use the dice or cubes based on suggestions I've offered and your own ideas.

In terms of logistics, there are many ways to prepare:

- You can make your own cube out of bond paper. If you conduct an Internet search for "cubing" or "make a paper cube" you will find a template.
- You can buy wooden dice from a craft or teacher supply store and write the prompts on them. If you use this method, be careful not to use a fat-tipped permanent marker on the wooden die because it will bleed.

- You can download my prompts from Figure 7.3 in the companion website and cut and affix them onto a cube with double-sided tape. As an option, you might then decoupage these prompts onto the cubes so they are securely stuck to each side. I did this using wooden cubes, and it worked out rather nicely in climates that are not humid! I found that when I travelled in the summer and presented in highly humid areas, the cubes stuck together. That technicality never dawned on me!
- You can also type prompts onto mailing labels and then cut them out and stick them on paper or wooden cubes.

Even though this section focuses on making cubes or dice, you might decide to merely copy the prompts from Figure 7.3 onto 100 lb. paper, which is the thickest that can go through a printer. Then cut these cells out to use as cards. Students can pull a card from a hat, or place several cards face down for them to choose.

Option 2: The Question Designer

How Do You Use the Question Designer?

This activity also involves rolling dice or cubes; however, prompts are not featured on them. Instead, students use a combination of a question word and a helping verb on a pair of dice or cubes as frames for fashioning their own questions around targeted subjects. They then respond to what they create. This strategy is a vehicle for students to probe more deeply into the content of literature or nonfiction text, or even into a particular topic, issue, or idea. We pose questions to students so often; it is important that they master the skill of fashioning their own levels of questioning, too.

To devise these frames, first write or affix question words on each of the six faces of a die or cube: *who, what, where, when, how, why.* On another die or cube, write or affix these six words on each of the six faces of this die or cube: *is, did, can, would, will, might.* Make enough pairs of dice or cubes so that students in your class can play individually or in pairs, trios, or foursomes. You can make your own cubes or buy wooden ones, as described in the previous section.

Once your preparations are complete, follow the directions below to model and execute this strategy:

1. First model the exercise by presenting some sort of content, such as reading a text, featuring a video or guest speaker, or lecturing. Or you might designate a topic or concept, identify an individual or character, or show a demonstration. Roll the dice or cubes on a document camera or in front of the class. Let's say *how* and *did* are face up. Use the think-aloud strategy to fashion questions about a topic. For example, *How did Confucius influence others?* Or *How did Confucius believe government should be run?*

2. Ask students to volunteer other questions with the frame of *How did . . . ?* Roll again and use the think-aloud strategy to show how you use what is rolled to frame and respond to questions. Students need to be clear about the quality and types of questions and what represents factual knowledge versus high-order thinking and deeper analysis. You want a combination of both, so hold a discussion around this point. Show different examples of queries and what you expect, including text-dependent questions.

3. After modeling and discussion, arrange students in pairs or small groups. Distribute dice or cubes, prepare differentiated subject matter or text for students to use as the basis for this activity, and instruct them to take turns rolling.

4. The student who rolls generates and answers a question based on targeted informational or literary text, topic, or idea. Once finished, the question is open for discussion from other group members.

5. As students generate and discuss questions, have them record selected ones on Figure 7.4, "Question Designer." There are far too many spaces, so don't require students to fill in the entire figure. Rather, have students discuss and write down selected higher-level questions.

6. You might instruct students to determine four of the questions on Figure 7.4 that represent deep thinking and get at the root of the topic and submit these—along with their answers—to you as a formative assessment. Determine whether or not each individual needs to turn in a sheet.

7. Conduct a whole-class debriefing exercise in which each group leads a discussion based on its selected questions.

Question Designer

	is	did	can	would	will	might
Who						
What						
Where						
When						
How						
Why						

FIGURE 7.4

Source: Glass (2012).

How Can You Differentiate the Question Designer?

Because students can generate questions based on a text, topic, or issue, this is a natural way to differentiate:

- If pairs or small groups are reading different materials based on readiness levels, then these students will create questions based on the varying levels of text readability and even content sophistication.
- If students are focusing together on interest-based topics and issues, they can continue to work in these interest groups to formulate questions.
- For struggling students, provide adult assistance to help them create appropriately probing questions that span the breadth of the text, topic, or issue. This support is important so that students do not continuously create lower-level questions in which responses are found directly in the text. Students should also be prompted to create questions that foster inferential thinking, as well.

INSTRUCTIONAL STRATEGY: USING MANIPULATIVES

During math lessons, manipulatives abound—especially in the younger grades. Teachers use pattern blocks, tiles, cubes, spinners, tangrams, and more. In other content areas, as well, teachers can customize and differentiate manipulatives so students can engage with learning in tactile and kinesthetic ways. Cubing is one such way to use manipulatives.

This section provides myriad ways to constructively use other manipulatives to enhance learning and engender more participation from kids physically and intellectually across content areas. Unlike rolling a cube or die, though, which are solely tactile activities, the manipulative ideas presented here can be used tactilely *or* kinesthetically:

- When designed as a tactile activity, students lay out various pieces individually, in pairs, or in small groups and maneuver them on a table, desk, or the floor in accordance with directions the teacher communicates based on learning goals. You should prepare these pieces, gather them in a set, and consider placing them together in an envelope. Tactile activities are more controlled, as students manipulate several pieces in one location.
- As an alternative, kinesthetic activities using manipulatives involve giving each student, or sometimes a pair, one card or strip. Individuals or partners then circulate around the room to find another student or partnership that satisfies the directive. The kinesthetic approach requires more movement, of course.

Whichever method you employ, consider that students need several manipulatives in repetition in order to grasp a skill or concept. Both are engaging, add variety, and appeal to students with different learning styles. The dynamics and necessary classroom management strategies are different for each, so teachers should establish ground rules for students to know, practice, and follow before engaging in these activities.

What Types of Manipulatives Can You Use, and How Can They Be Differentiated?

Always be aware of your desired lesson outcomes and students' needs to determine if this strategy would be effective at some point during instruction. Teachers can conduct manipulative activities both informally and formally and as a preassessment and formative assessment. Before or during instruction, have the unit and lesson guiding questions visible and communicate them orally so students are aware of the purpose for the activity. An exception occurs if you want students to discover on their own the relationships between, or common attributes of, the manipulatives to arrive at an understanding. For example, you might have students sort cards of personification examples and nonexamples to determine if they can ascertain the reason for grouping certain cards together. (See the cell for "Concept Attainment" in Figure 6.2.) The directive would be as follows:

> *Students, I will give each group a set of cards with sentences on them. Your job is to study all the cards carefully and see if you can determine a recurring pattern among some of them. Place the cards that have shared attributes together and put the other cards in their own pile. Be ready to explain what you found the grouped cards have in common.*

After students sort through their cards, proceed as follows:

- Have them discuss and analyze the common features among the sentences they grouped together during a class discussion. Agree on and articulate the shared attribute(s). For instance, *All of these sentences grouped together include examples of personification.* Or *All of these sentences use strong verbs associated with a thing, such as* wind whistled *and* feathers danced.
- Pose the guiding question so they continue their learning with this purpose top of mind. For instance, *What is personification?*
- Arrive at a class definition for the term. Have groups then verify whether or not it applies to all of the cards that they deem have commonalities.
- Instruct each group to provide its own examples to add to the grouped sentences, and share these with the class for confirmation that each example is indeed an example of the selected term.

The previous explanation is just one of many ways to use manipulatives. What follows are a variety of differentiation ideas for using manipulatives in your instructional program. Although I write as if educators always find or produce the manipulatives, certainly consider asking students to make them a part of their learning. When you conduct an activity using materials you make, a by-product is that students then have a sample to use as a model. So give them different resources as the basis for making their own manipulatives. This opportunity can help further their learning as they research, read, and amass information to use for an activity. After teachers check for understanding and correctness, classmates can use these student-generated manipulatives.

Before I itemize the manipulative activity options, here are six pervasive differentiation techniques; use some in combination, as appropriate:

1. *Level of adult assistance.* Some students might need more support than others, so offer additional instruction to struggling learners, as needed. By the same token, check in with all students to ensure they are being effectively challenged and taking appropriate risks to learn and grow.

2. *Power of observation.* Observe students informally as they work individually, in partnerships, or in small groups. Consider if certain students are struggling to complete

a task, finish it too quickly, ask too many questions, and so forth. Also review any formal work (e.g., graphic organizers, quizzes, quick writes) you assign to determine if you need to gather a small group for reteaching or enrichment.

3. *Learning style.* Determine if you want to conduct a tactile or kinesthetic activity based on your learning goals and the composition of your students. The activities detailed in this section are written as tactile; however, any of them can be altered to accommodate a kinesthetic activity.

4. *Readiness.* For tactile work, distribute sets of cards or strips to groups based on readiness so each group receives appropriately challenging material. Also consider the quantity you give each group to provide the right number of manipulatives.

5. *Color-coding.* Color-code manipulatives for the different levels of learners. For example, customize a game of bingo for learning vocabulary by color-coding the bingo cards and clues. Specifically, high achievers could have a blue bingo card, at-grade-level students a yellow card, and struggling students a green card. Write clues on blue, yellow, and green cards to match the bingo cards that reflect readiness levels. Give struggling students a hint before playing bingo to listen carefully to clues read from a green card. You can also create various sets of cards to use for other games—concentration, matching, sequencing, or other activities—and color-code each set to reflect readiness levels.

6. *Grouping.* In some activities, group by readiness or interest. Other times, though, allow students to choose to work independently or with a partner they select. Offering this choice responds to differentiation by learning style.

Specific ideas for using manipulatives, along with ideas for differentiation, are itemized as follows:

- *Matching.* Create pairs of manipulative cards for students to match vocabulary words with definitions, terms or concepts with examples or pictures, characters with their personality traits, animals with their habitats, causes with effects, passive with active voice, and so forth. As with all of these manipulative ideas, matching can be used as a preassessment or formative assessment, or even used for both. See Figure 7.5 for various simile and metaphor cards that you can use. For example, *Her teeth are as straight as* is one card and the matching card reads *white picket fences.* I am a firm believer in using examples students are exposed to, so create your own manipulatives by pulling similes and metaphors from text students are reading so they see authentic application. However, you can use Figure 7.5 as a model for students; then they can create their own sets from their fiction or nonfiction text.

  o *Differentiation.* See the six general ways to differentiate listed previously. For struggling students, you might color-code the cards so that the word, character, habitat, or whatever category is being matched is in a color and the corresponding card is in white. This way, students can lay out the pieces into two separate columns and match them more easily. For advanced students, create all white cards instead of color-coding them. For a figurative language activity, find various similes and metaphors that show a range of sophistication so you give the appropriately challenging cards to groups of students to match. You'd be surprised at the range that exists within one particular literary or nonfiction work, so use an appropriately challenging example in a text they are reading if you conduct this activity.

Simile and Metaphor Cards

He is as intelligent as	Albert Einstein.	Her teeth are as straight as	white picket fences.
The baby's hair was as soft as	chenille.	The shot hurt as badly as	a sharp pencil poke.
Her eyes were as blue as	the azure sky.	Her fingers expertly danced on the computer keys like	a concert pianist's.
The dog's bark is guttural like	an old man with croup.	His shirt is blood-red like	a persimmon.
The cat savagely attacked the mouse like	it was its last meal.	The plane took off effortlessly like	a bird taking flight.
My heart is	stone, sitting empty and cold.	The glistening pool called me like	a soft-spoken mother beckoning her child.
A drink of lemonade on a hot summer's day	is a refreshing dip in the pool.	Tulips are	tiny teacups for fairies.
Sarah, our soccer team's goalie,	is a wide barricade on a highway.	The baby's persistent cries on the crowded flight	were nails on a chalkboard.
Anything written on the Web is	a public announcement.	She radiates the room with her presence because she	is sunshine all day long.

FIGURE 7.5

- *Sequencing.* Ask students to manipulate sentence strips to reflect the sequence of a story, events in history, or steps in a process or experiment. Encourage students to lay the strips out in a shape instead of a linear sequence, as appropriate (e.g., basic inverted check or more sophisticated design for a story). When they have finished arranging strips, ask them to identify and defend which strip represents the central conflict or climax in a story, turning point of a historical event, or key step in a process.

  o *Differentiation.* As with all manipulative activities, consider the six general differentiation ideas previously listed. For sequencing, see the literature example in Figure 7.6 for Isaac Asimov's short story "Rain, Rain, Go Away." To differentiate, prepare and create a different set of strips for the same text that vary by sophistication and distribute the appropriate level of challenge to each group. Another way to differentiate is to have students read different texts based on interest and readiness and ask them to write accompanying sequencing strips to use with classmates.

- *Card sort.* As opposed to matching, have students sort cards to categorize them based on the lesson goal. They can sort nonexamples of imagery (*I like my crazy pet dog*) and imagery examples (*My rambunctious dog, Titan, jumps on any surface in sight: the green marble kitchen counter, the smooth felt of the pool table, or the coffee table cluttered with leftover snacks*). If you are studying parallelism, create cards with sentences that show this syntax from the literature or informational text you are reading and sentences void of this structure for students to sort. They can sort cards with examples of renewable and nonrenewable energy or contributions, leaders, events, and artifacts of particular ancient civilizations. Also, students can sort cards with more than two categories, such as sentence beginnings (e.g., those that begin with adverbs, dependent clauses, prepositional phrases, etc.), excerpts from literature by the method of characterization (e.g., what a character says, what a character does, what a character looks like, etc.), or examples of the different states of matter.

  o *Differentiation.* There are boundless examples of sorting students can do that can be differentiated by the sophistication and number of items to sort. If you have students group themselves kinesthetically, give high achievers the lead cards so when they walk around the room, they can help to seek out students with the associated cards who might need support. For example, a lead card might read *gerund* with these associated cards: *dancing, swimming, sharing.*

- *Identification cards.* Use the cards in Figure 7.7 that show the elements of an argument paper with an arrow. Ask students to place each card with its arrow pointing to the appropriate place on a student or published sample showing where the author employed each element. For papers without a particular element present, the student does not use a specific card, which itself becomes a discussion opportunity. Give duplicates of certain cards such as *transition* and *evidence.* Of course, this strategy can be used with any genre by creating element cards specific to a writing type (e.g., setting, plot, character, point of view, theme for literature). Or create identification cards of literary devices (e.g., tone, mood, foreshadowing, etc.) and have students place each card where evidence of the method exists. In science, create and use cards for science lab reports (e.g., methods, introduction, results, etc.).

  o *Differentiation.* Distribute different student or published samples to student groups based on interest or readiness to use as the basis for this activity. For an extension, have students use identification cards to point out these elements in their independent reading books or rough drafts of a writing assignment.

Sequencing Strips

The Sakkaros move in next door to the Wrights. The Wrights often talk about their neighbors' strange habits.

Mrs. Sakkaro won't let her son play outside with the Wright boy because she is afraid it will rain.

When Mrs. Wright visits the Sakkaros' home, she is surprised that the house is so clean and immaculate. Mrs. Sakkaro doesn't even allow water to touch the sink when she gets a drink for Mrs. Wright.

At Murphy's Park, the Sakkaros eat nothing but cotton candy and M&M's. Mrs. Wright offers Mrs. Sakkaro an orange drink but she refuses.

The Sakkaros are unusually concerned about weather conditions. They listen to the radio on their way home from the park.

Once the Sakkaros get out of the car from the park, they get very nervous and run quickly to their house.

Unfortunately, the Sakkaros get wet and begin to melt.

The Wrights finally discover the mystery of the Sakkaros—they are made of sugar.

FIGURE 7.6

Argument Identification Cards

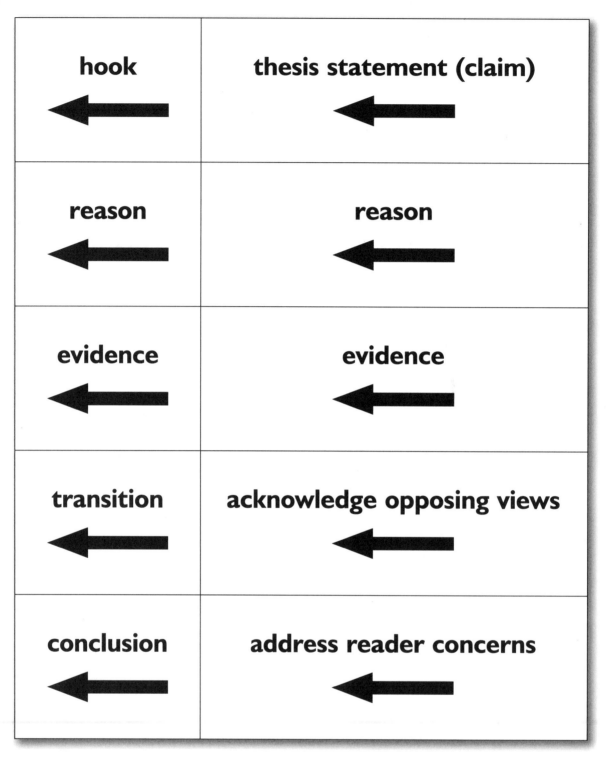

FIGURE 7.7

What Activities Can You Implement Using Manipulatives?

Prior to conducting a manipulative activity, you can prepare students for learning by stating the guiding question, making a connection to a previous activity, or conducting a mini-lesson. For example, before I had students categorize sentence strips based on their beginnings, I led a short lesson where I read an excerpt from Louis Sachar's *Holes* and posed the question, *What do you notice about the sentence beginnings in this excerpt?* The excerpt is as follows: "He dug his shovel into the side of the hole. He scooped up some dirt, and was raising it up to the surface when Zigzag's shovel caught him in the side of the head. He collapsed. He wasn't sure if he passed out or not. He looked up to see Zigzag's wild head staring down at him" (Sachar, 1998, p. 78). The discussion that ensued set the stage for the manipulative activity that focused on various types of sentence beginnings. (By the way, I made sure to communicate to students that authors take creative license in their work and that the lack of sentence beginning variety can be used for effect. We then discussed what Sachar hoped to achieve by his use of repetition.)

After students perform a manipulative activity, augment it with continued formative assessments such as students engaging in oral discussions, making their own manipulatives, finding evidence of the skill they learned in literature and informational text, and so forth. They have worked with partners or in small groups, so give them an opportunity to think and process what they learned and demonstrated independently. Ask them to implement the skill. For instance, after a manipulative activity on varied sentence beginnings, instruct students to hunt for such examples in published work and then practice writing paragraphs using a combination of different sentence beginnings. Ultimately, expect them to demonstrate understanding of this skill in a longer writing piece of their own.

How Can You Prepare and Store Manipulatives?

When I use this strategy, I copy all of my manipulatives on 100 lb. paper. Not all office supply stores carry this thickness, so go to the larger chain stores. This weight will go through your computer printer. After copying, you might laminate the sheet for durability and reuse, and then cut out the pieces. To create sets of manipulatives, you can place them in regular business envelopes or coin envelopes. (I am amazed at the different sizes of coin envelopes office supply stores provide at our fingertips!) I store my envelopes in plastic shoe boxes with labels on the front for categories, such as "Narrative Unit," "Parts of Speech," "Steps in a Lab Report," the title of a literary or informational text or unit title, and so forth.

CONSTRUCTING YOUR OWN DIFFERENTIATED INSTRUCTIONAL STRATEGIES

At this point, you might have completed all of the columns of your unit map, or you might have been waiting to do so until after reading this chapter. In either case, the resources and information provided in the exercise below will help you incorporate differentiation in your unit map.

EXERCISE 7: HOW CAN YOU INDICATE DIFFERENTIATION ON YOUR UNIT MAP?

In the multiple pages of Figure 7.8, "Ideas for Differentiating Instruction," you will find many ways to plan for and employ differentiation for your activities, resources, and assessments. As you review this figure, revisit your exercise from the previous chapter to ensure that differentiation is reflected in these components, as appropriate. Since differentiation is an expansive category filled with numerous resources, you might choose to build your professional repertoire in this area. I've included some titles in the reference section of this book, but there are certainly other books that you can read, videos you can watch, and online or face-to-face seminars you can attend to advance your knowledge of this important topic.

LOOKING AHEAD

Now that you've filled in your overall unit map, we'll turn to the topic of the next chapter: lesson design. While the key aim of this book has been to guide you on your journey to creating a unit map, doing so primes you to craft effective and engaging lessons. It is the lessons that make a unit map come alive. Read further for comprehensive, differentiated lesson examples along with specific suggestions for the entire curriculum design process—creating a unit map, designing lessons, piloting, and revising.

Ideas for Differentiating Instruction

Ideas for Differentiating Instruction: Readiness

Content	Process	Product

• Provide **resources and supplemental materials** at varying levels of readability, such as the following:
  ○ various textbooks
  ○ newspaper articles
  ○ magazine articles
  ○ short stories
  ○ novels (chapters)
  ○ diaries or historical journals
  ○ technical manuals
  ○ computer software
  ○ websites
  ○ speeches
  ○ documents
  ○ lab reports
  ○ science periodicals
• Consider the **amount** of reading.
• Adjust **what** material students are taught.
	• Provide **word labels.**
	• Provide **vocabulary lists** at varying levels of challenge for individuals to incorporate in their writing or speaking.
	• **Modify or extend directions.**
	• Partially complete a **graphic organizer.**
	• Assign appropriately challenging **graphic organizers, templates,** and **frames.**
	• Create an assignment using **cloze procedure.**
	• Create **tiered assignments** that vary by level of challenge. (As a management tip, use color-coding or symbols.)
	• Consider the **amount of writing.**
	• Allow **extra time** to complete assignments.
	• Consider **pacing adjustments** to eliminate instruction of skills and concepts that students have previously shown to have mastered.
	• Provide **reference materials** at varying levels of readiness (e.g., capitalize on different kinds of thesauruses, online resources, and dictionaries).
	• Create or find **games** and appropriately assign them to individuals, pairs, or groups based on readiness.
	• Assign particular **computer software.**
	• Assign **jigsaw** reading to groups based on readiness levels.
	• Assign students to specific **learning centers.**
	• **Teach or reteach** a skill, concept, or topic for selected students in need of honing targeted learning.
	• **Enrich learning** to higher achievers ready for more sophistication or extensions.
	• Issue multiple levels of **questioning.**
	• Assign **homework** at varying levels of difficulty.
	• Assign varied **journal prompts** according to readiness.
	• Preselect websites and assign to students as they investigate a research question (WebQuests).
	• Issue appropriately challenging sets of **manipulatives** and **cubing prompts.**
	• Provide tiered **RAFT** assignments (role-audience-format-topic).
		• Create **tiered products** that vary by level of challenge.
		• Create and issue **RAFT** (role-audience-format-topic) products based on readiness.
		• Create **rubrics** for different levels of learners, keeping in mind satisfying standards.

Readiness		

FIGURE 7.8 (*Continued*)

Ideas for Differentiating Instruction: Learning Profile

Content	Process	Product
• Use **gestures, facial expressions, and articulation** when reading or orally presenting new information. • Show **props, artifacts, visuals,** or extra visuals to further help students comprehend text or information. • Invite students to choose to **read text individually or in partnerships.** • Allow students to **access content** in a way that addresses their learning styles, such as the following: ○ computer software ○ videos ○ audio ○ interviews ○ speeches ○ demonstrations ○ texts (textbook, articles, poems) ○ PowerPoint presentations ○ artwork or photographs ○ graphic representations	• Have **directions read aloud or on a recorded device,** and in writing. • Offer **read-aloud or independent reading** as an option, when appropriate. • Allow choice of **graphic organizers.** • Offer **technology** as an option when working on a project with peers (e.g., Google Docs, classroom blog, etc.). • Allow students to **type or handwrite** their work. • Provide **choice** in how students **learn new words or facts** (e.g., flashcards, graphic organizers, songs, etc.). • Be flexible about **where students work** in the classroom (e.g., in a chair, on the floor, at a table, near the window). • Be flexible about **how students work** in the classroom (e.g., working with a partner or alone, using noise-canceling headphones, standing at an upright desk, etc.). • Create or find different kinds of **games** and allow students to choose which to play. • Use a combination of **tactile** and **kinesthetic** activities, as well as the more common **auditory** and **visual** ones. • Create and issue **RAFT** (role-audience-format-topic) or other assignments during formative assessment with choices that appeal to **multiple intelligences.**	• Allow students **choice** in how they demonstrate knowledge for a summative assessment, such as writing an article or poem, performing a skit or interview, using multimedia (e.g., PowerPoint or iMovie), drawing, using music, and so on. • Create and issue **RAFT** (role-audience-format-topic) products from which students choose.

Learning Profile

Ideas for Differentiating Instruction: Interest

	Content	Process	Product
Interest	• Provide **resources** with various topic choices (e.g., in a unit on the Renaissance, allow students to choose a topic that interests them—architecture, music, literature, etc.). • Provide different **reading genres** (e.g., biography, autobiography, etc.) and **media formats** to learn about a topic. • Conduct **literature circles.** • Use **student-generated questions** in lecture.	• Allow students to choose a **computer** program. • Conduct **jigsaw** activity based on topic of interest. • Allow students to choose or create **interest centers.** • Create or find **games** and appropriately assign them to individuals, pairs, or groups based on interest. • Assign varied **journal prompts** according to interest. • Preselect **websites** for students to choose from as they investigate a research question. • Create and issue sets of **manipulatives** and **cubing** prompts based on interest. • Allow students to choose **subtopics** within a greater unit (e.g., for colonial life, choose an individual or topic—clothing, art, religion—as the focus for an activity; in math, create a scale drawing of a self-selected object).	• Work with student(s) to devise an **independent study** that culminates in a product; provide criteria for quality of product and clear work expectations. • Assign students to collect a sampling of their best work in a **portfolio.** • Allow students to determine a community need and create (or participate in) a **service-learning project.** • Provide student choice in a **topic of interest** as the basis for a culminating project. • Allow students to select and respond to an **essay question** to demonstrate understanding.

Additional Differentiation Support

- *Adult assistance.* Work (or have another adult work) with individuals or small groups to provide further explanation, reteaching, or enrichment.
- *Extra modeling.* Provide extra modeling before individual, pair, or small-group work.
- *Peer support.* Assign peers to help further explain a task or explain it in a different way; be mindful not to overuse peers as tutors, as these students need to continue on their own learning paths.
- *Flexible grouping.* Arrange students in groups based on a variety of factors (e.g., purpose of task, topic, resources, projects, group goals, student needs).
- *Preview.* Preview an assignment at school before it is taught to the whole class, or send an activity home for parents or older siblings to review with a student in advance.
- *Language.* Provide instruction in a student's native language or allow students to work with an adult who speaks the same language to clarify content, lead text-based question discussion, or help summarize material.
- *Enrichment.* Provide opportunities for students to extend learning and explore a topic or concept with more depth and complexity.

FIGURE 7.8

8

Lesson Design

> *Beyond learning about a subject, students will need lessons that enable them to experience directly the inquiries, arguments, applications, and points of view underneath the facts and opinion they learn if they are to understand them. Students have to do the subject, not just learn its results.*
>
> —Grant Wiggins and Jay McTighe (1998, p. 99)

Although this book primarily focuses on the process of creating a comprehensive unit map, this chapter explains how and where lesson design fits within that overall process. In the pages ahead, you'll find a lesson template along with many examples of lessons that follow the template format. After reading this chapter and using the resources in this book, you should have a firm understanding of lesson design and a sense of the steps you may need to take as you further develop your expertise in this area.

LESSON COMPONENTS

To maximize student achievement, it is not enough to create the unit map and launch into teaching. The unit map serves as the guidepost for students' conceptual understanding and factual knowledge, but to have students glean what you intend, you must do more. The work you have accomplished in previous chapters has already provided you with the overall framework you need to engage in the process of creating detailed, step-by-step directions for each lesson in a given unit. Effective lesson design includes its own elements, of course, but it is guided by the tenets of sound unit design that are now familiar to you. Lessons set the stage for students to answer guiding questions as they learn factual information, hone skills, apply concepts, and seek understanding. In Wiggins and McTighe's (1998) seminal work on backward design in *Understanding by Design,* the authors call this

"Stage 3, the curricular activities and teachings—the design work at the heart of everyday teaching" (1998, p. 98).

To teach students in accordance with the goals expressed in the unit map, you need to find or create lessons that are differentiated, employ engaging and thoughtful teaching methods and instructional strategies, contain a range of assessments to inform your instruction, and more. Just like a curriculum unit map has a template with components, so do lessons. The lesson template featured in Figure 8.1 will guide you through the process of incorporating all of the aspects of sound lesson design. Some of what you see on the curriculum map will undoubtedly appear on the lesson template. However, lessons also include many more details; these are explained in the template and illustrated in the lesson examples throughout this chapter. Use this template to support you in your endeavors to design effective and meaningful lessons that will resonate with your students. Or, if you have existing lessons, edit them to ensure that they include these components:

- essential unit and lesson guiding questions
- lesson overviews
- standard(s)
- resources/materials (including options for differentiation)
- estimated timing
- step-by-step lesson details (including options for differentiation)
- extensions (optional)
- assessments (including options for differentiation)

The lesson template should serve as a reminder for you of not only *what* to teach, but *how* to teach it. *What* you are teaching is embedded within the essential understandings, guiding questions, knowledge, and skills as they emanate from the standards. These are some of the *how* questions that should be folded into the design of each lesson. You will notice that some questions overlap with other components on your unit map (e.g., activities, differentiation, etc.):

- *How will it be differentiated? What will be differentiated?*
- *How will students be grouped?*
- *How will the teacher deliver the information?*
- *What will students be expected to do?*
- *How will the teacher collect information informally and formally to plan instruction?*
- *What varied resources are needed? How will these resources be presented and used?*
- *When is the lesson taught within the unit, and how long is it?*
- *How do teachers bridge from lesson to lesson so this one makes sense and flows with the others?*
- *Are there extensions that make sense? If so, for whom?*

SAMPLE LESSONS

In this chapter, there are several lessons aligned to the Common Core that you can use if they are in accordance with your unit goals. Read the guiding questions to help you determine if the focus of a lesson is relevant to the material you teach. You might adapt aspects of the lessons to meet the needs of the level of students you instruct, or you might use the

Lesson Design Template

Essential Unit Guiding Question #_____: _____

Lesson Guiding Question #_____: _____

Written by:_____

Lesson Overview

Write a succinct overview of the lesson.

Standards

Write the actual standard(s) and associated identification letters/numbers or simply write the identification letters/numbers.

Resources/Materials (differentiation opportunity)

- Include a bibliography, as needed.
- Indicate whether or not the needed resources are already provided as part of the lesson by listing the resource and the word *provided* in parentheses after it.
- Punctuate appropriately, so teachers know the kind of resource to which you are referring. For example, put shorter works such as titles of short stories, poems, magazine articles, handouts, or songs inside quotation marks; set longer works, such as the title of a book, play, artwork, magazine, newspaper, or CD in italics.
- Indicate specific resources that are used for *differentiation* purposes.

Note: It is not necessary to list basic school supplies, unless you are using them for a special project.

Estimated Timing

- Include details about how long the lesson will take to conduct (e.g., *two 50-minute class periods*).
- Specify where in the unit this lesson should be taught (e.g., *teach this lesson after reading Chapter 2,* or *revisit parts of this lesson about conflict and cooperation throughout the unit as shown in the lesson details*).

Lesson Details (differentiation opportunity)

- Number each detailed step so the lesson is easy to follow.
- Begin each detailed step with a verb phrase (e.g., **Practice** *multiplication,* **Identify** *examples of figurative language,* **Complete** *a graphic organizer*). It might help to consider a

FIGURE 8.1 *(Continued)*

FIGURE 8.1 (Continued)

hypothetical sentence starter for each verb phrase such as *The teacher will . . .* or *The student will. . . .* Either is fine, but be consistent. Put each verb phrase in bold type and underline it so your eyes immediately go to it.

- Follow each verb phrase with detailed directions for conducting the lesson. Describe both your role and the students' roles. These directions should include the specific instructional and teaching strategies you will use to conduct this learning activity.
- Describe *differentiation* strategies.
- Include grouping plans.
- Refer to any resources or materials that are listed above in the "Resources/Materials" section. The lesson details need to explain what you will actually do with these resources and how they will be incorporated into the teaching of the lesson. By the same token, if the lesson details include something you need to conduct the activity (e.g., handout, prop, article, etc.), then go back and check to make sure it is listed in the Resources section.

Extension (differentiation opportunity)

Explain any relevant parameters of the extension, such as the following:

- individual or small groups
- mandatory or optional
- for some or all students
- homework or in-class activity
- necessary materials
- time estimates for each suggested extension activity

Assessments

- Express assessments as nouns or noun phrases (e.g., *observation of participation; "What method of characterization?" handout; written journal response*).
- List assessments by specific name if it's a handout, quiz, assessment, and so forth (e.g., *"Sensory Details" graphic organizer, Causes of the American Revolution journal write*).
- List informal assessments (e.g., *observation during class discussion or group activity*).

FIGURE 8.1

strategies within the lessons and revise the content to accommodate what you teach. Also, remember that each lesson is just that—a lesson that is meant to be couched within the context of an overarching unit. In other words, there are lessons that would need to come before and after the ones that are featured, and they would all play off of and work in conjunction with one another to help students meet entire unit goals. So when you create lessons, do so in the sequential order in which you mapped them out in the unit template. That way, you can bridge learning from one lesson to the next and also situate all of the lessons in such a way that students are given previews to upcoming lessons within your unit.

Below is a list and brief description of the lessons included in this chapter:

Lesson 1. In Grades 4–12, students are expected to make inferences, so this lesson can be used in many grades with appropriately challenging text. The guiding questions *What are inferences?* and *How do I make inferences about this text?* are addressed through a scaffolded approach, as the teacher first introduces inferences with a short text, then uses a think-aloud strategy with a lengthier text. This work prepares students ultimately to make inferences on their own. This lesson not only includes a detailed definition of inference, but also shares specific ways that readers can concretely hunt for inferences in literary or nonfiction texts. The Common Core does not endorse teaching reading strategies in isolation; therefore, weave this lesson into instruction associated with a complex text where inferring enhances comprehension.

Lesson 2. In this two-part lesson guided by these questions—*What is characterization? How do authors use characterization to create and develop characters?*—students first define methods of characterization (e.g., what a character looks like, says, does, etc.) and then hunt for text examples. To initially guide students to define these methods and find examples, I use the story "Eleven," by Sandra Cisneros, and include text-dependent questions for this suggested reading selection. Students then apply what they learn in the whole class session by finding examples of characterization in their own novels. Although I focus on methods of characterization around a shorter text as a model for a novel, teachers should augment the lesson to include other elements of literature (e.g., setting, plot) and literary devices (e.g., foreshadowing, dialect, tone) to promote close reading of the text. Additionally, this formative assessment can prepare students for a possible culminating activity in which they write an argument paper tied to a character. As an example, students can stake a claim by asserting that a character exhibits a certain personality and then use evidence from the novel to defend it.

Lesson 3. I had the good fortune of collaborating with Tasha Bergson-Michelson on a Google Inc. project that encompasses a series of research-based differentiated lessons that align with many ELA Common Core Standards. They are designed for teachers, librarians, technology staff, and anyone else who supports students in their quest for online information for various research tasks in any content area. The lesson I include in this chapter focuses on assessing the credibility and accuracy of sources used for a project. It is one among a series of lessons under the umbrella of the unit guiding question *How do I evaluate the credibility of sources to determine which sources to use for a task?* Other Google Inc. lessons can be found here: www.google.com/insidesearch/searcheducation/lessons.html.

Lesson 4. This lesson will help you put into practice what you learned about assessments in Chapter 5. It shows you how to present students with a checklist, instead of merely handing it out to them. Try this lesson to engender buy-in for a given writing assignment. This lesson's guiding question—*What are the expectations for my finished argument?*—is obviously geared to argument writing; however, you can adapt the strategy in the lesson to any writing type. The important factor is that students are fully aware of writing expectations prior to sitting down to compose their first drafts. You will conduct this lesson about a week or so into the unit, so it serves the dual purpose of checking for understanding and identifying clear criteria for writing. You can even adapt this lesson by applying the strategy to a project other than writing.

Note: In addition to what is featured in this chapter, I provide suggestions for how you might fashion a lesson around text-dependent questions. You'll find these suggestions in Chapter 3 in the section "Designing Text-Dependent Questions for Complex Text."

NEXT STEPS AFTER DESIGNING LESSONS

Designing lessons is a natural subsequent step to unit mapping. However, after you create lessons, there are a few more steps in the process. To give you a context for where lesson design fits into the overall curriculum plan and what you might do after you've written or found lessons, see the following sequence:

1. *Create a unit map.* When you arrive at lesson design, your unit map should be complete with these components:

   - grouped standards
   - knowledge
   - essential understandings
   - essential unit and lesson guiding questions
   - culminating assessment with criterion
   - differentiation
   - activities and evidence of assessments
   - skills
   - resources

2. *Design lessons.* This is the focus for this chapter.

3. *Pilot the unit.*

   - After you complete your lessons, you are ready to pilot the unit. When doing so, take detailed notes. If you and your colleagues are teaching the lesson concurrently or within the same school year, take notes separately in preparation for the reflection that you can do together. Determine the best system for taking notes: in a journal, on the computer, e-mailed notes to yourself, Google Docs, or whatever works best for your learning style. Your notes should be specific to each lesson and include answers to these types of questions:

     o Did the grouping work out?
     o Is there another way I could have differentiated?
     o What worked really well? What did not work so well and should be nixed?
     o Were the instructional activities and teaching strategies varied enough? Were they successful in engaging students?
     o Were there classroom management issues I need to address by editing a lesson?
     o Is there an extension activity I could add? A lesson I should add?
     o Was the timing correct, or did the lesson go on too long or not long enough?
     o What differentiated resources or materials should I add or delete?
     o Were the unit and lesson guiding questions right on, or should I add, delete, or revise any of them?

o Should I include additional preassessments for lessons or formative assessments?

o Is there suitable rigor in the lessons? Were the text selections complex enough for each learner?

o Did I make sure that students focused on the text thoroughly to glean information and use it to pull textual evidence to support claims and information?

o Are there other options for summative assessments that might work?

- You can now ask certain students if you can keep original samples of their formative or summative work or make copies. You can use these student samples as a means for your own reflection and also as samples for students to critique during the following year within a formal lesson. To this end, collect weak, on-target, and strong samples. If you don't have a lesson that includes reviewing and critiquing student samples, I suggest adding one, as it's an invaluable way to help students improve their own work. I caution against critiquing the work of your current students in the same class. This is because peers can be too generous and hesitate to offer the insights needed to revise for fear of hurting feelings; on the other hand, they can also be unnecessarily harsh. It is a safer route to use samples from a different class or the year prior and delete students' names.

- With this arsenal, you can enter into reflection and then revise the unit accordingly.

4. *Reflect and then revise lessons.* This is the ideal time to convene with colleagues who taught the same unit or, if you taught the unit on your own, to carve out your own time to engage in reflection. Come to this meeting with your notes and student samples to prepare for discussion. You might have one teacher facilitate the meeting to keep your group on task and organize a plan for your time together. Specifically, you might use the questions delineated in Step 3 as the basis for discussion. Furthermore, you will undoubtedly find that lessons will need revision, so have a plan for this step, which might entail dividing duties among colleagues and assigning due dates for reviewing one another's lessons and offering feedback. If you work alone, come up with your own timeline for revising these lessons. Even though you will not teach this unit until the next school year, you'll find that time has a tendency to creep up on you.

5. *Reteach.* The next time you teach this unit there should not be many changes beyond those you incorporated from Step 4, but there could be some. Take notes and make these changes, so the unit is intact and ready for the following year.

6. *Create a unit map for another unit.* And so the cycle goes; it is time to gear up for another unit of study and begin the process again. Eventually, with time, you will have a library of effective and meaningful units of instruction.

7. *Create a grade-level yearlong curriculum map; articulate across grade levels.* Curriculum mapping is defined in this book's Introduction. To briefly reiterate, the unit map constitutes one piece—albeit critical—of a unit you teach within your school year. In addition, it is an altogether worthwhile and useful endeavor to create a yearlong curriculum map of your entire school year if you haven't yet undertaken

such a project. I suggest you embark upon drafting a yearlong map for your grade level that delineates all of the units you will teach and accounts for all of the standards you are responsible for covering in a given school year. It can also include unit map components such as essential understandings, guiding questions, and skills. Then share and discuss your map with others in your school or district to uncover gaps and unnecessary repetition among the grades. Together, create a map that articulates units of study across grade levels. Your grade level and district might already have such mapping documents or have plans to create or revise them based on the new Common Core Standards. If not, there are many books and software programs to help with such a project. My book *Curriculum Mapping: A Step-by-Step Guide for Creating Curriculum Year Overviews* (2007) is one such resource you may wish to consult.

As you can see, the process of creating a unit map, designing lessons, piloting, and revising for each unit taught in a school year is intense. It is an ongoing effort and may take several years, so do not expect that within one year you will have completed comprehensive unit maps and accompanying lesson plans for everything you teach. For some of my long-term clients, I collaborate with them to produce one comprehensive unit of study a year. That might be a viable goal for you, too. Capitalizing upon the strengths of colleagues is strongly recommended, and to be as efficient as possible with time, you might collaborate on a curriculum map and then divvy up lesson design, offering feedback and ideas along the way.

A FINAL NOTE

[M]ost students have, at best, a partial view of the work that teachers do because so much of this work occurs when they are not present to witness it. . . . [T]he classroom performance of effective teaching is reliant on extensive preparation, which itself is based on extensive thinking.

—Anne Reeves (2011, p. 199)

This is the last chapter, so aside from the following lessons and these final words, I take leave. It is no easy task to plan engaging and effective curriculum. Educators who embrace this work are doing their charges an enormous service because these students will glean so much more than factual knowledge from a given unit. They will be given the opportunity to go way beyond that—to transfer information, make infinite connections, think critically, and experience complexity. Using the Common Core or other standards to foreground key concepts and essential skills, crafting guiding questions to frame learning, and delivering instruction in an engaging way are all powerful forces in helping students to grow intellectually and to ignite their excitement in learning. As you continue your efforts and develop lessons around your unit map, remember that you are doing important work. Once you catch the fever—which I, of course, have—you will find that there are endless opportunities to teach under an umbrella of profound meaning and purpose. So you should commend yourself for the work you've accomplished as you have tackled the chapters in this book. Go forth with a renewed spirit and a more elevated way of thinking, and be the awesome teacher and mentor you were destined to be.

LESSONS

LESSON 1: What Are Inferences? How Do I Make Inferences About This Text?

ESSENTIAL UNIT GUIDING QUESTION

How can readers make inferences to gain more insight into a text?

LESSON GUIDING QUESTION

What are inferences? How do I make inferences about this text?

> **LESSON OVERVIEW**
>
> Students cement the definition of inference in their minds as teachers provide them with opportunities to apply inferential reading strategies to various texts. First, students practice making inferences with a short text, then with a teacher-selected longer piece, and finally with passages they have chosen from a novel or nonfiction reading selection. Students are continuously asked to support their conclusions with evidence from the text and, as appropriate, with other pieces of evidence or facts from previous texts.

STANDARDS

- Read closely to determine what the text says explicitly and to make logical inferences from it; cite specific textual evidence when writing or speaking to support conclusions drawn from the text (2010a, R.CCR.1).

RESOURCES/MATERIALS

- "Hi, Marge! Letter" (Figure 8.2)
- "Conclusions: Peg" (Figure 8.3)
- Various texts
- Student journals or large sticky notes (optional)

TIMING

Approximately one 50-minute lesson. Embed this lesson during instruction around complex text.

LESSON DETAILS

Preparation for activity. Copy Figure 8.3 ("Conclusions: Peg") onto cardstock, laminate it, cut out strips, and place a set of strips in an envelope. Prepare one set for each pair or small group of students.

1. **Connect to previous learning.** Say to students: *Earlier we reviewed pictures and discussed how we can make inferences through details in images. Today we will take it a step further and practice using textual evidence to make inferences. Making intelligent inferences during and after reading can make you better readers. It is important to note that effective readers use information from an author to draw conclusions and form interpretations so that their inferences are supported by words in the text.*

Post the lesson guiding questions on the board and point to them as the purpose for this lesson.

2. ***Review definition of* inference *and practice making inferences.*** Remind students of the definition presented in a previous lesson: *Inference means the process of drawing logical conclusions from factual knowledge, sound reasoning, or evidence. It is an assumption or conclusion that readers logically make based on textual evidence (words on a page) or known facts. To make an inference requires readers to go beyond what the words on the page state to uncover what the author implies.* Explain to students that you will guide them in making inferences first. Then they will make inferences on their own with a novel or nonfiction piece they have each been reading. Here is the way to conduct the initial, guided activity:

- Tell students you will read a letter to a girl named Marge from a classmate named Peg. Distribute a copy of the letter (Figure 8.2) so students can follow along as you read it aloud.
- After reading the letter aloud, distribute a prepared envelope consisting of strips from Figure 8.3 "Conclusions: Peg" to each group. Tell students to empty the contents and read each conclusion together to decide which ones seem most appropriate. Return the strips that do not apply to the envelope.
- Students focus on the possible conclusions they have selected to narrow down the best one. To do this, they answer the questions at the bottom of the letter in Figure 8.2 for each possible conclusion to discover the one or two statements that a reader might infer from the letter. These questions call on students to support an inference using the text, so remind them to center their conversations around the contents of the letter that lead them to their conclusions.
  - ○ ***Differentiation.*** Ask high-achieving students to create their own inferences instead of using the ones you have prepared on strips. They should still test their conclusions against the same set of questions the others used. Also, be mindful to distribute an appropriate number of conclusion strips (Figure 8.3) to students based on their readiness levels—do not give all twelve strips to struggling learners; select four or five for them to study carefully. Provide adult assistance to groups, as necessary.
- When all groups have identified one strip, compare them as a class to isolate the one or two valid inferences. Have students articulate how these inferences are logical and how they are based on textual evidence.

3. ***Identify types of inferences readers can make.***
- Now that students have practiced making inferences with a short piece, use the think-aloud strategy on a more challenging text to prepare them for making inferences on their own with a longer work. Select an appropriately challenging text that lends itself to making inferences. It does not have to be a literary selection, as readers can make inferences with nonfiction, as well. Make sure students have a copy of what you are reading.
- First, explain that making inferences can be tricky because the author is not explicitly hand-delivering readers the information. Rather, readers draw inferences using the information from the text to draw conclusions and make knowledgeable interpretations. As you conduct this exercise, think aloud not only to explain your thought process as you make inferences, but also to describe how you select portions of the text that are conducive to making inferences. It is helpful for students to have concrete ways to make inferences, which is what Kylene Beers has provided in her book *When Kids Can't Read.* Following are some of her suggestions for types of inferences that skilled readers might make (Beers, 2003, p. 65). I've added parenthetical notations for use with nonfiction text. Introduce these items and zero in

on pertinent ones when you are thinking aloud. Explain the rationale behind your choices to your students.

- o Understand the intonation of characters' words (or identify the tone the writer takes).
- o Identify the characters' (historical figures', leaders', noteworthy individuals') beliefs, personalities, and motivations.
- o Understand the characters' (historical figures', leaders', noteworthy individuals') relationships to one another.
- o Provide details about the setting (environment, location, geographical features).
- o Provide explanations for events or ideas that are presented in the text.
- o Understand the author's (writer's) view of the world.
- o Recognize the author's (writer's) biases.
- o Offer conclusions from facts presented in the text.

- Close this activity with a discussion around the question: ***How do inferences help readers gain insight into a text?*** The art of making inferences enriches readers' experiences because it enables them to arrive at new insights after examining the text critically. Re-emphasize the point that one way readers infer is through making reasonable conclusions based on hints the author provides.

4. ***Make inferences independently.*** Ask students to make inferences on their own or with a partner who is reading the same text. Instruct them to complete a graphic organizer that shows the quotes they have pulled and the associated inferences they have made. This could be in the form of a T-chart or double-entry journal. Or you might have students place large sticky notes next to text they feel is worthy of referring to and then write their inferences on these sticky notes.

   - o ***Differentiation.*** Differentiate by readiness level so that students are reading appropriately complex material from which they can make inferences. If you are using a class text, then scaffold appropriately by helping struggling students choose inference-worthy portions of the text. Also, you might provide them with a shortened list of ways to make inferences (see second bullet in Lesson 3, above).

ASSESSMENTS

- participation in discussions and activity
- written inferences

Hi, Marge!

I'm awfully sorry to hear you've been sick and in the hospital for two weeks. I've been meaning to come see you—I really have—but I've been terribly, *terribly* busy. Did you know I replaced you in the school play? Rehearsals are a blast!

I suppose you're living a life of luxury—nurses to wait on you hand and foot, good-looking doctors to watch over you. Gee, some people have all the luck! I guess a healthy little nobody like me just doesn't rate.

I hope you don't mind, but Eddie asked me to the prom. I saw him the other day and asked him who he was taking—I knew you couldn't go. You probably won't be able to do

FIGURE 8.2 *(Continued)*

FIGURE 8.2 (Continued)

much more than rest and take it easy for months. Anyway, he said he'd asked Gloria. Now, I know you wouldn't want him to take *her*—you'd probably never see him again (ha, ha). So, I convinced him to take me. I'm sure you'd prefer that he took a friend of yours.

Could I ask you a tiny little favor? Could I wear the dress you bought for the prom? After all, it won't do you any good just hanging in the closet. And pink is the color that looks best on me.

Seriously, I hope you get better soon.

Do you think you'll be able to rejoin the cheerleading squad this year?

Love,

Peg

After Reading

1. Is the conclusion statement clearly supported in the letter?

2. Is this conclusion statement something a reader would guess from reading the letter?

3. Does this conclusion statement seem untrue from reading the letter?

4. Is there anything in the letter to support whether or not this conclusion statement is true or false?

5. What is a character trait to describe Peg? What evidence do you have from the letter to support this trait?

FIGURE 8.2

Source: Pooley, Daniel, Grommon, & Niles (1967).

Conclusions: Peg

1. Peg is really concerned about Marge's illness.
2. Peg is jealous of Marge.
3. Peg has probably never been in a hospital.
4. Peg has no sympathy for others.
5. Peg would like to be in a hospital herself.
6. Peg is very shy with people.
7. Peg is forward with other people.
8. Peg thinks of herself as not very important.
9. Peg would like to be important.
10. Peg is very practical and doesn't like to see anything go to waste.
11. Peg takes advantage of her friends.
12. Peg would like to replace Marge as a cheerleader.

FIGURE 8.3

Source: Pooley, Daniel, Grommon, & Niles (1967).

LESSON 2: What Is Characterization? How Do Authors Use Characterization to Create and Develop Characters?

ESSENTIAL UNIT GUIDING QUESTION

How do authors develop characters?

LESSON GUIDING QUESTIONS

What is characterization? How do authors use characterization to create and develop characters?

LESSON OVERVIEW

This two-part lesson focuses on the ways in which authors develop characters through methods of **characterization,** specifically through revealing what a character looks like, says, does, thinks and feels, and what others say about the character. Additionally, students will gain practice with making inferences. Teachers first model examples of methods by using the text "Eleven," by Sandra Cisneros (or another reading selection). After modeling, students identify textual examples of characterization in a longer work. Text-dependent questions around the story "Eleven" are included in this lesson so students can experience close reading of the text to examine story facets other than characterization.

STANDARDS

- Read closely to determine what the text says explicitly and to make logical inferences from it; cite specific textual evidence when writing or speaking to support conclusions drawn from the text (2010a, R.CCR.1).
- Analyze how and why individuals, events, and ideas develop and interact over the course of a text (R.CCR.3).
  - ○ Analyze how particular elements of a story or drama interact (e.g., how setting shapes the characters or plot) (RL.7.3).
  - ○ Analyze how particular lines of dialogue or incidents in a story or drama propel the action, reveal aspects of a character, or provoke a decision (RL.8.3).
  - ○ Analyze how complex characters (e.g., those with multiple or conflicting motivations) develop over the course of a text, interact with other characters, and advance the plot or develop the theme (RL.9–10.3).
  - ○ Analyze the impact of the author's choices regarding how to develop and relate elements of a story or drama (e.g., where a story is set, how the action is ordered, how the characters are introduced and developed) (RL.11–12.3).

PART 1: MODEL WITH STORY

RESOURCES

- "Methods of Characterization" (Figure 8.4)
- "Characterization for ＿＿＿＿" (Figure 8.5)
- "Characterization: *Rachel*" (Figure 8.6)

TIMING

This lesson occurs in approximately two 1-hour class periods.

LESSON DETAILS

1. *Pose guiding questions and set the stage for the lesson.*

   - Remind students that there are five elements of literature: *theme, plot, setting, point of view,* and *character.* Tell them that as they read, they will focus on the element of *character.*
   - Ask students to brainstorm answers to these guiding questions: ***How do authors develop characters? What does an author do to help readers learn about characters?*** Record students' responses so they are visible to the class. Then introduce (or review) the definition for characterization: **the term for the methods an author uses to create or develop a character.** Distribute Figure 8.4, "Methods of Characterization," and feature it on the document camera or overhead. Have students compare this figure with the class brainstormed list. Discuss differences and validate similarities. Tell students that they will be focusing on various methods of characterization as they listen to and read the story "Eleven" (or another featured text). Explain that later they will individually investigate methods of characterization for a longer work of literature.

2. *Reveal examples of each method of characterization.*

   - To illustrate how Cisneros uses methods of characterization, tell students you will read the story "Eleven" aloud. Students can read it again silently. Then together you will record examples that are used for the character Rachel onto Figure 8.5, "Characterization for___." For this exercise, place this figure on the document camera or make a transparency of it for an overhead. Since you will focus on Rachel, write her name in the blank after "Characterization."
   - Begin recording text excerpts onto the figure by first using the think-aloud strategy. Then solicit students to contribute text examples for each method and record their information. If students are reluctant to share, refrain from calling on just a few students. Rather, involve more students in the discussion by isolating one method of characterization at a time and asking students to work in trios to find text examples before sharing with the whole class.
   - "Characterization: Rachel" is a teacher resource and includes examples of partial entries you and your students might make. There are other ones, as well, so in each row that is applicable, record several examples on Figure 8.5 during the collaborative class activity. When completing the sheet, note that there are not as many examples of physical appearance or what others say about Rachel. At this point you will leave the third column for "Personality Traits" blank.

3. *Infer personality traits from recorded text examples.*

   - Explain to students that they will use what they have gleaned from the quotes they identified about Rachel to make inferences about her personality. Explain that making inferences can be tricky because the author is not explicitly presenting readers with information. Rather, readers draw inferences by using the information from the text to draw conclusions and make knowledgeable interpretations. The art of making inferences enriches readers' experiences because it enables them to arrive at new insights after critically examining the text.

- Review the various examples of quotes from the story that are recorded for each method on Figure 8.5, "Characterization for_____." After each method—except for the first one, on physical appearance—focus on the impression readers glean from the textual information about Rachel. To do so, reread each example from the story and ask students to talk in trios to answer the following question: **What personality trait can you think of to describe Rachel based on this quote from the story?** Encourage them to use additional text evidence that is not on the characterization sheet in order to make their inferences. You might first review personality traits to remind students that they are expressed as adjectives. Rattle off a few examples to get them thinking: caring, responsible, conceited, parsimonious, rude, loyal. You might choose to use the traits listed in Figure 8.7 during this part of the lesson. It is acceptable to assign more than one personality trait for a particular method of characterization if there is enough evidence to support this.

- Invite trios to share and support their impressions of assigned traits of characters using textual evidence. Discuss commonalities among students' input and arrive at a class consensus on the personality traits associated with Rachel. Take this opportunity to explain and discuss how words have shades of meaning. Extend the conversation to other characters in the story: Mrs. Price, Sylvia Saldivar.

- Make the point that through methods of characterization, readers get an overall impression of a character. This is similar to the way that people in our lives develop an overall sense of other individuals based on what they say or do.

4. *Engage in discussion using text-dependent questions.* After discussing characterization, instruct students to read "Eleven" independently again (if needed). Then engage students in an activity using the following text-dependent questions; revisit Chapter 7 for ideas.

- *What is the significance of counting backward from eleven? Why is this such an important age for Rachel?*
- *Why does Rachel not want to claim the sweater?*
- *Why can't Rachel be honest with Mrs. Price about the sweater? Why is she so shy and reluctant?*
- *Why does Cisneros use the hyperbole of one hundred and two?*
- *What are examples of simile that Cisneros uses in "Eleven"? What are the comparisons in each example? How does each example of simile convey information about Rachel's character?*
- *What are examples of repetition in "Eleven"? Identify and examine specific words and phrases that are repeated. What effect does repetition serve in the story?*
- *From whose point of view is "Eleven" told? How does this particular point of view create a more impactful story than it would if it were told from a different perspective?*
- *Cisneros uses the metaphors of an onion, rings of a tree trunk, and stacking dolls to describe growing old. Reread that paragraph and rewrite it in your own words.*
- *Why does Rachel write in the second-to-last paragraph: " . . . it's too late"? What tone is conveyed in this paragraph?*
- *The story is a combination of interior monologue and dialogue. Does one device carry more impact than the other?*

Add other questions focusing on the standards that would be relevant to this lesson.

Methods of Characterization

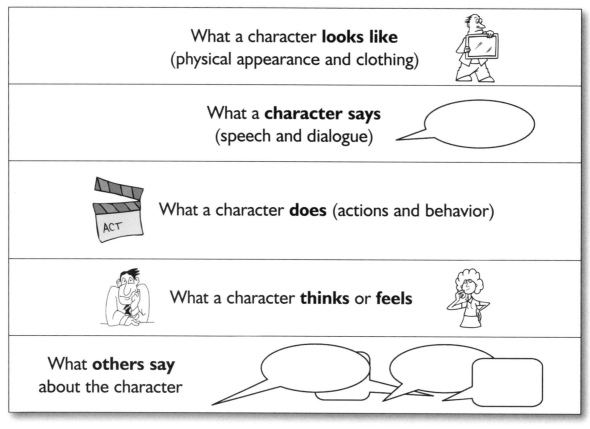

FIGURE 8.4

Characterization: _____
How Do Authors Develop Characters?

Method of Characterization	Example	Personality Trait
What a character looks like		
What a character says		
What a character does		
What a character thinks and feels		
What others say about the character		

FIGURE 8.5

Characterization: *Rachel*

How Do Authors Develop Characters?

Character Method	Support	Personality Trait
What the character looks like (describe the character's physical traits)	*Maybe because I'm skinny . . .* ("Eleven" by Sandra Cisneros, 1991, p. 7)	
What the character says (report the character's speech and dialogue)	*"That's not, I don't, you're not . . . Not mine," I finally say in a little voice that was maybe me when I was four.* (Cisneros, 1991, p. 7)	
What the character does (report about the character's actions and behavior)	*I move the red sweater to the corner of my desk with my ruler. I move my pencil and books and eraser as far from it as possible. I even move my chair a little to the right.* (Cisneros, 1991, p. 8)	
What the character thinks and feels (reveal the character's thoughts and feelings)	*In my head I'm thinking how long till lunchtime, how long till I can take the red sweater and throw it over the schoolyard fence, or leave it hanging on a parking meter, or bunch it up into a little ball and toss it in the alley.* (Cisneros, 1991, p. 8)	

FIGURE 8.6

♦　♦　♦　♦　♦　♦

PART 2: INDEPENDENT WORK WITH LONGER TEXT

RESOURCES

- Novel (or short story)
- "Characterization for _____" (Figure 8.5)
- "Character Traits" (Figure 8.7)—three versions: ♥ struggling learners, ♣ at grade level, ♠ high achievers

TIMING

This lesson occurs in approximately a 1-hour class period.

LESSON DETAILS

1. *Connect to previous learning in Part 1.*

- Say to students: *During the discussion around the story "Eleven," you were introduced to methods of characterization. We examined quotes from the story that support methods of characterization for Rachel and then we used those text examples to infer personality traits. Now you will do the same for characters in a novel as we continue to address the guiding question:* **How do authors develop characters?**

   ○ *Differentiation.* For this part of the lesson, students examine how authors develop characters using a class novel, one they are reading in literature circles, or a novel they read independently. If students select novels based on interest, ensure that the novels they have chosen are appropriately challenging in terms of readability and sophistication, so that they can all wrestle with complex texts to improve their reading competencies.

2. *Identify examples of characterization for a character in the novel; infer personality traits.*

- Distribute a copy of Figure 8.5 "Characterization for ____" that was used in Part 1; feature it on the document camera or overhead, as well. Tell students to find examples for each (or most) of the five methods of characterization for a designated character in their novels and record their findings on this figure. This is an ongoing exercise, so make several copies of this figure available for students to use as they experience their novels.

- As before, have students identify personality traits that are associated with pertinent methods of characterization. Let them know they will have to defend their impressions of these characters with classmates based on textual evidence. You might distribute "Character Traits" in Figure 8.7 and conduct exercises around these words so students expand their inventory of vocabulary and use these and other words to identify a character's personality.

   ○ *Differentiation.* Instruct all students to complete the "Characterization for ____" handout for the novel's protagonist. For more advanced students, assign additional characters that are appropriately challenging. Scaffold support for struggling learners by preparing some quotes in advance that they can match to methods of characterization. For personality traits, distribute a "Character Traits" sheet to students based on readiness levels: ♥ struggling students, ♣ at grade level, and ♠ high achievers.

3. *Discuss entries and claims.* This is an ongoing assignment for the duration of the novel. Periodically set aside class time for students to hold discussions in various grouping configurations (e.g., pairs, small groups, whole class) about quotes they entered and their impressions about characters. Their discussions should center on textual evidence as they support the claims they make.

   ○ *Differentiation.* If students are reading books in literature circles, group them based on their selected novels. If they are reading different books, they can still work in groups to share their impressions and cite evidence. It might prompt them to read one another's books as they learn about characters in various reading selections.

4. *Write a brief argument.* For a formative assessment, have students write a brief argument of a paragraph or two in which they use textual evidence from the novel to address any of these prompts:

- Defend a trait a character possesses and evidence to support it. Include a counterclaim of a different trait that others might assign to this character.
- Argue for how a particular action a character takes impacts the plot.
- Give your rationale for why the author included a particular section of dialogue and how it affects the plot.

As is the purpose of formative assessment, use students' responses in this paper to inform your instruction. At the end of this novel study, students can write a more formal argumentation essay as a summative assessment.

ASSESSMENTS

- Participation in paired, group, and class discussions
- "Characterization: _____"
- Argument paragraph

Character Traits

♥ **CHARACTER TRAITS** ♥			
adventurous	cowardly	hopeful	secretive
bashful	cruel	innocent	sincere
bossy	distrustful	loving	skillful
careful	foolish	loyal	stubborn
careless	gentle	moody	ungrateful
clumsy	helpful	practical	wise

♣ **CHARACTER TRAITS** ♣			
aggressive	fierce	knowledgeable	thrifty
capable	heroic	modest	timid
clever	humble	overbearing	trustworthy
comical	impatient	reasonable	unfaithful
confident	insincere	sociable	vain
energetic	irresistible	suspicious	wholesome

♠ **CHARACTER TRAITS** ♠			
aloof	gullible	nonchalant	sentimental
anxious	haughty	optimistic	spontaneous
apathetic	humane	passive	treacherous
bitter	imaginative	pessimistic	unruly
boisterous	incompetent	radiant	unyielding
dignified	ingenious	rebellious	villainous
exceptional	inventive	resilient	vivacious
frail	morbid	sarcastic	vulgar

FIGURE 8.7

LESSON 3: What Factors Help Me to Evaluate the Credibility of Sources?

ESSENTIAL UNIT GUIDING QUESTION

How do I evaluate the credibility of sources to determine which sources to use for a task?

LESSON GUIDING QUESTION

What factors help me to evaluate the credibility of sources?

LESSON OVERVIEW

In this activity, students first zero in on the author of research information. Specifically, they determine who wrote the information, the date it was written, and if the information can be verified. Students either go on a scavenger hunt or play a game using a targeted Internet site and then answer questions pertaining to the authorship of the information. They then use what they find to make an evaluation about credible sources for their own research tasks.

STANDARDS

- Write arguments to support claims in an analysis of substantive topics or texts, using valid reasoning and relevant and sufficient evidence (2010a, W.CCR.1).

  o Support claim(s) with clear reasons and relevant evidence, using **credible sources** and demonstrating an understanding of the topic or text (W.6.1b).

  o Support claim(s) with logical reasoning and relevant evidence, using **accurate, credible sources** and demonstrating an understanding of the topic or text (W.7/8.1b).

- Gather relevant information from multiple print and digital sources, **assess the credibility and accuracy of each source,** and integrate the information while avoiding plagiarism (W.CCR.8).

RESOURCES

- Internet access and computers
- Teacher pre-selected website links differentiated by interest and readability level
- "Scavenger Hunt Record Sheet" (Figure 8.8)
- "Source Sleuth Game" (Figure 8.9)
- Game pieces and number cards
- "How Do I Identify Credible Sources?" (Figure 8.10)
- Google search lessons (teacher resource), www.google.com/insidesearch/searcheducation/lessons.html

TIMING

This activity is approximately one or two 50-minute class periods.

LESSON DETAILS

1. *Set the stage for learning.*

- Tell students that in this and other lessons, they will learn about tools to help them identify credible sources to use for their research tasks. They will address the guiding question: *What factors help me evaluate the credibility of sources?* Explain that identifying the author can help determine the credibility and truthfulness of your source. Ask students what questions they would want to know about an author. Possible answers: *Who wrote this information? When did he or she write it? Is this person reliable?*

- Tell students they will engage in an activity in which they delve into the kinds of questions they just generated about the author of an information source. Explain that not all of the information they seek will be available for every source. This activity is intended to show them the kinds of information they might see. Make these points to students or use them for your own edification when teaching:
  - o Recognizing credibility is not cut and dry. With web sources it is hard to determine credibility, but considering the questions posed in this activity will help.
  - o Information sources that are missing answers to some of the questions posed does not necessarily mean that they are entirely unreliable. Therefore, use the activity questions subjectively to determine credibility. These questions are not a checklist. Rather, they are designed to give you an opportunity to practice locating, identifying, and processing this kind of information.
  - o Other factors to consider when assessing credibility include the date when an article was written and whether or not the source can be verified. For certain topics, how old the information is can impact its reliability and accuracy. Some examples of information for which the date is important include presidential elections, Olympic Games, latest scientific findings, or current events. The date might not be as important when students are researching historical topics such as King Tut's tomb or the Trail of Tears, or when they are seeking information about a person from the past like Helen Keller, Albert Einstein, or Julius Caesar. The caveat is when these events or people become a current event because of a new finding. Ask students to provide their own examples of when they think the date of a research source may or may not be important.

2. Investigate the credibility of sources.

- I offer two group activity options described below as a means for students to practice carefully critiquing a site's authenticity. They then use what they learn to evaluate the credibility of their own sources for research projects they are conducting. You might choose to skip the group activities, though, and merely distribute Figure 8.8, "Scavenger Hunt Record Sheet," for students to complete for examining their own research.
- For either activity option, do the following: (1) Invite students to select a topic of interest from a list you have prepared. (2) Arrange them into groups according to their selected topics and also their readability levels. I suggest having students select a topic on one day so that you can then spend time that evening forming the appropriate groups to be announced the following day. (3) Issue a website address to each group.
  - o **Option 1: Conduct a scavenger hunt.** Once students are situated into groups, distribute Figure 8.8, "Scavenger Hunt Record Sheet," to each student. Instruct them to work together to discuss and complete it based on their assigned site. Although they are working in groups, each student should complete the handout.
  - o **Option 2: Play a game.** Students play a board game using Figure 8.9, "Source Sleuth Game," to investigate information about the author of material on a website. To start the game, students put a game piece on the "Start" box. This can be a collection of pieces you or students provide, such as beans, pennies, buttons, macaroni, metal rings, or paperclips. In addition, provide duplicate number cards with a 1, 2, and 3-point value for students to place face

down. Assign students a website and ask them to open the link next to their prepared game cards. Students determine who goes first. This person turns over a number card and moves to the spot on the board indicated by this number. Using the source information on the website, the student answers the question. Other group members must agree on a correct answer before it is the next student's turn. Repeat so that students continue to move around the game board answering and discussing questions based on the website. The game is over when the first person (or all students) reach the "End" spot.

- o *Differentiation.* To prepare for either of the two group activity options, determine a list of topics that might interest your students such as sports, animals, art, or music. Find several sites that span readability levels and record these website links. Ask students which topics they are each interested in and arrange them into groups based not only on topics of interest but also on readability levels. Assign appropriate website links to each group and work with groups that need additional support. Note: Please do not choose hoax sites, as it is difficult to transfer these skills from fictional topics to information on topics students will actually encounter.

3. *Debrief with classmates.*

- Invite groups to share one or two key findings about what they found or didn't find on their sites. Use the following as a springboard for discussion based on either the questions on the scavenger hunt sheet or the game board: *Is it important to be able to answer every question? Why or why not? What do we do when we find sources where there are a lot of unanswered questions? What do you think about the credibility of your site after investigating answers to these questions?*

  - o To close this lesson, have students complete a sentence starter. You might say: We have *started to learn about what makes a credible source.* Using what you learned in this lesson, complete this sentence starter in your journals: **"When we research, it is important to. . . ."**

  - o Have volunteers share their sentences and come to a class consensus based on responses. Guide them to respond with something close to this: *When we research, it is important to find and use credible sources. To help determine credible sources, researchers need to know about the author, when the article was written, and how this source can be verified.*

4. *Recognize and apply credibility factors.*

- Make copies of Figure 8.10, "How Do I Identify Credible Sources?," for each student. Before distributing it, show and read only the top paragraph on a document camera or overhead. Explain that this handout will be a resource for them as they consider credible sources to use for their tasks. Remind them that it is not a checklist, but rather a set of ideas to get them started. No website will meet all of these criteria, and some websites that do may have other factors that make students suspect them. Then uncover the whole sheet and show them that they have already focused on the top four rows. Explain that in subsequent lessons, you will lead them in lessons to tackle the other aspects of credibility.

- Option: You might have students complete Figure 8.8, "Scavenger Hunt Record Sheet," for a particular site they use for their research tasks if they have not done so already.

ASSESSMENTS

- Participation in group and class discussions
- "Scavenger Hunt Record Sheet" (Figure 8.8)
- Participation in "Source Sleuth" game (if played)

Scavenger Hunt Record Sheet

Search Topic: _____ **Site Address:** _____

Group Members: _____ **Class Period:** _____

Directions: Review a site and answer these questions and prompts. You may divide this task among group members.

Who wrote this information?	
What is the author's education, training, or experience as it relates to this content?	
Does s/he have a professional title or is s/he recognized as an authority? Identify the title.	
Is the author connected with an organization? If so, can you determine if it is a respected organization? Name the organization.	
Can you contact the author or company? How?	
If the author is unnamed, can you take extra steps to find information about this author? What steps did you take?	
When was the article written?	
Does the author include a date for the information written? What is it?	
Is it important that the information be current, or are you researching a topic from long ago?	
Do the links on the site work, or are they outdated?	
Can the information be verified for accuracy?	
What sources does the author of this information use? Name one.	
Are these sources listed in the article?	
Does the author include a works cited list or other links to provide additional resources or original source information? Identify one.	
Are there identified sources for any data or statistics in the content? Write one statistic and its source.	
Can you find other sources that share the same information, or is this the only source? Name the other source you accessed.	

FIGURE 8.8

Reprinted from Google Search Education—Lesson Plans (© 2012 Google), www.google.com/insidesearch/searcheducation/lessons.html.

Source Sleuth Game

Directions: Sit with a partner and access your assigned information page on the web. Take turns playing this game. When you land on a square, answer the prompt based on the source information on your site. Discuss each of your answers so there is agreement before taking the next turn.

			END
			Do you feel this source is credible? Why or why not?
			Can you find other sources that share the same information? Which sources?
			Are there identified sources for any data or statistics in the content? Show one statistic and its source.
What is the author's education, training, or experience?	Does the author have a professional title? What is it?	Is the author connected with an organization? Which one?	Does the author include a works cited or other links? Identify one.
Can you contact the author or company? How?		Is the author unnamed? How can you find the name?	
Does the author include a date for the information? What is it?		Is it important that the date is current? Why or why not?	
Do the links on the site work?		What sources does the author of this information use?	
START		Are the sources the author uses listed in the article? Where?	

FIGURE 8.9

Reprinted from Google Search Education—Lesson Plans (© 2012 Google), www.google.com/insidesearch/searcheducation/lessons.html.

How Do I Identify Credible Sources?

When collecting evidence for a research project, information report, argument paper, or similar task, it is important to use factual information. For an argument paper, it is true you want to sway your reader and will have a clear position and perspective. However, basing your evidence on facts will be more convincing to your readers. For a research project or report, you will want to include accurate and reliable facts and information. Consider the following when you collect evidence so you can use credible sources.

Does the writing seem too good to be true?

Sometimes content seems so amazing that it makes a reader wonder if it's true or not. Beware of this as it can indicate unreliability and inaccuracy. Ask these questions to help you determine if the writing might be largely untrue: *Does this information seem unbelievable? Does it make sense to you or others? Does what you read conflict with something you already know to be true? Does the writing seem like hyperbole where something is grossly exaggerated? Is there a way to check this information out so you know whether it is true or not?*

Who wrote this information?

Identifying the author can help you determine the credibility and truthfulness of your source. Consider these questions: *What is the author's education, training, or experience as it relates to this content? Does he or she have a professional title or is he or she recognized as an authority? Is the author connected with an organization? If so, can you determine if it is a respected organization? Can you contact the author or the company? If the author is unnamed, can you take extra steps to find information about this author?*

When was the article written?

For certain topics, how old the information is can impact the reliability and accuracy. *Does the author include a date for the information written? Is it important that the information be current or are you researching a topic from long ago? Do the links on the site work, or are they outdated?*

Can the information be verified?

To check the accuracy of information, you might consider these questions: *What sources does the author of this information use? Are these sources listed in the article? Does the author include a works cited list or other links to provide additional resources or original source information? Are there sources identified for any data or statistics in the content? Can you find other sources that share the same information, or is this the only source?*

How might the tone or style of the writing reflect its credibility?

The design of the website will not necessarily mean it is unreliable. What is most important is the actual writing. The way in which an article is written can reveal clues about its credibility. Consider the following: *Does the article have several grammar, spelling, punctuation, or capitalization errors? Is the writing emotional and does it include language that has a bitter, critical, or demanding tone? Is the writing so informal that it seems hard to trust? Does it seem unfair or extremely slanted or biased to a particular point of view? If it is biased, are there facts to back it up or other sites to verify what it states? Does it seem like it would anger or manipulate people?*

Why does the author write this information?

Sometimes people write articles for reasons that contribute to unreliability, bias, and untruths. This doesn't mean that an individual writing an article about something he or she is passionate about will necessarily be unreliable, or that a person who writes a persuasive piece is completely biased. Argument papers are by nature meant to persuade a reader, so take this into account while reading. As you read sources, use your judgment and the clues about credibility to make sure you access the information you need to satisfy your task.

FIGURE 8.10

LESSON 4: What Are Elements of an Argument Paper? What Are the Expectations for My Finished Argument?

ESSENTIAL UNIT GUIDING QUESTION

How can I organize and develop a logical argument with clear reasons and relevant evidence?

LESSON GUIDING QUESTION

What are the elements of an argument paper? What are the expectations for my finished argument?

LESSON OVERVIEW

Students brainstorm what they think a strong argument entails based on what they have learned so far in the unit. Students compare their brainstormed list with a teacher-prepared checklist. As they compare their list with the teacher's list, students reinforce their understanding of the components needed for a strong argument and have an opportunity to study the writing expectations.

STANDARDS

- Demonstrate command of the conventions of standard English grammar and usage when writing or speaking (2010a, L.CCR.1).
- Demonstrate command of the conventions of standard English capitalization, punctuation, and spelling when writing (L.CCR.2).
- Write arguments to support claims in an analysis of substantive topics or texts, using valid reasoning and relevant and sufficient evidence (W.CCR.1).
- Produce clear and coherent writing in which the development, organization, and style are appropriate to task, purpose, and audience (W.CCR.4).
- Gather relevant information from multiple print and digital sources, assess the credibility and accuracy of each source, and integrate the information while avoiding plagiarism (W.CCR.8).
- Acquire and use accurately a range of general academic and domain-specific words and phrases sufficient for writing at the college and career readiness levels (L.CCR.6).

RESOURCES

- "Argument Writing Checklist" (Figure 8.11)
- "Let's Review" (Figure 8.12)
- "Suggestions for Using a Checklist" (Figure 8.13)—teacher resource
- "Revision Sheet: Argumentation" (Figure 8.14)

TIMING

This activity is to occur a few days into your unit on argumentation so that students are already aware of the elements that comprise this writing genre.

LESSON DETAILS

Note: Presenting a writing checklist to students early in a unit will serve to explain to them what the summative assessment will entail and how they will be assessed. This lesson is designed to give students a formal orientation to a writing checklist. When students are made aware of expectations for writing or for any project in advance of working on it, they have a higher likelihood of producing better results. If you continuously use checklists in your classroom—which I recommend—students may not always need a lesson as formal as this one to engender ownership of items on the list. For older students, you can use a rubric in lieu of a checklist and follow pertinent suggestions in this lesson to introduce the rubric. For your reference, see Figure 8.13, "Suggestions for Using a Checklist," along with the detailed explanation and examples of revision sheets included at the end of this lesson.

1. ***Connect to previous learning.*** Say to students: *We have spent time reading many argument papers, and you now know that you'll each write an argument. In order to write the best one you can, I want you to clearly understand the criteria now so you can be thinking about writing expectations.*

2. ***Explain group task.***

   - Explain to students that when they write their arguments, they will be well aware of what you expect *before* they write. This way there are no surprises and they can work hard to meet clear expectations. Use the analogy that when they bake chocolate chip cookies or order a pizza, they have a clear sense of what these food items taste and look like before they actually eat them.

   - To set students up for success in writing, properly orient them to Figure 8.11, "Argument Writing Checklist," before passing it out. Give them the opportunity to discuss what elements they think might be included in an argumentation essay and recall the tenets of strong writing in general. To do this, tell students they will brainstorm in groups to generate a list about possible criteria. They will then compare a student-generated list of criteria with the checklist you will give them. To prepare them for this task, you might say:

     We have been studying about elements of argumentation and have read several examples in class. Think about what makes a strong argument. You will talk in your groups and make a list of those features that contribute to a sound argument and a strong piece of writing in general.

3. ***Brainstorm list using roundtable strategy.***

   - Tell students to work in groups to write a list of what is important to include in an argument essay by addressing the prompt: **What are expectations for my finished argumentation essay?** It's important to make it clear that you want a list of both features specific to this writing type (e.g., thesis, reasons, evidence, counterclaim, etc.) and those for strong writing in general (e.g., proper spelling and grammar, transitions, etc.).

   - Use the roundtable strategy for students to generate this list. See directions in Figure 8.12 to see how this strategy is conducted. (Note: You can use this strategy for another lesson when students need to generate a list. To do so, merely change the prompt.)

   - To help students begin brainstorming, merely remind them of what they learned so far during this unit. While students brainstorm, casually visit each group and gently guide them. Their lists will probably just contain features of argumentation at first. You also want line items about what makes all writing strong. Provide additional hints by saying, *Your list is impressive because it includes elements of argument that you learned. But what if I can't read your work? Remember what all good writing includes and put it on your list.* Typically, the student who is a weak speller writes down *spelling,* and then it opens it up to a new burst of energy.

4. ***Create a class list.***

- Once the brainstorming is complete, have groups report out to the whole class. Write down their responses on butcher paper or the whiteboard so you have a comprehensive class list. Remind students to avoid duplications by looking at what was recorded before contributing new items to the list.

- Then show Figure 8.11, "Argument Writing Checklist," on a document camera or make a transparency of it. Have students do an item-by-item match of what they brainstormed with what you have on the checklist. Applaud them for the points that are similar; there will undoubtedly be overlap, and that's good. Seeing this overlap reminds students that what they thought you planned to assess them on is something they knew. It reinforces what they have learned about this genre's features.

- Let students know that as they write their arguments, their checklist should be constantly visible. It is a vehicle to guide them *while* writing and not something to use when the paper is done so they can randomly check each box. Remind students that you will assess them against each point on the checklist; hence, you will teach many lessons to assist them in satisfying most line items. Review which items you have introduced so far in the unit.

- Distribute a checklist to each student. Students can store the checklists in a writing folder for easy reference. As you teach specific lessons, have students retrieve their checklists so you can highlight a particular line item that is the basis for that lesson and explain how it ties to a targeted lesson guiding question. This keeps the purpose for learning center stage.

  o ***Differentiation.*** When students write their papers, consider creating tiered versions of the argumentation checklist and distribute appropriate ones to individual students based on readiness. You can have two or three levels of challenge, but make sure you still align to standards.

ASSESSMENTS

- Participation in brainstorming
- Group brainstormed list

Argument Writing Checklist

Directions: Use this checklist to guide you as you write an argument about a debatable topic.

Ideas and Content/Organization	Voice
☐ I include an **original title**. ☐ My paper focuses on **one claim** without getting off-track. ☐ My paragraphs are **indented** appropriately. ☐ I use appropriate **transitions** to link sections of my text and create cohesion so my paper flows.	☐ I understand my **task, purpose, and audience**. ☐ I write in a **consistent point of view**; I do not write in second-person point of view. ☐ I maintain a **formal style**.

→Introduction

☐ My *introduction* provides a context for my argument and draws in the reader.

☐ I clearly stake my claim about one issue through a *thesis statement*.

→Body Paragraphs

☐ Each of my body paragraphs includes the following:

	1	2	3
Topic sentence—Each topic sentence includes a *logical and specific reason* that supports my argument and connects to the thesis.			
Support—I support each reason/topic sentence with *relevant and accurate evidence* including facts, data, and examples that are not common knowledge.			
Interpretation—I *interpret or comment* on my evidence to explain what it means.			
Concluding sentence—I *restate the topic sentence* without repeating it exactly.			

☐ My pieces of evidence are in a *logical, organized sequence* and are not in a list.

☐ I save my *best argument* for *last*.

☐ I use at least *three separate sources* of evidence.

☐ I *address reader concerns* with a counterargument that states why the other point of view is weak.

→Conclusion

☐ I have a strong ending; my conclusion *sums up my most important points*.

☐ I suggest ways that readers can *take action*.

Sentence Fluency

☐ I have *no run-on sentences or fragments*.

☐ My *sentences begin in different ways*.

☐ I use a *variety of sentence structures*: simple, compound, complex, and compound-complex.

☐ I use appropriate *transitions* between sentences to show how ideas relate.

Word Choice

☐ I use *specific and accurate words* to support my argument.

☐ My *writing does not repeat* itself or have unclear language.

Conventions

☐ My *grammar* is correct. I make sure I use consistent verb tense and active voice.

☐ I use correct *capitalization*.

☐ My *punctuation* is accurate. I make sure to punctuate in-text citations correctly.

☐ My *spelling* is correct; I use references, if needed.

☐ I include a *works cited* list and correctly format it.

☐ I use *proper formatting*: My *title is centered* and I include a *proper heading*. I use Roman or Arial font and double-space with 1-inch margins, 12- or 14-point black type, and a proper heading.

FIGURE 8.11

Let's Review

1. Take out one piece of paper per group.

2. Each group member is to have a pen or pencil.

3. Raise your hand if your birthday is closest to George Washington's birthday. You are first. The person on your left is second so that the paper moves clockwise.

4. Starting with the first person, write down one word or phrase that answers this question: *What do strong argument essays include?*

5. Continue to pass the paper clockwise entering one word or phrase that answers the prompt. Write a bulleted or numbered list instead of sentences.

6. Read all the previous entries before writing yours, so there are no duplications.

7. Time limit:_____

FIGURE 8.12

Source: Glass (2012).

Suggestions for Using a Checklist

1. ***Establish frequency and familiarity.*** Orient students to the notion that checklists are a way of doing business in your classroom. Sometimes they will help create checklists and sometimes students will be given one to use. Either way, they use these checklists as a guide. You might create a checklist as a one-shot deal for a specific assignment, and you might have one checklist that is used repeatedly. For example, you might create a checklist for a quick write or journal prompt to use each time they respond to this type of assignment.

2. ***Present a checklist to students.*** Avoid passing out a checklist without properly introducing it. That will undoubtedly overwhelm kids. Instead, engender ownership by having them brainstorm what they think might be included in a checklist before you distribute your prepared version. Chances are they will have a pretty good idea of what you expect before the formal assignment is issued, since you have conducted lessons all along. After you pass out the checklists, have students work in groups to compare what they collectively generated in their brainstorming with your checklist and highlight what is missing from their brainstormed list. Students might even add to your prepared checklist because they have brainstormed something pertinent that the class agrees needs to be added.

3. *Use the checklist to state objectives and find or create lessons.* Make sure you teach to most elements on the checklist. That means that you constantly refer to the checklist as you state the objective(s) for the day (or week). To do so, make an overhead of the checklist or feature it on a document camera. Also, copy it for students on colored paper so it's easily found and accessible. And certainly make sure that you have lessons for each point on the checklist or refer to past lessons for some items, like grammar or conventions. The items on the checklist should align with your guiding questions, so point out to students how they are connected.

4. *Establish as a way of doing business.* Remind students frequently that they will use the checklist to guide them while writing. This means it needs to be visible as they write. They will also use the checklist in the editing and revision stages.

5. *Include a revision sheet.* Make an accompanying revision sheet so students are led through the process of systematically tending to each line item on the checklist. Once they become more experienced writers, they will hopefully not need such a detailed method of utilizing a checklist. Through a prepared revision sheet, students see that every item on the checklist needs to be satisfied as a way of policy in your class.

6. *Final thoughts.* Use the checklists routinely. If you use a checklist once in a while, it won't have the same effect and impact as if you use it frequently and follow these suggestions. Teachers who use checklists wisely and effectively get improved student results. A caveat, though, is that you do not need to follow each of these suggestions every time you issue a writing assignment. You will undoubtedly have short assignments in which a brief checklist is needed. If kids are familiar with these suggestions, they will use the checklist successfully for these small assignments, since they have been used and introduced properly before.

FIGURE 8.13

TEACHER RESOURCE: SUGGESTIONS FOR USING A REVISION SHEET

Figure 8.13, "Suggestions for Using a Checklist" (teacher resource), refers to a revision sheet that is an effective instrument to assist students in producing their best work. It works in tandem with a checklist because oftentimes a checklist alone won't be altogether successful in supporting students as they work to their potential. The reality is that some students merely disregard a checklist. Or they use it after writing instead of as a guide to remind them of the criteria during the writing process. You can help address this problem and pave the way for all students to be successful. To do so, instruct them to write a first draft and then self-assess using a genre-specific revision sheet like the one for argumentation in Figure 8.14. The entries on the sheet will provide guidance for revision and mirrors the items on the checklist. Then peers and even family members can assess using the same sheet and provide additional comments for a subsequent revision. Teachers should also give students feedback. Note that a revision sheet is primarily for revision—as the name indicates—and not for editing (i.e., grammar and conventions). Here is how to introduce and use this tool as part of your instructional program:

- Say the following: *You will carefully review your rough drafts and make sure that each item on the checklist is satisfied. To do this, you will look at your paper and complete boxes on a revision sheet.* Show students a copy of the revision sheet on the overhead or document camera. This revision sheet contains items from the checklist, so what is on it is not a surprise.
- Tell students that they will use this revision sheet to look at their own work, so they know what revisions to make. After they make necessary revisions, a classmate will give them comments on a clean copy of the revision sheet. They will then be given time again to revise further.
- Model how to use the revision sheet by filling one out using a student sample from a previous year (or from another teacher's classroom). Explain that there are three choices for completing the revision sheet, so show how this works: (1) Some spaces on the revision sheet cannot be filled in because the paper doesn't include a particular expectation or expectations. If this is the case, leave these spaces blank so the writer knows where to revise. (2) If a portion of the paper is weak, students fill in the appropriate spaces on the revision sheet and mark these spots with a highlighter so the writer has an indication of what he or she should spend time revising. (3) For sections or examples in the paper that are strong, enter the associated words or phrases on the revision sheet and put in an asterisk.
- Let students know that they will follow this revision process:
  1. Self-assess using the revision sheet.
  2. Revise their papers based on their self-assessment.
  3. Give their papers to a peer, who will read their second drafts and complete a clean copy of the revision sheet.
  4. Revise again based on peer comments.

Also, you should review students' papers and give specific comments with or without the revision sheet to provide students with clear guidance for improvement. Point to line items on the checklist or revision sheet to direct them where to spend their time revising. Students can take their revision sheets home for parents or older siblings to complete. This is a helpful home-school connection. It also serves to redirect some adults who might otherwise make intrusive or unwelcome notations on students' papers. Make it clear to parents that they are not to mark on the student's papers; all comments are to be on the revision sheet in response to student work. Let students know they might use these comments to revise again as part of the writing process before it gets to the publishing step.

Revision Sheet: Argumentation

Descriptors	Circle	
The writing demonstrates **argumentation.**	Yes	No
The paper **stays on topic and focuses on one claim.**	Yes	No
There are no **grammar or conventions** errors and the **paper uses proper formatting.**	Yes	No
Proper **indentation** is used for each paragraph.	Yes	No
There is an original **title.**	Yes	No
The paper maintains a consistent **first- or third-person** point of view.	Yes	No

Descriptors	Ideas/Organization	
The **opening** provides context and draws in the reader.	Write a sentence from the introduction that compels the reader to keep reading:	
There is a clearly stated **thesis** to stake a claim.	Write the thesis statement:	
The writer states three logical and specific **reasons** to support the thesis. The reasons are expressed as topic sentences.	Write three different reasons to support the claim: 1. 2. 3.	
The writer supports each reason (topic sentence) with **evidence.** There is **commentary** to explain the evidence.	Write selected evidence: 1.	What is the commentary for the evidence?
	2.	
	3.	
There is **relevant evidence** throughout the paper to build a logical argument. Write any **comments** here:	Check all that apply: ☐ There is relevant evidence in all body paragraphs that relate to the claim. ☐ There is evidence, but it doesn't always connect to the claim. ☐ More evidence would make the paper stronger. ☐ There is explanation or commentary for the evidence to make it clear why this evidence is incorporated in the paper. ☐ More explanation or commentary is needed to explain why certain evidence is included. ☐ The strongest argument is saved for last.	
Transitions connect ideas so the paper flows.	Write an example of at least three transitions (no need to write complete sentences; just record transitions):	

FIGURE 8.14 *(Continued)*

FIGURE 8.14 (Continued)

Descriptors	Ideas/Organization
The opposing viewpoint is addressed by a **counterargument**. The writer states why the other point of view is weak.	State a counterargument:
	Write how it is addressed:
There is a strong **conclusion** that sums up the major points of the argument.	Write one sentence of the conclusion that is original and leaves the reader with a lasting impression:

Descriptors	Voice
The paper maintains a **formal style.**	Write two sentences indicating a formal style:

Descriptors	Sentence Fluency
Sentences begin in different ways.	Write two sentences that each begin in a different way: 1.
	2.
There are a variety of **sentence structures.**	Write two sentences that each have a different structure: 1.
	2.

Descriptors	Word Choice
The paper includes **accurate and strong words** to support the argument.	Write at least four strong words relevant to the argument:

FIGURE 8.14

References

Achieve. (2010). *On the road to implementation: Adding to the Common Core: Addressing the "15%" guideline.* Retrieved from www.achieve.org/files/15PercentGuideline.pdf

Anderson, L. W., Krathwohl, D. R., et al. (Eds.). (2001). *A taxonomy for learning, teaching, and assessing: A revision of Bloom's taxonomy of educational objectives.* Boston: Allyn & Bacon.

Aronson, E., Blaney, N., Stephan, C., Silkes, J., & Snapp, M. (1978). *The jigsaw classroom.* Beverly Hills, CA: Sage.

Beers, K. (2003). *When kids can't read.* Portsmouth, NH: Heinemann.

Black, P., & William, D. (1998, March). Assessment and classroom learning. *Assessment in Education, 7*–74.

Bloom, B. S., & Krathwohl, D. R. (1956). *Taxonomy of educational objectives: The classification of educational goals, by a committee of college and university examiners. Handbook I: Cognitive Domain.* New York: Longmans, Green.

Bruner, J. S., Goodnow, J. J., & Austin, G. A. (1956). *A study of thinking.* London: Chapman & Hall, Limited.

California Department of Education. (2009). *History-social science content standards for California public schools, kindergarten through Grade 12.* Sacramento: Author. Retrieved from www.cde.ca.gov/be/st/ss/documents/histsocscistnd.pdf

Calkins, L., Ehrenworth M., & Lehman C. (2012). *Pathways to the Common Core: Accelerating achievement.* Portsmouth, NH: Heinemann.

Carmichael, S. B., Martino, G., Porter-Magee, K., & Wilson, W. S. (2010). *The state of state standards—and the Common Core—in 2010.* Retrieved from www.edexcellence.net/publications-issues/publications/the-state-of-state.html

Cisneros, S. (1991). *Woman hollering creek and other stories.* New York: Random House.

Coleman, D., King, J. B., Jr., & Gerson, K. (2011). *Common Core in ELA/literacy: Shift 4—text-based answers.* (Video interview.) Retrieved from http://engageny.org/resource/common-core-in-ela-literacy-shift-4-text-based-answers/

Coleman, D., & Pimentel, S. (2012). *Revised publishers' criteria for the Common Core Standards in English Language Arts and Literacy, Grades 3–12.* Retrieved from www.corestandards.org/assets/Publishers_Criteria_for_3–12.pdf

Council of Chief State School Officers. (2011). *What we do.* Washington, DC: Author. Retrieved from www.ccsso.org/What_We_Do.html

Daniels, H. (1994). *Literature circles: Voice and choice in the student-centered classroom.* Portland, ME: Stenhouse Publishers.

Davenport, T. H. (2005). *Thinking for a living: How to get better performances and results from knowledge workers.* Boston, MA: Harvard Business School Press.

DuFour, R. (2004). What is a "professional learning community"? *Schools as Learning Communities, 61*(8), 6–11.

Duke, N. K., & Bennett-Armistead, V. S. (2003). *Reading and writing informational text in the primary grades.* New York: Scholastic.

Dunn, R., & Dunn, K. (1978). *Teaching students through their individual learning styles: A practical approach.* Reston, VA: Reston Publishing Group.

Erickson, H. L. (2002). *Concept-based curriculum and instruction: Teaching beyond the facts.* Thousand Oaks, CA: Corwin.

Erickson, H. L. (2007). *Concept-based curriculum and instruction for the thinking classroom.* Thousand Oaks, CA: Corwin.

Finn, C. E., Jr., & Petrilli, M. J. (2010). *Foreword.* In S. B. Carmichael, G. Martino, K. Porter-Magee, & W. S. Wilson (Eds.), *The state of state standards—and the Common Core—in 2010* (p. 1). Retrieved from www.edexcellence.net/publications-issues/publications/the-state-of-state.html

Fisher, D., & Frey, N. (2012). *Engaging the adolescent learner: Text-dependent questions.* Retrieved from www.missionliteracy.com/page78/page72/assets/FisherFrey%20Text%20Dependent%20 Questions%20April%202011.pdf (International Reading Association)

Fisher, D., Frey, N., & Lapp D. (2012). *Text complexity: Raising rigor in reading.* Newark, DE: International Reading Association.

Fountas, I. C., & Pinnell, G. S. (2001). *Guiding readers and writers grades 3–6: Teaching comprehension, genre, and content literacy.* Portsmouth, NH: Heinemann.

Gardner, H. (1993). *Multiple intelligences: The theory in practice.* New York: Basic Books.

Glass, K. (2007). *Curriculum mapping: A step-by-step guide for creating curriculum year overviews.* Thousand Oaks, CA: Corwin.

Glass, K. (2009). *Lesson design for differentiated instruction, Grades 4–9.* Thousand Oaks, CA: Corwin.

Glass, K. (2012). *Mapping comprehensive units to the ELA Common Core, Grades K–5.* Thousand Oaks, CA: Corwin.

Google Inc. (2012). *Lesson plans.* Mountain View, CA. Retrieved from www.google.com/insidesearch/searcheducation/lessons.html

Jacobs, H. H. (1997). *Mapping the big picture: Integrating curriculum and assessment K–12.* Alexandria, VA: Association for Supervision and Curriculum Development.

Kadushin A., & Harkness, D. (2002). *Supervision in Social Work (4e).* New York: Columbia University Press.

Kendall, J. (2011). *Content knowledge: A compendium of standards and benchmarks for K–12 education* [Online edition]. Retrieved from www.mcrel.org/standards-benchmarks

Kober, N., & Renter, D. S. (2011). *Common Core State Standards: Progress and challenges in school districts' implementation.* Washington, DC: Author.

Literacy Design Collaborative. (2011). *Template task collection 1.* Retrieved from www.literacydesign-collaborative.org/wp-content/uploads/2012/02/LDCTemplateTasks.pdf

Massachusetts Department of Education. (2003). *Massachusetts history and social science curriculum framework.* Malden, MA: Author. Retrieved from www.doe.mass.edu/frameworks/hss/final.pdf

McTighe, J., & O'Connor, K. (2005, Nov.). Seven practices for effective learning. *Educational Leadership, 63*(3).

National Assessment Governing Board. (2008). *Reading framework for the 2009 National Assessment of Educational Progress.* Washington, DC: U.S. Government Printing Office.

National Governors Association (NGA) Center for Best Practices, & the Council of Chief State School Officers (CCSSO). (2010a). *Common Core State Standards for English language arts & literacy in history/social studies, science, and technical subjects.* Washington, DC: NGA Center and CCSSO.

___. 2010b. *Common Core State Standards for English language arts and literacy in history/social studies, science, and technical subjects: Appendix A: Research supporting key elements of the standards.* Washington, DC: NGA Center and CCSSO.

___. 2010c. *Common Core State Standards for English language arts and literacy in history/social studies, science, and technical subjects: Appendix B: Text exemplars and sample performance tasks.* Washington, DC: NGA Center and CCSSO.

___. 2010d. *Common Core State Standards for English language arts and literacy in history/social studies, science, and technical subjects: Appendix C: Samples of student writing.* Washington, DC: NGA Center and CCSSO.

National Governors Association (NGA). (2011). *Who we are.* Washington, DC: Author. Retrieved from www.nga.org/cms/about

New York State Department of Education. (1999). *Social studies resource guide with core curriculum.* Albany, NY: Author. Retrieved from www.p12.nysed.gov/ciai/socst/pub/ssovervi.pdf

New York State P-12. (2011). *Common Core State Standards for English language arts and literacy.* Retrieved from www.p12.nysed.gov/ciai/common_core_standards/pdfdocs/nysp12 cclsela.pdf

Pooley, R. C., Daniel, E., Farrell, E. J., Grommon, A. H., & Niles, O. S. (1967). *Projection in literature.* Glenview, IL: Scott, Foresman and Company.

Reeves, A. R. (2011). *Where great teaching begins: Planning for student thinking and learning.* Alexandria, VA: Association for Supervision and Curriculum Development.

Sachar, L. (1998). *Holes.* New York: Dell Yearling.

Spandel, V. (2001). *Creating writers: Through 6-trait writing assessment and instruction* (3rd ed.). New York: Addison, Wesley, Longman.

Spandel, V. (2012). *Creating writers: 6 traits, process, workshop, and literature* (6th ed.). New York: Pearson.

Sternberg, R. J. (1996). *Successful intelligence: How practice and creative intelligence determine success in life.* New York: Simon & Schuster.

Strickland, C. A. (2009). Tools for high quality differentiated instruction: An ASCD toolkit. In C. A. Strickland (Ed.), *Professional development for differentiated instruction: An ASCD toolkit.* Alexandria, VA: Association for Supervision and Curriculum Development.

Strickland, C. A., & Glass, K. T. (2009). *Staff development guide for the parallel curriculum.* Thousand Oaks, CA: Corwin.

Tomlinson, C. A. (2001). *How to differentiate instruction in mixed-ability classrooms* (2nd ed.). Alexandria, VA: Association for Supervision and Curriculum Development.

Tomlinson, C. A., & Eidson, C. (2003). *Differentiation in practice: A resource guide for differentiating curriculum.* Alexandria, VA: Association for Supervision and Curriculum Development.

Tomlinson, C. A., & McTighe, J. (2006). *Integrating differentiated instruction + understanding by design.* Alexandria, VA: Association for Supervision and Curriculum Development.

Tomlinson, C. A. et al. (2002). *The parallel curriculum: A design to develop high potential and challenge high-ability learners.* Thousand Oaks, CA: Corwin.

Wandberg, R., & Rohwer, J. (2010). *Teaching health education in language diverse classrooms.* Burlington, MA: Jones and Bartlett Learning.

Wiggins, G., & McTighe, J. (1998). *Understanding by design.* Alexandria, VA: Association for Supervision and Curriculum Development.

Wiggins, G., & McTighe, J. (2005). *Understanding by design* (2nd ed.). Alexandria, VA: Association for Supervision and Curriculum Development.

Index

CORWIN
A SAGE Company

The Corwin logo—a raven striding across an open book—represents the union of courage and learning. Corwin is committed to improving education for all learners by publishing books and other professional development resources for those serving the field of PreK–12 education. By providing practical, hands-on materials, Corwin continues to carry out the promise of its motto: **"Helping Educators Do Their Work Better."**